Lethbridge Community C

"the JOY of RAISING OUR KIDS in the 21st CENTURY!"™

A pastor, father of six, and a
researcher, father of four, explain
how to raise and teach our children
while growing up in these difficult times.

Gilbert H. Goethals
&
L. Raymond Hayes

BRUIT PUBLISHING COMPANY, INC.™

Manufactured in the United States of America
First Edition
Library of Congress Cataloging in Publication Data
Goethals, Gilbert H.
Hayes, L. Raymond

"The Joy of Raising our Children
in the
21st Century!"
1- Parenting
2- Parent and Child
3- Parent and Child - Study and Teaching
4- Parenthood
5- Children, Raising
6- Children, Teaching / Instruction

SAN 298-069X
LC# 93-73668
ISBN 1-884420-03-6 Hard Cover
ISBN 1-884420-04-4 Paperback

Testimonials

"Thank you for your book on child rearing. Our daughter is eight months old, and we know it will help us to be better parents."
Marty and Linda Jenkins

"Just a few lines to let you know how much I have enjoyed your book. Thus far, I am about half way through it now and looking forward to what I'll learn in the last half." E. Pollock,

"Thanks a million for sending me your book. Also, thanks for writing this book and making it available to us! There is no question about it being helpful! Thanks too for being at Hammond, Louisiana last week and your part in the seminar."
Sid Botelee

"I really have enjoyed your book on child rearing. It has helped me to better understand how to go about properly training children. I have a son 51/2 and he is very strong. Thank you." Mary Rice

"Thanks for your truly inspiring book. Even though I am not married, your book has brought tremendous insight in my understanding of how to be a right parent. Thanks sincerely for your hard work." G. Robertson

"The book is great - I hope you sell a million copies! P.S. So was your sermon... Thanks," Florence Lillengreen

Table of Contents

Chapter:		Page:
1	It takes More Today to be a Parent than it did Yesterday or the Day Before!	1
2	The Assembly Line Concept!	9
3	It's All about Time!	19
4	The HUMAN MIND and a KID's Brain! Are they One and the Same?	33
5	The Importance of COMMUNICATION!	41
6	PARENTING! What went wrong?!	57
7	GRANDPARENTING TODAY!	69
8	Raising Children by a Single Parent!	87
9	How to Help Your Kids Make Wise Decisions!	99
10	Youth & Leadership! The Qualities of Having Both!	113

Chapter:		Page:
11	Something to Consider about the Mind of a Child!	135
12	What in the World is SUCCESS?!	139
13	DISCIPLINE!! A Very Controversial Subject!	161
14	Teaching Children all about MONEY!	185
15	How NOT to Provoke your Child to Wrath!	205
16	DATING: That particular fearsome time when a parent's mettle is sorely tested!	231
17	ANTICIPATION! For Our Children's Welfare and Success!	271
18	Especially for the CHILDREN: "How to Raise Your Parents!"	283
19	For the PARENT: Some Final Thoughts	303
20	PARENTING: A Very Special PERSPECTIVE!	329

About the Authors

GILBERT H. GOETHALS

While Gil has no advanced degree in child psychology, he has something just as meaningful...hands-on experience! And, a lot of it! Along with his first wife Nancy (deceased), Gil successfully raised six children (3 boys and 3 girls). And, he is also the proud grandfather to twenty-three very active grand-children!

Gil was not content to rear just his own children. In his youth, he rose to the rank of Eagle Scout, having trained with the Boy Scouts of America; and this experience helped prepare him for a major part of what he was to do later in life...being a youth camp director for the past 25 years. He has worked with and taught children at camps in Washington, Minnesota, Texas, Arkansas, and Scotland. This type of experience has given him a deep understanding and appreciation for children from all walks of life.

As a full-time pastor, Gil has had the opportunity to work and counsel with happily married parents, single parents, divorced parents, and their children...children of every race, color, creed, and background.

Over the years, Gil has acquired the type of judicious wisdom and knowledge needed to help so many moms and dads who love and care for their children enough to seek practical, down to earth, sensible, and intelligent guidance for the purpose of learning how to become better parents; the type of guidance and training parents need today if they are to succeed in the most challenging and compelling task and responsibility given to them by God...that of being Loving, Caring, and Devoted Parents - *Real Parents* - to their Children!

L. RAYMOND HAYES

After graduating from the USAF Air University (engineering), Raymond attended several schools on a part-time basis until he discovered the joy and challenge of writing music and screenplays, creating business enterprises, working within the entertainment industry and managing international companies. During his travels to many foreign countries, he began to realize that almost every society on earth today is experiencing a serious decline in the family structure...families are in trouble worldwide!

Raymond has explored both academic and theological studies during the past 18 years regarding God's plan for mankind which includes the rearing of children, overcoming this world, studying humanities, and succeeding in life. He worked hard to achieve "the great American dream"...the desire for material and physical *things* that only success can buy. And, he also paid a price for his worldly success.

In his twenties, Ray fathered two boys and adopted a boy and a girl. Yet, because of his overwhelming drive to succeed in business - including his relentless desire to create and develop companies - he, like so many other men and women in business management today, failed as a parent.

"My children have turned out to be really great kids. Not because of what I did, but rather because of how their mothers raised them. I was too busy trying to make a place for myself in the business world. I was so busy that I sorely neglected to properly train and instruct my children and I failed to give them my unconditional love.

"As I watched Gil raise his kids, I often coveted his family and the love they have for one another. I can attest that when parents, such as myself, fail to build a solid relationship with their children - a type of relationship that includes deep devotion, trust, quality time, and love, such as Gil and Nancy gave their children - there will be a fracture in the relationship between parent and child even if a child grows up to be kind, caring, and successful. And my experience tells me that it takes a long time for this fracture to heal.

"When I finished writing this book with Gil, I realized that where Gil succeeded as a father, I failed. I can tell you, the reader, that I am living proof that if you don't apply what is written in the following pages, chances are you will also fail as a parent. I only wish I had had a book like this to study before I became a father. I hope this book will help you raise your children in a positive manner and that you will succeed as a parent!"

"They get their exercise and ten cents a bottle,
and I get ALL the rocks out of my garden.
Isn't life WONDERFUL!?"

A Statement
by the
Authors

GILBERT H. GOETHALS

I believe God was the inspiration for my writing this book. I thank Him and praise His Righteous and Holy Name for having given me the wisdom, understanding, experience, and courage so my wife and I might successfully raise six wonderful and loving children. I thank God for having provided me with a wonderful, lovely, and most caring wife...a helpmate, mother of my children, sweetheart, and friend. And, I also thank Him for my grandchildren.

I love children and I enjoy watching them grow, their minds filled with hope, desire and love. As a counselor to both parents and children, I hate it when I witness young lives being ruined due to lack of understanding and improper training by their parents. The purpose of this book is to help you gain a deeper understanding and insight from my experiences so that you can become a more loving, exemplary, and caring parent.

I hope and pray this book will help you understand the tremendous importance and responsibility we parents have been given in the raising of our children. If you approach child rearing with love, care, dedication, resolve, and deep, heartfelt prayer for guidance and direction, I promise you, no strings attached, you will experience great joy and success as a parent!

I want to personally thank all those who encouraged me to finish this book: To my first wife Nancy, who died of cancer but not before she had given so much of herself in raising our children. Nancy was a wonderful lady whose support and encouragement are greatly missed. And, thanks to my six children for their help and love; for being such devoted and caring children, not only while they were young and growing up, but today as adults!;

To my wife, Leta Ray, for her encouragement and support especially during the most difficult times. She is a true advocate, sweetheart and friend;

To all my friends who keep asking, "When is your book going to be finished? I want a copy!" I couldn't let them down, and believe me, this certainly helped give me the strength to continue writing;

To Mrs. Marion Loring who deciphered my early notes (which meant hours and hours of work!); and, special thanks to Mr. and Mrs. Mark S. Carroll;

To my friend and coauthor L. Raymond Hayes. This man coauthored this book and then edited it in such a way that I know it will be a very meaningful tool for parents who have such great responsibility - the most important endeavor imaginable...*Successfully Raising Their Children!* ;

And, most of all, I thank God for the strength, knowledge, experience, wisdom, and courage He has provided throughout my life, which is the basis for my having written this book.

L. RAYMOND HAYES

When Gil Goethals asked me to look at the first draft of his notes which were the basis for this book, my years of studying about the decline of the family and how children were being affected in very negative ways told me that there was a definite need for this type of information, and that he was certainly the person capable of instructing the reader as to how to become a successful parent.

I have known Gil and his family for many years. I have known him as a teacher, pastor, father, older brother and friend. I had the great pleasure, indeed the honor, to watch him and Nancy raise their six talented and devoted children. So, it is not without a certain degree of humility and a sense of sobriety on my part, that when asked to help write this book, by my friend Gil, who I have the greatest respect and love for, I felt it a great blessing, responsibility and honor.

It is also with sobriety that I went before God daily to

ask for His guidance and direction with this writing, for what Gil and I have put to print in this book is based on the Holy Scriptures and teachings of Jesus Christ!

Writing this book took time and energy and there were moments when I questioned how my wife and I were going to survive financially. However, our faith that God would protect us and direct our hearts and minds to do this work gave me the strength and courage to continue. Being blessed with a wife like Marlyne was the other most important factor in this effort. This remarkable lady not only fought off those who felt the need to scoff at what it we were trying to accomplish but also worked at a job that wasn't the most creative or fulfilling so that we could eat, pay the rent; and obtain the tools necessary to complete this work.

I also want to thank my Mother, Evelyn Hage, for her tremendous encouragement and for the financial support she so often and willingly provided; my son, Kenneth, for the early use of his Mac computer; my good friend, Henry Z Jones, for his help and understanding; my friends and very talented business partners, Hal and Julane Mirka; and, most of all, I want to thank God, my Father, and Jesus Christ, my Lord and elder Brother, for their guidance, inspiration, protection, direction, faith, and mercy. And also for the talent and ability given to me so that I might help write and finish this book.

WE WISH TO GIVE SPECIAL THANKS TO:
LARRY RAY, Art/Graphics/Text Director
JULANE MIRKA, Photography
ROBERT HOWARD, Cover Design/Graphics/Preproduction
JERRY BALLINGER, Illustrations
THERESA GOETHALS, Back Cover Photography
M.C. BERG, Editing
JO MOREHOUSE, Editing
HAL MIRKA, Editing

Note: Unless otherwise noted, Scriptures from the Holy Bible are from the New International Version, New King James Version, and The Living Bible.

Introduction

After years of counseling parents and children regarding family relationships, including marriage, child rearing, child abuse, parent abuse, teenage rebellion and the many other facets which affect children and parents alike, and recognizing the great need parents worldwide have for help regarding how to properly teach and instruct their children, we decided to take the time to sit down and write this book. We hope what we have written will help you as parents realize that with a determined effort - including prayer and fasting, devotion, discipline, daily support, quality time, personal commitment, and most of all, LOVE for your children - you will indeed experience great Joy in Raising Your Kids in the 21st Century! And, you know, the 21st Century isn't that far off!.

As most parents raising children throughout the world today begin to recognize that there are certain overwhelming conditions and problems facing our societies like never before, we begin to also realize that many of these terrible and negative problems seem to surround those whom we so dearly love...our children.

Teenage suicide, street gangs, rape, murder, unwanted pregnancies, drug abuse, child abuse, carjacking, muggings, robbery, theft, and other crimes of violence are on the rise. Each new day, international, national and local statistics indicate a worsening of this global problem. Why?

Could a large part of the answer be that as parents we have missed the mark in teaching, training and instructing our children as to how they should act and behave? How they should live their lives? Do we parents understand that when we do not properly teach and train our children, we fail to prepare them for adulthood? Do we really understand that our kids are the adult leaders of tomorrow, and they had better be prepared for the challenge if our civilization is to continue?

We believe the effects of not having properly taught our children right from wrong, or how to live their lives without so much selfishness and greed, underlie the reasons why our kids are in serious trouble! Our society is in serious trouble! We parents are in serious trouble! Unless we get our act together as parents and become more diligent in our quest to turn things around, our society's ills and problems are not going away...they are only going to escalate!

Perhaps it is time (hopefully your children are still young enough to be taught) that you take a moment and ask yourself: What do I really want for My Children? How can I Help my Kids Succeed in Life? What really is Success? How can I provide the type of encouragement that will allow my kids to overcome the many temptations they face every time they leave the house? Do slogans like "Just Say No!" really work? What can I do to help my Kids say, "NO!"? How can I really help my children make right decisions? Isn't parenting really MY responsibility and not the teacher's or some other person to whom I have entrusted the care of my child? We hope to help you answer these and many other questions as you read this book.

Some of what you will read might upset you if the meaning behind the written words hits a nerve or two, but that's okay. In fact, we hope what we have written will strike a nerve that will cause you to take the time to look deeper into your life; to the way you treat and instruct your children; to the possibility that you may not be handling things at home as well as you would like; to a better understanding of what correct discipline means; to an acceptance that you may need to learn more about how to properly raise your children; and to the fact that the leaders of tomorrow are in your care today.

By writing this book, it is our intention to help parents take back control and responsibility for the overall teaching, instruction, discipline, and training of their children.

You *DIRECT* their lives!   **You** *COUNSEL* them!
You *DISCIPLINE* them!   **You** *ENCOURAGE* them!

Wait a minute! Did we just use the big "D" word? Did we actually say, "You *DISCIPLINE* them!" You bet we did! However, we are NOT suggesting the type of so-called discipline (child abuse) we often witness today. Certainly, parents should never "beat" or "abuse" their children. The type of discipline we write about is DISCIPLINE with love and compassion, using the Word of God as a guide and foundation for the way in which we instruct and chasten (discipline) our children.

In fact, before you begin reading the following material,

why not go to God in prayer and ask Him to help guide your understanding, and to increase your discernment and judgment as you read each chapter. Then, after reading something that captures your interest, take a moment and meditate about what you just read - consider the understanding and wisdom behind the instruction given to you - and put yourself into the situation you just read about.

Ask yourself, "How do I see myself as a parent regarding what I have just read?" "Am I giving my child all that I am able to give? All that he or she really needs to succeed in life, indeed all that my child hungers for?" "Do I show my little boy or girl love...a very special unconditional love that only I, as a parent, can give?"

We pray that you will be able to answer these and other questions throughout this book in the affirmative, and that what you read in the following chapters will help you become the type of parent you desire to be...a successful parent!

Gilbert H. Goethals
L. Raymond Hayes

"Train your CHILDREN in the way
they should go,
and when they are old
they will not turn from it"
(Proverbs 22:6 Paraphrased)

WHY IS IT SO IMPORTANT
THAT WE PARENTS
TAKE THE TIME
TO READ AND STUDY
THIS BOOK?

HERE ARE A FEW STATISTICS REGARDING WHAT'S HAPPENING TO OUR CHILDREN TODAY!

The federal government has spent almost $3 billion of our taxes since 1970 to promote contraceptives and "safe sex" among our teenagers. What have we gotten for our money?

Here are the facts !

- The federal Centers for Disease Control estimate that there are now over 1 million cases of HIV infection nationwide.

- 1 in 100 students coming to the University of Texas health center now carries the deadly virus.

- The rate of heterosexual HIV transmission has increased 44% since September 1989.

- Sexually transmitted diseases (STDs) infect 3 million teenagers annually.

- 63% of all STD cases occur among persons less than 25 years of age.

- 1 million new cases of pelvic inflammatory disease occur annually.

- 1.3 million new cases of gonorrhea occur annually; strains of gonorrhea have developed that are resistant to penicillin.

- Syphilis is at a 40-year high, with 134,000 new infections per year.

- 500,000 new cases of herpes occur annually; it is now estimated that 16% of the U.S. population ages 15-74 is infected, totaling more than 25 million Americans. Among certain groups, the infection rate is as high as 60%.

- 4 million cases of chlamydia occur annually; 10-30% of 15-19 year olds are infected.

- There are now 24 million cases of human papilloma virus (HPV), with a higher prevalence among teens.

- To date, over 20 different and dangerous sexually trans- mitted diseases are rampant among the young. Add to that the problems associated with promiscuous behavior: infertility, abortions and infected newborns. The cost of this epidemic is staggering, both in human suffering and in expense to society; yet epidemiologists tell us we've only seen the beginning!

Source: Focus on the Family ©1992

CHAPTER ONE:

"It takes more today to be a parent than it did yesterday or the day before!"

"Teach my words to your children,
talking about them when you sit at home
and when you walk along the road, when
you lie down and when you get up!"
(Deu. 11:19 NIV)

In today's society, I have discovered that very few adults actually stop to think about what it takes to be a successful parent. The tragic result is that so many young people have never been given the opportunity of being properly taught by mom and dad, and when a crisis or temptation suddenly appears, they often blow it! And the effect can be most harmful!

An example today might be: when two young people on a date find themselves caught up in the heat of the moment and conception occurs. This means that nine months later when a little baby arrives on the scene (if it isn't aborted), it's a little late for them to ask each other, "What kind of parent will I be?" And, studies show that neither the boy or girl believe that she will become pregnant after having casual sex especially if it's "just once!" It just "seems to happen," yet suddenly they're going to be "parents!"

Most young people want to marry "someday" and later have children but never ask themselves, "What does it really take to be a parent? Can I handle the great responsibility that comes with marriage and caring for a baby?"

Today, parents often go through hell on earth as they realize they can do little more than stand back and watch their offspring heading for the many pitfalls which often destroy a marriage, children, or even the young people themselves. Certainly Mom and Dad, witnessing the effects of having inadequately prepared their children, now wish they could stop and start all over again. When children reach the age when we, as parents, no longer have relevancy or control over them, it is heartbreaking to watch those we dearly love commit indiscretions which may possibly destroy them. We then have little alternative other than to conclude that we didn't give them enough quality time, the benefit of our experience, loving parental discipline and a "whole lotta love." By then, however, it is often too late to rectify the situation - truly a sad situation. This can break the heart of a parent and most often does!

How many parents today put forth the time and energy to teach their children how to become effective moms and dads when the time comes? Is this important information taught in our high schools? Is it taught at day care centers? What about at the college and university level? Is it even taught at home? Sadly, all indications and studies point to the fact that, for the most part, teaching a child how to become a successful and caring parent is not being taught in our schools, at home, or anywhere!

So, why isn't this type of information being provided at school? The only answer I can come up with is that teachers cannot teach something they don't really understand themselves. So, how can parents instruct children about something they themselves don't always completely comprehend? Remember parents, children are going to learn from what you *do* and how you *act* more than from what you *say*...and from *you* more than from any other person!

Can it be that many parents never were taught themselves how to become successful parents? Take a moment and think about this. Who taught *you* about life? Who taught you about what it takes to be a winning parent or how much you would have to give up of yourself so that your child can progress, succeed, and grow? Who took the time to explain to you about the great responsibility a parent must commit to before bringing a child into the world? And as the world becomes more complex and dangerous, who is presently teaching your children about life, sex, child rearing, and so many other problems and situations they will face today and tomorrow?

If we parents are ever going to be able to answer these questions (and so many other vital questions that will pop up from time to time), we must diligently begin seeking the answers today...answers which must be mined as if seeking precious gems; fought for with persistence, toil, and zeal.

So just what does it take to be a parent? When does it begin? Does it begin when two people come together sexually and nine months later a new little baby is born? Certainly part of the answer to this questions is a resounding, "Yes!" For there is little doubt that when a couple has a baby they definitely fall into the classification as having become "parents!"

But, just because these two are now quite literally "parents," do they know the first thing about what "being a parent" - actual parenting - really means? Did their parents teach them or prepare them for what should be a most blessed event (having a baby)? Did their life science teacher instruct them in how to be loving, giving, and caring parents? Or, did the teacher only inform this young mother how to change a diaper or prepare a bottled formula? Did either one of these two enthusiastic young parents have real role models to follow while they were growing up? Does this new Mom or Dad really know what to do now that they have a baby to care for? I'm sorry to report that my experience tells me, "The answer is probably a resounding NO on all counts!"

Webster's dictionary tells us that a parent is "one exercising the functions of a father or mother." Wow, what an in-depth statement about what being a parent is all about!

What are the functions of a "father?" What does being a "mother" mean? What does the word "function" mean? Do these "functions" simply mean feeding the baby or providing it with shelter, changing its diapers, or sending it off to school, or perhaps even establishing a few "do's" and "don'ts" by which it should live?

Many parents today assume they are providing their children

3

with basic essentials just because they help get their kid ready for school, provide lunch money, buy some new clothes, rent the latest video, purchase the most recent video game or provide their youngster with an allowance. Still, in reality, the parents who only provide the material necessities for their children are not preparing them for what lies ahead...what we call "real life".

Of course we all need material accouterments to help support our daily lives...those things that make life more interesting and provide us with certain types of entertainment. Obviously, there is so much more to being a parent than simply providing physical things (and I realize that when parents have poor paying jobs or no jobs at all with a whole lot of debts and very little money to make ends meet, it can be very difficult to provide just the basic physical needs!). However, what I am suggesting doesn't cost the parent one cent! What is it? Read on.

Being a parent today is much different than when our parents were raising us! And, for many of us, this includes when we were raising *our* kids.

Over the years we have come to understand that merely providing for our children's physical necessities will most often produce, at best, a child with an indifferent personality and, at best, an insipid attitude.

What parent really has a burning desire for his or her child to be like every other child...to be considered merely average? All loving parents want to raise their children so they will have every opportunity possible to surpass the physical, mental, and spiritual levels they, as parents, sought to achieve. But if young parents don't understand the fundamentals of what it truly means to function as a parent - how to raise a child properly, how to show love and concern when a child is hurt or discouraged, or how to instruct, teach, and discipline a child when he or she needs to be admonished or corrected - then how in the world will these new moms and dads ever succeed as parents? The answer is they probably won't!

4

Whenever I counsel young people for marriage, I always discuss the subject of what it takes to be a parent and the things they will need to do and know, separately and together, before becoming parents.

I find it very sad that so many of the young people I counsel haven't been taught about such important things such as sex, commitment, marriage, money management, faithfulness, and proper child rearing. No wonder so many young lives are completely messed up with bitter divorces, spouse abuse cases, child abuse tragedies and acts of violence coming before the courts every day.

I also try to explain to a young engaged couple that just as it took time and energy on their part, as students, to learn about science, math, language, or history, it takes a lot more time to learn about work, marriage, living with another person and raising children.

In high school, a student must first learn all about certain subjects before he or she can pass to the next grade year. During their senior year in high school, they must pass their SAT tests and college entrance exams before they will be accepted to an accredited college or university. Then, after they enter college, they must really buckle down and study, study, study. But for the most part, with all this learning and studying and staying up late cramming for the next day's big exam, our young students still haven't a clue as to the really important questions they will face once they leave college...how to properly live their lives, how to be successful in marriage, and how to be loving and understanding parents!

Survey after survey strongly indicate that our youth today are ill prepared and poorly educated for entrance into the job market and especially the enormous responsibility of becoming a parent!

The Bible tells us, *"My people are destroyed for lack of knowledge."* (Hosea 4:6 NIV) And, I might add to this, so are our children! Why is it most people don't or won't ask God for knowledge, help, or understanding?

Every newborn baby comes into this world conscious but mindful of nothing. This new arrival is just a bundle of joy and love

5

and very precious to its mother and father. During the first months and into the formative years, it has to be nurtured, fed, changed, trained, and protected every moment. We all know that the baby will soon die if its parents do not take care and give proper attention to its every need. So where then does this little darling get its knowledge, wisdom, direction, and understanding? How does our infant gain understanding as to why it was born? Or, how it will survive and flourish over the next 70 to 80 years? Or, what part he or she will play in the scheme of things surrounding the universe?

What is it that might cause this cute little bundle of joy to grow up to become a bloody killer? A con artist or thief? A man who rapes and mistreats women? An adult child who maligns and dishonors his or her parents? Or a woman who abuses her own children?

Or what might cause this child to grow up to be kind, courteous, gentle, wise, considerate, and loving? What is it this child needs, or indeed must have, if it is going to grow from infancy to mature adulthood with both proper knowledge, understanding, and righteous character?

It matters little about what you may think about yourself as a parent. Certainly for the sake of obtaining and encouraging healthy self-esteem, we should think well and positively about ourselves; Still, the fact remains that what our children grow up and become is based mainly on what they experience at home. School, clubs, and other social aspects in their life will have profound effects on their behavior, progress, and growth. But the environment in the home, combined with the quality leadership, teaching, and training which children receive from their parents will determine, to the greatest degree, how they behave, what they believe, how they grow, overcome weaknesses and mature, and what they will make of their lives.

That's right, parents. Your example in the home, your love and positive attitude will greatly determine your child's chances for success in life. And all of this begins the moment your cute little bundle of joy arrives from the womb!

Stop for a minute and ask yourself, "Am I setting a proper

6

example for my children regarding the way I live? The way I treat their mother or the way I respect their father? The way I act around our friends and relatives? Or the way I behave at home or when I'm away with my family?" The way we act and behave is what our children will emulate, because children are characteristically mimics. Remember, at birth a child knows nothing...you knew nothing. Our children learn and grow into adulthood from the environment we, as their parents, provide.

Truly our kids are "chips off the old block." And so often, much to our dismay, they most likely will retain many of the characteristics of the "old block!" - including the bad and the ugly parts of the " old block"! We are now beginning to understand the importance that our actions and words have on our children (as well as on those with whom we come into daily contact).

Parents often say to me, "I cannot understand why my child seems to hate me, or why he or she refuses to listen to me. They just won't obey what I tell them anymore. I mean, I've scolded and I've even spanked; I've done everything I know how to do! So now what do I do?!"

Wait a minute! Did you catch what this parent said? "I have done everything *I know how to do!*" That's the problem! In trying to help his child grow and mature, this parent did everything he knew, as a parent. But what he knew just wasn't enough! He knew how to physically respond, but he just didn't understand how to emotionally, spiritually, or intellectually manage the situation.

I realize that no one wants to admit to failure. Especially parents! We all want to think of ourselves as having common sense and the brains to know enough to figure out how to live our lives. However, the truth is that we do frequently fail...and, what makes it worse, we fail at those things that are so very important to us...our relationship with our kids, family and friends. And perhaps our greatest failure is when we are unable to show our love.

Certainly we try to do our best to accomplish those things which we believe are right and proper - to do the things we know

7

how to do! But in reality, what we know - what we *truly* know and understand - is not really very much at all! Perhaps this accounts for why we have such high crime in our cities and homes; such disrespect for others, including the elderly, minorities, teachers, and laws that govern the land; such disobedience toward parents and disregard for those in authority.

All parents yearn to have children who are polite, courteous and obedient.   Parents want to be proud of their kids and pleased with their overall development.   However, realizing the blessing from a caring and loving child will only come to pass once a parent truly begins to understand what being a parent really involves: taking on the responsibility for guiding and directing their child's fertile young mind, and becoming an honorable and sincere leader of the family.

To sum it up, more than ever before it takes a tremendous amount of energy, unconditional love, tolerance, respect and compassion to be a successful parent today!   To truly succeed at being a parent means having:

> The LOVE of God
> The FAITH of Abraham
> The PATIENCE of Job
> The DETERMINATION of Paul
> The WISDOM of Solomon
> The COURAGE of David and
> The LOVE and CARING of Jesus Christ!

Take a moment and ask God to give you the wisdom and understanding to be the type of parent (or grandparent) you yearn to be. And, we truly hope what is written in this book will help you become a more loving, patient, knowledgeable and understanding PARENT!

CHAPTER TWO

THE ASSEMBLY LINE CONCEPT!

"One little, two little, three little babies..."

I don't know if you realize it but parents are like production managers who have the responsibility of the assembly line management for each child's growth, education, broken bones, illnesses, financial support, and so much more. Indeed, the production manager is responsible for a child's very life! Using our assembly line scenario, once the product (child) is on the production line (life), it just keeps going at an ever quickening pace from start to finish. We parents (production managers) only have so much time to work with our children before it is time for them to leave home and enter their own personal world of work, marriage and life. Most parents have a tremendous desire for an extension of time because the accountability for the responsibility we have as parents is so great.

Everyday our children mature and become more perfected - heading toward becoming a finished product, a fully developed adult.

And as production managers for this priceless, perfectly designed and cherished product, we parents have total responsibility for how this product...our children...turn out. Mom manages the factory and Dad is in charge of quality control. Together each must carry out and oversee their individual responsibilities if their little ones are to mature and prosper.

What type of character and maturity will our children have when they finally roll off this hypothetical assembly line? Will they have defects and bruises? Or will they shine and glitter with brilliance and well-crafted distinction? Will they travel life's road in health and fitness? Or will they soon begin to sputter and fizzle out after traveling only a short distance? The answer really depends on how well Mom managed the factory and Dad the quality control...how well they both have done their jobs!

What if there is no Dad? Who manages quality control? Mom does! And what if there is no Mom? Who manages the factory? Dad does! We all know that we are living in a time when there are many single parents raising children. And if a child is being raised by a single parent, does this mean that his or her opportunities are limited? Just because there is only one parent at home, must the child receive instruction only in factory management or quality control management? By no means! If a child is being raised by only one parent, it is that parent's responsibility to help prepare his or her child with as complete an education as possible.

Perhaps another parable might help to better illustrate the importance of how we raise our children and demonstrate that there is a very obvious similarity between what we do at work and how we manage our home.

So let's look at the Parental Automaker: after considerable thought and a lot of planning by a whole lot of very talented, educated and capable people, a new automobile model is brought to the assembly line. Now, this new car is very complicated and still has many flaws and problems to sort out , but soon it is finally heading down the assembly line. It will proceed one step at a time until all parts, pieces, and assorted equipment have been assembled and the final unit is complete. After it rolls off the assembly line and all safety checks have been performed, hopefully it will be an automobile the new owner will be proud of.

Sometimes, after tens of thousands of automobiles have been driven off the dealer's lot, the manufacturing company discovers a serious problem with the car (it may be something to do with a failure to properly include a part or perhaps installing inferior equipment while the car was on the assembly line). After considerable debate and a review of the financial implications of having to repair so many cars, the company finally implements a procedure known as a "recall" to allow the dealers the opportunity to repair each malfunctioning automobile. The expense for all of this is enormous!

The automaker may recall all or part of that particular year's models for repair. And almost anyone who has ever bought a new, shining, great-smelling automobile understands what a "recall" is all about.

Cars are simply physical tools we purchase for transportation. However, unlike the automobile, when something goes wrong inside a child, how do we "recall" a seventeen-year-old boy or girl? How do we "recall" a child who no longer lives at home and is now out there somewhere breaking down? Unlike the art of manufacturing an automobile, raising a child provides a parent with only one chance to "put it together correctly!" We parents cannot make a lot of mistakes in raising our kids hoping that if we do, somehow we will be able to rectify our mistakes by some sort of mythical "child recall". Believe me, it just isn't possible.

We have to train and instruct (assemble) our children while they are young. And even though we cannot change the mold from whence they came, we can attach well-fitting emotional, intellectual, and spiritual parts and equipment throughout their youth.

However, if we neglect to properly educate and inspire our children while in their informative years, or if we fail to equip them with valuable parental knowledge, wisdom, and understanding, chances are they may end up with some very serious emotional, physical, and spiritual defects. The type of defects that can be more than harmful, they can be very destructive! What do I mean, "type of defects that can be destructive?" I refer to young adults today who are experiencing drug abuse, sexual disease (VD, AIDS, Herpes), unwanted and unplanned pregnancies, gang membership, murder, rape, every kind of abuse, and so many other negative entanglements that can ruin a young life.

What can we do about it?! The plural *WE* is important because it takes everyone involved to work through the problems and difficulties in raising children today. What we can do is formulate a plan (a blueprint) regarding what needs to be done and how best to accomplish the job of raising our children. We need to set attainable goals for both ourselves and our kids...goals that can be reached and performed one step at a time...goals that relate to family experiences, overcoming problems, educational achievements, overall performances, and schedules to be kept. And, we (parents with their children) need to prepare a list of family priorities such as prayer time, play time, study time, family time, time alone, etc.

Proper instruction of a child is probably one of the most frustrating yet most important and rewarding achievements we, as parents, will ever accomplish. It is very important that we teach our children how to be polite, honest, faithful, and caring; and we must also instill in our young people the values of being strong, compassionate, loyal, and trustworthy. It is also important that our kids grow up with a healthy respect for money and the knowledge of how to manage it intelligently and skillfully (more about this later).

We also want to make sure that our children have been well trained and cautioned about dating prior to the time when they begin one of the most significant encounters that will ever happen to them...an actual date with someone they have had their "eyes on for ages!" (more regarding this often nerve-wracking subject for parents later on).

Mom and Dad should spend quality time with an older child explaining the values, commitments, and principles of marriage, including the type of mate their child should desire (especially regarding character, attitude and disposition) before he or she actually begins thinking seriously about such a profound subject as matrimony.

Helping a child learn appropriate work habits is also very important if they are to enjoy a meaningful and productive career. How a young person performs on the job has everything to do with how well they advance (both financially and with job-related promotions) within their chosen career, and to what level of life-style they will rise.

It all comes down to helping prepare our children for life...helping them not make the same mistakes which we, their parents, made! And, also helping them not to make the same mistakes *our* parents made!

We realize that our parents probably did the best they knew how in raising us. However, today, our children face a totally different environment from what we or our parents experienced in our youth.

Isn't it strange that we seem to teach our children from only what we personally have experienced? After the turn of this century and on to the close of World War II, few individuals actually attended a four year college or university, and high schools didn't provide study courses on how to raise children. So most parents were only able to teach their children by what they personally experienced.

How can a person who walked "two miles to school every day, even in the winter when the snow was butt-high" really understand children having the luxury of riding a bus? And in the same way, how can an older person who walked to school on a safe country road understand what it is like for a young child to ride on a school bus often carrying a load of unruly and violent delinquents? Without really understanding the situation and having empathy for what their children face every day, the answer is that most parents just can't relate.

Certainly one way we can help our kids overcome many of the fears and anxieties we may have concerning their maturing process, is for us to pass on to our children what knowledge and understanding we possess regarding those fundamental components which make up most of what we refer to as "life." If we are to pass on wisdom, knowledge and understanding, then we must continue to seek it ourselves at every opportunity. We must seek additional education, wisdom, and instruction not only for our benefit but for the good of our children.

Some time ago, I spoke with a group of high school students who were very excited about the fact that they would soon be receiving their high school diplomas. After listening for awhile to their complaints about school and how much they were all looking forward to getting out, I told them that they would also soon be receiving another diploma. "Whatta ya mean, another diploma?!," they asked in unison. So, I proceeded to tell them about the next school they would soon be attending...the "school of hard knocks!"

I went on to explain that every individual attends this school after graduating from high school or college. I told them that unlike a four year high school or college, this school of "hard knocks" would last them a lifetime. Also, the diploma from this school was usually signed in blood, sweat, and tears instead of ink, and the deleterious portion that each student could look forward to was that it was going to be *their* blood, *their* sweat, and *their* tears!

After spending a couple of minutes trying to get these students back into a more positive perspective, especially after having hit them with such a realistic observation in regard to life after school, I closed my lecture by telling them that the reality of life is that almost every diploma their parents or anyone else achieved was signed in blood, sweat, and tears. As graphic as this may sound, nevertheless, it is true. I have often wondered why so many professional adults addressing a graduating class aren't more graphic with details about what actually awaits the unsuspecting graduate.

Again, we must teach our children every chance we get! (Deu. 6:7). And keep in mind, we only get one chance per child! Because before you know it, they're off the assembly line and heading out the door.

I know several fathers (and some mothers) who can relate with Harry Chapin's song, "Cat's in the Cradle," all too well. For

14

those not familiar with this song, it is a story about a father who was too busy to spend time with his son while the son was growing up. The son continues to want to be with his Dad, but ol' Dad is just too busy with work and building his career. Then suddenly one day, Dad looks around and Junior has left home. His son is now out of school and on his own. And, Dad? Well, poor ol' Pops now has time to spend with his son, but you know what? Junior is off the assembly line, out the door and starting to build his own career with no time for his Dad.

Of course, they both meant well. But, like father, like son! What a sad realization that a song like this would indict so many families today. And, by the way, if you haven't listened to this song in awhile, please do. It is certainly worth the time and effort. And don't be surprised, Dad, if it pricks your conscience just a little.

Most parents probably have some idea of what they hope their children will become...what they will be like and what they will do with their lives. They wish only the best for them. However, keep in mind that once the mold is set, it becomes nearly impossible for an unruly or disobedient child to change direction without experiencing some type of calamity or hardship.

Surely there are those who have made great changes in their lives, but usually not until they have experienced some type of significant and destructive circumstance. As an example: once a person is struck with AIDS, it's too late to undo the act that brought on the disease, and an early death is most likely to occur.

Don't most parents hope and pray that their children will be spared from having to experience the devastating effects of AIDS, drug addiction, an auto accident caused by a drunk driver, time in prison, or so many other evils that may result from not having been taught right from wrong during childhood?

Without question, many accidents that happen to us or our children are out of our control. Time and chance happen to us all. But what about the accidents and diseases we experience that are caused by a lack of forethought on our part? What about our selfishness and greed? Or the stupid things we do to ourselves and to others?

The Bible admonishes parents to teach and train their children during the children's youth. We are not to try and change them later in life...when it is too late. The Bible also explains that if properly trained, a child's chances of experiencing sexually transmitted diseases, being arrested for robbery, rape, or worse, or dying before their allotted three score and ten years, greatly decreases.

As parents we are not building cars or managing an assembly line. However, we are charged with a much greater responsibility. And, much in the same way as an automobile on an assembly line must reach certain levels of development within definite time frames, our children will also reach certain physical, emotional, and spiritual development levels within definite time frames. If we are not prepared to help our children reach each new plateau of development at the time it occurs, we will have lost a great opportunity, and more than this, we will have failed as parents.

The answer to the question, "How to become a successful parent" lies only in the faith, dedication, and resolve within the heart and mind of each parent. Ask God to grant you the understanding, wisdom, courage, guidance, strength, and instruction so that you can evolve into the type of parent (or grandparent) you yearn to be.

And may you become the greatest production manager, quality control manager, or factory manager imaginable; and, may your children grow to be victorious, prosperous, and successful because of the time you spent with them and the care, labor, and love you provided!

READ ON!
READ ON!
READ ON!

READ ON!
READ ON!
READ ON!
READ ON!
READ ON!
READ ON!

YOUR KIDS ARE WORTH IT!

BRINGING UP FATHER

"When I was a boy of 14, my father was so ignorant I could hardly stand to have the old man around. But when I got to be 21, I was astonished at how much the old man had learned in seven years."

- Mark Twain

CHAPTER THREE

It's All About Time!
It's All About Time!
It's All About Time!

Time and tide waits for no man, nor will they wait for you or me or for our children! Time passes by so quickly that before we know it the leaves have turned, the air grows colder, and gray fills the color of the sky. And just as the tide moves quickly forward, then out to sea, so go our children into the world!

One day my son and I were talking about something that must have been important to us both when suddenly he asked me, "Dad, with all the work you do, how did you find the time to be with us kids? I mean, you know, where did you get the time to talk and play with us?" After a moment he continued, "I want to spend more time with my family, but when I come home I'm really tired and I find it hard to find the time to stop and play with my kids like I want to. Like you did with us. What can I do?"

A very good question! *"What Can I Do?"* A question asked by so many working parents today. However, as difficult as this problem may be, and realizing that every family has different problems and priorities, there is an answer, and it must begin with parents realizing the *importance* of spending time with their children. If mom or dad doesn't consider taking time to play and talk with their children important enough to do it, then they have a real big problem. A problem that isn't going to fade away, nor is it going to be easily resolved. Taking time away from the self is often very difficult; However, if a parent is ever going to raise successful, intelligent, and loving children, giving quality personal time to their children is something that must be thought out and put into action.

When I was a young boy, I desperately wanted my dad to play with me. But he just never had the time; he always seemed to be at work. He never had the time to play ball, a game of cards, kick-the-can, or even sit down and talk with me. My dad felt that was just "kid's stuff." It didn't seem to interest him. And looking back, I realize I missed part of my youth that only my dad could give me. But, I've also come to understand that he also missed more than he realized. My dad's action (or perhaps a better word might be "inaction") toward me had a lot to do with how I felt as a child, about not wanting to be separated very far from meaningful conversation or sports activities with someone whom I cared deeply about; Also, as I grew older, I recognized the serious need children have in wanting to be close, both physically, and mentally, to their parents. And I promised myself that when I became a father, I *would find the time to be with my kids.* On this particular point I was determined!

"Hey, Dad. Ya wanna fly my kite with me? Okay?"

So I explained to my son that much of what we want for ourselves and others comes from what we experience as children. I desperately wanted time with my dad, but when he was not able to provide the time, I decided then that I would provide for my children what I missed in my childhood. It all comes down to desire, needs, commitment, priorities, and determination.

Another important point to consider is that we only have so much time to teach and train our children about God, His laws, His way of life, His Son, and His Word. There is only so much time to teach and train our children about the physical aspects of life: how to succeed in what they put their hand to do, how to date, who to date, what to look for in a mate, how to work, how to get along with others, how to accept disappointments, how to graciously accept praise and good fortune, how to manage money, how to overcome the many obstacles they will face daily, and so much more.

No responsible parent ever wants their child to enter society totally unprepared...falling short in education, having a negative attitude, lack of ability, and poor character when taking on the responsibility for marriage, employment, living socially with others, and child rearing. Yet, how can parents make sure their child will be prepared? By taking the TIME to *talk, instruct,* and *play* with their kids while they are young!

Before parents know it, their children are grown and beginning to date. And dating, as every parent realizes, often leads to marriage (or we hope it leads to marriage and not just two young people living together while denying certain basic commitments that can result in a family's failure). And marriage, more often than not, leads to the responsibility of having a family...babies born or adopted by the parents .

The question now becomes: "How is my daughter or son ever going to handle being married and taking on the responsibility of a family?" The answer lies to a large degree on how well you taught your child and if you spent enough quality time in conversation and play time.

Looking into the future, we can see why it is so important to properly teach and train our children at every opportunity; it is up to us to *make* each opportunity happen! And at the same time knowing "it ain't gonna be easy!" In fact, it will be very difficult! However, making each moment count and each opportunity happen is something we as parents must do if we ever expect to raise physically, mentally and spiritually successful children.

After we determine the importance of time and just how little there is of it, overriding thoughts occur such as, "How can I not waste any of my precious time? How can I teach my child with what little quality time I have? Where am I ever going to find the time?" All very good questions a parent will ask.

Time is more precious than silver or gold! If you don't believe me, go and ask a person lying in a hospice waiting to die just what they think about time. Or ask an elderly person who just can't believe how quickly time flew by - yesterday she was a young, beautiful mother and today she's an old woman in her late December years. Time is very precious indeed!

But time is one of the special accouterments we must pass on to the next generation...our kids. How do we get the time? Well, we make the time! So often we make the time by perhaps stealing time from some other place, and usually this other place connects only to us. You *give up* yourself and your precious time in order to *give* time to your child. It isn't easy, but it sure is important!

"How can I not waste any of my precious time?" Quality time spent helping a child is never wasted! It is the *quality* of the time that is so very important. If a parent only spends an hour each day with his child and the time spent is quality time, it is worth every minute - and is very precious indeed.

"How can I teach my child with what little time I have?" First of all, take the amount of quality time you have somehow uncovered (probably stolen from yourself) and prioritize what you want to do today with your son or daughter; i.e., we will go shopping, eat out, play ball, fix a toy, see a movie, read together, or just talk. The "just talk" part is really the most important part of quality time between a parent and child.

Also keep in mind "just talking" really means communication. And communication means both parties having the opportunity to speak, and both parties taking the opportunity to listen to what the other has to say. And, hold on to your hats, Mom and Dad! This also means when your little one asks, "why" over and over again, it's up to you to answer in an intelligent manner and not just put your child off with some casual and thoughtless reply. Remember, no one said it was going to be easy!

Using the instruction manual that our Creator gave us so that we might have the proper direction and answers for situations such as raising children, we are admonished, *"These commandments that I give to you today are to be upon your hearts. Impress them on your children (teach them diligently to your children). Talk about them when you sit at home and when you walk along the road, when you lie down and when you get up"*. (Deu. 6:6-7 NIV)

Through these commandments God is telling us something that is very important, and He is also instructing us as parents. He is telling us to take advantage of every opportunity we have to instruct and help mold our children. He is also letting us know that He has provided us with laws and commandments that will help us as parents and our children live fruitful and prosperous lives. If we parents hope to achieve true success in raising our children, we must put this knowledge and instruction into action...we must use it!

We cannot allow the advantage of growing closer as a family slip away. God admonishes parents to be with their children, to spend time with them and not follow the type of attitude that prevails today where so many parents give their kids a few bucks and then send them off to do whatever just as long as they don't pester ol' Mom or Dad.

Parents, above all else, don't waste your valuable time with meaningless activities and foolish projects that are time-consuming and will most likely be forgotten tomorrow. Rather, spend your time when you are away from your job with your kids. Take a walk or hike with them. Talk to them. Learn from them. Tell them about yourself, their grandparents and relatives; tell them how they looked and acted when they were little babies; help them get to know who they are and how much they mean to you. Make sure you always tuck your little ones in bed at night, tell them a story, and also teach them how to pray before going to sleep.

And by all means show them affection...kiss them and hug them and when they grow older never stop demonstrating your love toward them. The time will arrive when your child is going to become embarrassed when you outwardly express your affection for them. However, if you have shown affection and love to your children from the time they were little tots and carried it through into their teens, even though they might be somewhat embarrassed by an open demonstration of affection from Mom and Dad in front of their friends, they will nevertheless yearn for it throughout their lives. Ask yourself, don't you really appreciate receiving affection from your folks? Even today?

Just how much time do we have as parents to properly train and raise our children? From the time a child is born until age 18 we parents have approximately 216 months to prepare them for adulthood. (I mean, today, some auto leases seem nearly that long!) If we only teach our children one hour a day those things that are necessary in order for them to live, mature, and succeed in life (how to eat, what to eat, how to overcome, how to live, who or what God is, how to complete difficult studies at school, etc.), we have *less than one year of actual teaching time* to supply the knowledge and understanding, not just theoretical or academic reasoning, that will provide the type of support system they will stand on for the rest of their lives! What a sobering thought!

So, we are beginning to understand that we have little or no time to waste! We must talk with our children when they are in the house, when driving to the store, when they go to bed. And we must play with them at every opportunity. How do we find the time? We must look for...indeed manufacture if necessary...the opportunities to have enough quality time to teach, instruct, and play with our little loved ones. And above all, we must always let them be children - allow them to have their youth. And we must be a *real part of their lives!*

To drive this time subject home a little further: do you have any idea what the average amount of time each day parents living in the United States spend teaching, instructing, and playing with their children? Would you believe the average time spent with their kids is only 37 SECONDS A DAY! Unbelievable isn't it? Nevertheless, it's true!

24

With such an infinitesimal amount of time many modern-day parents spend teaching and playing with their kids, is it any wonder so many of them are failing school, dropping out, shooting teachers, abusing drugs, becoming involved in illicit sex, breaking laws, and causing harm to themselves and others? Does this type of upbringing give cause for a young person to merely exist by living a disobedient, rootless, and unstable life? Could this be the reason why so many young people are living dangerously on the edge, and why so many are also taking their own lives by suicide, drug overdose, or various other means of self destruction?

I realize that some readers don't, or won't, believe that in this world there is a great unseen power who desperately seeks to control your child's fertile mind and then instruct it his way. Who is this being? The god of this world is Satan.

Satan has plenty of time to attack and destroy our children, and he has all the tools and equipment necessary to do it. He provides our kids with idle hours so they can listen to certain types of negative and harmful music; hours of sitting alone watching television, videos, or films (often "R" rated or bordering on pornographic); freedom to run around with a gang of kids who have also been left alone and neglected and who, for the sake of boredom, can sometimes be very violent. Then he provides that big inducement that can cause a young person, male or female, considerable misery, pain, and suffering...that of being tempted to fall into a snare of immature sexual desire and passion. And, what do our kids have to help support and protect them against such temptation? **37 seconds a day** of guidance, play time, instruction, and involvement from their parents!

Many parents actually believe that an hour or so in church once a week will solve the problems they may be experiencing with their kids. Will it? Isn't there a little more to it than simply hoping or praying once in a while that everything will be okay and that given enough time junior will stop being so rebellious? Thinking about the problem is certainly a start, and praying about it is very important; however, if we are to actually ever resolve this problem, won't it take considerable action and involvement on our part as parents?

25

When children are left alone to come under the influence of Satan, is it any wonder they rebel against authority. Satan did! When so little time is spent teaching and instructing a child in the way he or she should properly live his or her lives, is it also any wonder that Satan's attitude and influence might have the ease of access to penetrate the minds of our children? If we only spend 37 seconds a day with our kids, we are allowing Satan the freedom to approach their minds and to persuade and sway them. It is our responsibility to not allow this to happen!

I remember some of the best times I ever experienced were the occasions when I talked with my children during family outings or on long hikes in the woods. One particularly beautiful area where we enjoyed hiking was about a mile's walk into the woods. Was it ever beautiful! Giant firs, cedars, and hemlocks completely surrounded us. These trees were so large that an adult couldn't stretch his arms around the trunk. All around us there was a clean, fresh fragrance that seemed to float in the air. And the area where we often camped had a wide stream that roared as it pounded over rocks and fallen logs.

As a family we would camp there several times a year. We would hunker around the campfire and talk about life, or we would sit on a large boulder in the middle of the stream fishing and talking about anything the kids wanted to discuss. Girls, boys, school, dates, fights, jobs, their futures, personal fears and desires, it didn't matter, we just talked. And you know what? Not only did my kids enjoy this quality time, but ol' Mom and Dad also took great delight and pleasure in every moment.

To this day my children remember those times and the things we all talked about. Did it make a deep impression on them? You bet it did! And just as important, did I personally gain from this experience? You bet I did!

Today, more than a few parents moan and groan about not having time to spend with their kids. They say, unlike a few years ago, times are different and there's more pressure now to do the job and perform at work. They swear there just isn't time to go into the woods or to the beach with the kids; not if they are going to work and support their family.

Indeed, times are different. But this doesn't mean they are better or even worse. It also doesn't mean parents ten or fifteen years ago didn't have hard times when raising their children. While I was raising my kids we had schedules to keep, work to perform, and a company that kept the pressure on. Still, I had to ask myself, "What is more important, a good paying job or my family?" I chose my family, and if given the same circumstance today, I would again choose to support and be with my family. The benefits my children and my wife and I received from my having opted to make less money and to spend more time with our kids far exceeded any new house, luxury car, latest model TV or stereo component, expensive wardrobe, or any jet setting experience could ever provide.

Today, most adults have opted for the wealth and pleasure of physical objects and the desire to be viewed by their peers as being materialistically prosperous and academically successful. Although material wealth and academic learning are not of themselves wrong, what is wrong is when this wealth and affluence comes at the expense of neglecting and ignoring the greatest achievement and blessing known to man...the proper raising of our children! The care and training of God's little ones!

Parents who dearly love their children want more than anything for each child to grow and succeed to as great a level of spiritual and mental competency as possible. We parents also hope and pray that our children will grow to be loving and understanding parents themselves; that they will have a strong and compatible marriage...be a devoted and faithful husband or wife to a loving and caring spouse; and that they will take the time to raise happy and respectful children. We also want our children to succeed far above whatever meaningful accomplishments we were able to achieve.

A parent asks, "When is my child ever going to be ready to be out on his own? When is he going to be prepared to fight off all those problems and difficulties I know he is going to face in life?"

The answer was given to parents hundreds of years ago when they asked the same questions: our children are only going to be prepared for life "when we teach them at every opportunity, when we walk with them, when we talk with them, when we sit in the house, when we lie down, when we put them before our very self...." then they will be prepared to go out; then they will be prepared to overcome and lead a successful life.

Remember, again, time and tide waits for no man. It is no different when it comes to raising our children. Time flies by, while the tide pushes us toward the grave. So let's not let our children be washed out to sea where they could drown with the cares and dangers of this world. Provide them with that special life preserver that will help keep them safe from suffering and destruction...give them your time beginning TODAY!

The Time Is Brief

Because the longest life is brief
I must be swift in keeping
The little trysts with kindliness,
Before the time of sleeping!

I must be swift in reaching out,
To those whose hearts are yearning;
O, swift indeed to love them much
Before the long road's turning!

Before a sudden summons comes,
I surely must be saying
The words that I have failed to say -
The prayers I should be praying.

Grace Noll Crowell

A SIMPLE LIST
for
MOM and DAD!

Here is a list of suggested things you might consider doing with your children.
(see if any of these have gone unnoticed.)

Grade yourself!

		Good	Fair	Poor
1-	Talking with my child:	____	____	____
2-	The entire family at the dinner table:	____	____	____
3-	Quality time with my child when he comes home from school:	____	____	____
4-	Tucking my little one in bed:	____	____	____
5-	Evening prayer and talk about God, family, friends:	____	____	____
6-	Play time (together):	____	____	____
7-	Watching television (together):	____	____	____
	Listening to music (together):	____	____	____
	Playing a video game (together):	____	____	____

		Good	Fair	Poor
8-	Playing games outside the house (together):	___	___	___
9-	Taking a walk together:	___	___	___
10-	Going on a hike, to the beach, or to the woods with my child (just the two of us):	___	___	___
	(as a family):	___	___	___
11-	Teaching my children to do the chores:	___	___	___
12-	Working in the yard together:	___	___	___
13-	Doing school activities together:	___	___	___
14-	Helping with school work (if I can understand how):	___	___	___
15-	Fishing together:	___	___	___
16-	Hunting together:	___	___	___
17-	Sewing together:	___	___	___
18-	Letting my child help me cook dinner:	___	___	___
	Letting my child cook the dinner:	___	___	___
19-	Setting the table;	___	___	___
	Washing/drying the dishes:	___	___	___
20-	Picnicing together:	___	___	___
21-	Washing the car together:	___	___	___

		Good	Fair	Poor
22-	Shopping together:	____	____	____
23-	Doing hobbies together:	____	____	____
24-	Flying a kite together:	____	____	____
25-	Supporting my child in his or her sports:	____	____	____
26-	Teaching my teenager to drive:	____	____	____
27-	Talking with my child while driving:	____	____	____
28-	Giving my child a big part of my life!	____	____	____

There are only 28 suggestions listed above; but, if you stop for a moment and think about it, I'm sure you'll come up with several more ways to spend time with your children.

Don't tell yourself this is just "kids' stuff." There are so many important lessons and good times that can be experienced in every activity a parent and child share together. Establish a pattern early on while your children are still young and growing and have such receptive and fertile minds; where and when you talk together, play together, cry together, laugh together, and learn together; then relate with them on all those important issues and even the nonsensical and sometimes foolish ideas and notions that a child comes up with. The magnificence and splendor of this amazing adventure will remain with you forever as a major achievement in both your and your children's lives!

What Would You Take?

What would you take for that soft little head
Pressed close to your face at time for bed;
For that small, dimpled hand in your own held tight,
And the dear little eyelids kissed down for the night?
What would you take?

What would you take for that smile in the morn,
Those bright, dancing eyes and the face they adorn:
For the sweet little voice that you hear all day
Laughing and cooing - yet nothing to say?
What would you take?

What would you take for those pink little feet,
Those chubby round cheeks, and that mouth so sweet;
For the wee tiny fingers and little soft toes,
The wrinkly little neck and that funny little nose?
Now, what would you take?

Good Housekeeping

CHAPTER FOUR

The Human Mind
and
a Kid's Brain!
Are they one and the same?

The human mind is a fabulous piece of inspired creativity and perfected workmanship. Nothing in this world can compare with it...nothing ever has and never will. Computers are highly sophisticated, mechanical devices that stagger the imagination, and they can accomplish objectives for the good and the not-so-good of society . With today's super computers we can send rockets to the moon, pinpoint ballistic artillery projections, keep a hundred million dollar jet fighter on course, tabulate this country's national debt, and manage or control many other highly technological operations. And yet, let's not forget that the computer was created, researched, and developed by the power and intellect of the HUMAN MIND. Some power!

What is really interesting is this great brain power (what we call the "mind") was also created. God created it just as He did the nervous system, respiratory system, vascular system, vision, hearing and every other function of the human body. The brain with its amazing abilities, including reasoning and creativity, is part of our body when we are born. It comes free of charge, but with a very interesting and profound obligation attached. We are responsible for how we manage our mind and what we do with it.

So often when we don't have to pay for something, we don't always see the value in it. I suppose that if we had to pay a million dollars for our brain, we would probably take better care of it...we certainly would provide it healthier nourishment, exercise it daily, and no doubt do all that we could to carefully evaluate what enters into its memory banks. We would also make sure our brain was kept in good working order...clean from dust, cobwebs, and any type of sludge or grime, just as we do with our computers and other expensive technical equipment.

This brings up an interesting question: are we doing everything possible to guide, protect, and keep healthy the minds of our children? As parents and guardians, are we not responsible for the material and information that enter into our children's minds? As we consider their expanding brains (physical) and forging minds (spiritual) to be of such value and importance, should we not truly seek to safeguard them at all costs?

Let's take a moment and explore a folksy, down home, easy to understand example: when a child is born, unless there has been some type of physical brain damage due to something happening prior to birth or during the birthing process, the brain is much like a fertile, yet uncultivated field. The baby's mind has been prepared by the One who created it to produce fruit...to develop intellect and creativity.

Now, just as the uncultivated field doesn't know what is going to be planted into its soil, neither does an infant know what is going to be planted into it's mind. The baby doesn't look up at Mom or Dad and simply ask, "Hey folks, like, whatta ya putting into my gray matter today?" Like the analogy of the field, the baby just lies there waiting for the parents (the farmer) to begin planting its (his or her) seeds.

After waiting for the ground to clear and the weather to warm (the baby's birth), the farmer begins planting. Let's say that the farmer decides to plant wheat and nightshade. Wheat for human consumption and nightshade which is a deadly poison. The soil certainly doesn't know the difference between a rich food product or a deadly poison. In fact, it's strictly up to the farmer as to what goes into his soil and what doesn't.

If properly watered and cultivated, both seeds will grow and mature. One for food, the other for poison. And just as the heart of a tiny baby nurtures the body, the soil will also nourish and strengthen

34

both the wheat and nightshade seeds.

A child's mind can be viewed as being similar to the farmer's field. It never asks, "Hey, what kind of seed are ya putting into my field?". It doesn't understand what good seeds are and what kind of crop they will produce, nor does it understand what kind of damage a bad seed can cause.

Ask yourself, "What kind of seeds am I allowing to go into my young child's mind? Are these seeds, which I realize will soon begin to grow and mature and directly affect my child's life, pure? Are they toxic or nontoxic? Are they healthy? Are they the type of seeds that I want going into my child's brain?"

When a seed is planted into the soil, it takes considerable time for it to grow, mature, and finally produce fruit. If a seed is immature or poisonous, it may not only bear poor fruit but may also damage the good fruit. It's the same with the mind of a small child. The type of *fruit* (deeds, ability, character, honesty, etc.) your child will produce greatly depends on what type of *seed* (outside influences including music, films, education, TV, friends, etc.) you, as the child's guardian (the farmer), allow to enter into his or her mind. This is a great responsibility that God has placed in our trust, and one that we must take very seriously. How our kids turn out later in life has everything to do with how we manage and control what goes into their minds today .

Right about now I can hear some readers thinking to themselves, "Hey, wait a minute! I'm not going to suppress my kid's growth by controlling what he views or dictating what she participates in! I mean, we left the Victorian era (attitude) years ago!"

Well, to this reader all I can say is you're absolutely right. We did leave the Victorian age years ago. And its true, much of what was going on during that time in history wasn't all that great...especially for the young people. However, look around at society today. Why do you think we parents are having so many problems with our children? Why is there such lawlessness, crime, and disobedience with so many of our kids? Don't you think that just maybe the way parents have neglected their responsibilities toward raising and providing their children COMPASSION, DIRECTION, UNCONDITIONAL LOVE, GUIDANCE, and DISCIPLINE might have something to do with the way things are? By not properly training them, which may also mean having to gently yet firmly admonish or punish them when he or she seems to be heading the wrong way...could this indeed be part of the reason for the severe problems we and our children are now facing?

What do you do when your child is going to touch a hot stove? What about the day when you see him going into a street after you have told him several times not to? Do you take him aside and try to explain in a calm and intelligent manner, as you might an adult, that he had better not do that because some big ol' nasty car might run over his little body and kill him? And if you do, how do you respond when junior looks up at you and says, "Daddy, what does kill mean?" Do we parents really believe that our young tots are able to reason in such a manner that they have no need for either admonishment or punishment, or that a small child is actually able to think out all the different ramifications that might result from an immature and thoughtless act?

I believe - and my experience with counseling young people and their parents supports this belief - that we have come to a point where society has put so much negative pressure on the parents not to punish or discipline their children that little or no discipline is being administered in the home.

There are parents who abuse their children. This is wrong! It is harmful and destructive! There is absolutely no reason for a parent to ever physically or mentally abuse a child. However, it is also wrong for a loving and supportive parent to allow the way some misguided parents treat their children to influence the way in which they admonish, discipline and train their children! (More about this subject later).

The Bible gives us an interesting illustration regarding how things that go into our minds influence our actions. In other words, how we react to an experience.

For example: we have been taught that Adam and Eve were the first humans God created (no Junior, I don't care what your teacher says, we didn't come from an Ape or some swinging Orangutan!) These were our first parents. We also remember how Satan's deception led Adam and Eve to sin. Somehow these two near-perfect human beings became influenced by some rotten seed entering their minds! In this case, it was the seed of deception!

And just as Adam and Eve fell into disobedience and sinned, so did one of their sons, Cain. Did you ever wonder why Cain killed his brother Abel? Who planted the seed that infected Cain's mind to the point where he would commit the very first murder? Who caused Cain to become so jealous and angry that he would do such a terrible deed? Who was responsible for protecting Cain, for guiding his life, for teaching him the ways of God, for showing him love, for instructing him as to how to live his life in a proper and appropriate manner? The answer is, it was the only other humans alive...his parents, Adam and Eve!

Let's put ourselves into a more modern "Garden of Eden" situation: here you are, a very prosperous man or woman and you own a very large farm. The soil is the richest and most fertile in all the county. You also have several winning race horses and more farm machinery and equipment than all your neighbors combined. And let's not forget the boat, plane, and luxury cars. You have everything your heart desires, yet a problem remains...it's not paid for!

Without notice, the day comes when your spouse loses his job and within a very short period of time your family loses everything. I mean everything! What do you do? Cry? Yell? Hit something or someone? Scream profanities? Become very bitter? Run and hide? Want to kill someone? Maybe your spouse? Maybe yourself? Or, maybe your brother?!

Could it be that after Adam and Eve lost everything because

37

of their sin, they failed to teach their firstborn son Cain the correct way to live? The proper way of serving and showing love and compassion toward his parents and brother? Could it be that both parents were so caught up in their own failed lives that they neglected the needs of their older son Cain? Not only had they planted into their oldest son's mind hostile and corrupt seeds, they apparently were not aware of the negative seeds which were also being planted into Cain's mind by a very evil force. The same force that had deceived both Adam and Eve! The question is, are we ever like Adam and Eve in this regard? Do we let what happens to us affect the way we treat others? Or, the way we treat our kids?!

"What you allow to be sown is what you will also reap!" (Paraphrased). This is telling us that whatever we allow to grow and mature in our child's mind is what will be produced sooner or later: for good or for evil. And just like the wise farmer who understands that reaping a high yield on his crop is what will keep him and his family from bankruptcy and possible starvation and death, and that the only way to reap a high yield is to plant healthy seeds, we parents must also plant good, healthy seeds into our children's minds so that there is simply no room for negative and rotten seeds to take root.

Make sure you know what your child is watching on television, seeing at a movie, or listening to on the radio or tape machine. Know who your children's friends are and get to know them and their parents well enough to decide if there is common ground for nurturing a solid and decent friendship. Oversee your children's activities. And remember, not everything in this world is lovely, safe, or decent.

Some parents say that it is impossible to protect children from all the evil that is perpetrated against them today. Perhaps we can't protect our kids from all the filth and garbage they will come into contact with; however, a rotten seed has a better chance to take root and grow when someone other than the parent is doing the planting. So what if we can't protect our kids from all the bad stuff out there, we can protect them from the really harmful and destructive trash

38

and rubbish that seems bent on destroying them. But only if we have a mind to, and then we do it!

Finally, just how receptive is a young person's mind? How active is a kid's brain?

One of my sons is raising two young boys, and I'm somewhat proud to boast that my son and his wife work daily with their children planting healthy seeds (quality information and expressions of love) into their young minds.

My grandsons each have a set of flash cards their parents developed to help teach them. The cards have a variety of large and small lettered words printed on one side. Well, by the time both boys were between the age of 2 and 4, they fully understood each word and what it meant (do I sound like a proud grandfather?!). A young active mind is one powerful piece of creation! Not every mind will develop into a mathematical genius nor every child become a computer programmer; however, with all the data and information regarding the brain and its awesome complexity and great potential, even children born with mental disabilities are now being taught how to use their minds...how to let the brain function to its full potential!

Each and everyone reading this book started out as a baby with a tiny brain and very little in it. Some of you have gone through hardships and difficult times that might not have been necessary had someone planted positive and healthy seeds in your mind when you were small...when your mind was fertile and very receptive.

Some reading this book had parents who took the time and energy to protect and filter what went into your mind. You were fortunate because your parents planted fertile and healthy seeds. And they cultivated those seeds in order that each one would grow and mature so that you might avoid having to experience self-induced hardships or mental problems. If you are one of these readers, you must agree that what is planted in the mind of a young child will have a very special impact on the way a child matures, behaves, and succeeds in life.

PLANTING SEEDS in OUR CHILDREN

If you desire successful children, plant a successful SEED.
If you want obedient children, plant the obedient SEED.
If you want your child to become a leader in society, plant the leader SEED.
If you want your child to be courageous, decent, and kind, plant courageous, decent, and kind SEEDS.
If you want your children to know and love God, plant righteous and loving SEEDS!

So, Mom and Dad, keep your eyes and ears open regarding your children and their place on this Earth. Be sure to take full responsibility of overseeing and managing the planting of only good, healthy seeds into your children's most fertile and precious possession...their Minds! Take good care of your Kid's Amazing Brain!

"TO EDUCATE A MAN IN MIND
AND
NOT IN MORALS
IS
TO EDUCATE
A
MENACE TO SOCIETY!"

Theodore Roosevelt

CHAPTER FIVE

The Importance of Communication!

I cannot over emphasize the tremendous importance of communicating WITH your children on a daily basis. And as a word of caution, be prepared for what comes out of the mouths of little babes today. In this modern day of high technology and instant communication via television and the satellite dish, children have an incredible variety of influence and mental stimulation more than ever before. We parents for the most part accept the fact that two plus two equals four; however, our children not only understand basic arithmetic, they also want to know the reasoning behind the equation. "Why does two plus two equal four?" "Prove it!" And, if you decide to try and prove it using today's modern math methods, I wish you well!

The best way to really get to know our children is by talking *with* them, never *to* them. Of course, there is a time and place for everything. There is a time when talking *to* your child is important...like the time Junior disobeyed Dad and decided to run out into the street. A time to talk *to* your child? You bet it is! No time like the present! Still, even during times of punishment and reproof, communication plays a very important part in child rearing.

Little Johnny dashes into the street where he nearly gets hit by an oncoming bus. Well, as soon as Dad's heart stops pounding and he is able to breathe again, he immediately decides that punishment is the order of the day. Communication (verbal interaction between the father and son) now comes into play because it is very important that little Johnny understands why he is going to be punished. He needs to know what the punishment is going to be, how long the punishment will be, and most important, that Dad still loves and cares for him very much.

41

"You mean you also had bad days when you went to school?!"

Just what does communicating really mean? What does talking *with* a child mean and how is it so different from talking *to* a child? When parents talk *with* their children, they must be willing to *listen* to what *they* are saying. This is as important as parents telling their children what is on *their* minds. Communication goes both ways...listening and speaking!

Remember the scenario about little Johnny running into the street? What if little Johnny really didn't disobey his dad on purpose? What if he saw a small puppy about to be run over by the bus and he thought he might be able to save the dog? Wouldn't understanding the circumstance from his son's point of view help dad refrain from becoming overly emotional and possibly punishing his son more severely than might be necessary? Unless dad takes the time, even while emotionally stressed out, to listen to his son's explanation as to why he did what he did, ol' Dad just might make a harmful mistake in the manner in which he punishes his child. Little Johnny should not have ran into the street no matter what the reason. However, after listening to his son, dad can now see that his intentions were well meaning...and in order to be fair, he now realizes he must give his son points for "well meaning intentions!" This then translates into a lesser type of punishment which is good for both little Johnny as well as his dad.

An important part of communication is trusting the other person. Unless little Johnny feels that his parents will really listen to him (and this is only going to happen if both parents have a solid track record of listening to their son or daughter), he is not going to trust them and will probably make up a story about what happened or just simply remain silent. And it's so much better when our kids want to tell us the truth. By communicating their mistakes, their hopes and feelings without fear that we'll make fun of them or put them down, children learn to trust us, and they don't feel the need to lie whenever they imagine they are going to be punished by mom or dad.

As a minister and parent, many young people come to me with a need to talk. And, sad to say, some of these kids really don't have anyone else to whom they can go.

I recall one young person in particular who said, "I can't talk with my Mom or Dad! I mean, you know, they appear to listen, but they really don't hear what I'm sayin'. It's like I'm just some dumb kid that's too young to know anything worthwhile listenin' to. Don't they know what I have to say is also important...to me anyway!"

Too many parents have the attitude that the only important problems are the problems that lie directly on their shoulders...that they are the only ones in a family who face difficult situations on a daily basis. These parents just don't seem to realize that kids are little human beings who sometimes have very big problems.

"I need someone to talk with!" "I need someone who will listen to what I have to say!" "Oh, sure. Mom and Dad expect me to listen to them, but how can I when they just yell and holler at me?!" "It's getting to the point where I just don't want to hear what they have to say anymore; and besides, why should I? I mean, they never listen to me!" These are just some of the comments I hear so often from teenagers. And as I take a moment to reflect on what I see and what I hear from so many troubled kids, I see a terrible situation looming ahead for our country, indeed, for almost every nation. The character, disposition, apathy, and attitude of so many of our youth today, unless transformed soon, will only produce a society that worsens with each generation.

One young teenager I spoke to had tears in his eyes as he cried out to me about how he desperately wanted to communicate with his parents. But, he felt he couldn't because they wouldn't listen to him. They just wouldn't take the time to *hear* what their son was trying to tell them. It takes time, compassion, and a "whole lotta love" to communicate with a young person. And, yet, when this young person is our very own child...why is it so often we won't listen to what he or she has to say?!

Over the past several years, I have heard so many stories like the one this young man confessed that when I realize the pain felt by a boy or girl whose parents just don't seem to care, and that there is little I can do to remedy the situation, it just breaks my heart!

Take a moment and ask yourself, "When was the last time I really sat down and talked with my son or daughter, or grandchild?" Or, "When was the last time I told my kid that I really cared about how he was doing in school and that I loved him and I was thankful to be his parent, and I also wanted to be his friend?"

Also ask yourself, when you were young and impressionable, who was your closest friend? Who did you want to share your problems and those deep-seated feelings with? Wasn't it to that one person to whom you could bare your soul, a caring human being who wouldn't laugh or ridicule what you said or how you said it? Someone whom you could trust?

Sometimes, if you will take a moment to remember your youth, you will no doubt discover that just like you did, your children also experience an abundance of excitable emotions, deep feelings and serious problems. And just like you, they also have fears, anxieties and doubts; except today there is one major difference. Unlike the age when most parents reading this book attended school, our children go to schools where drug dealers roam the halls looking for unsuspecting prey, students carry guns and often use them on their teachers and peers, girls as young as ten and eleven years of age become pregnant. In some schools teachers have been found guilty of molesting their young charges, filthy and violent language is common place, and disobedience is a way of life. Unless a child is able to articulate his or her feelings and fears to someone who really cares, the possibility of ending up in prison, the hospital, or dead at a young age is very real!

Right about now you may be thinking, "Okay. I see the problem and I know I have to communicate with my child. But where do I begin?" Well, how about going back and rereading our previous chapter regarding time? First of all, you must understand that you have to make the time available before you will ever really be able to communicate with your son or daughter.

Next, you must realize that the problems your children are facing in this speeded up, hi-tech, morally decadent world are very real. Not only are these problems real to your child, they can be enormous! Remember, as a parent and adult, you have years of experience which helps you find solutions so that you are able to resolve most of your short term and long term problems. Granted it isn't easy, but your maturity and experience will help you through most situations. On the other side of the coin, your children have little or no experience with which to fight and overcome the problems they must face, and the problems they face can be very serious!

This is where listening becomes important. If you haven't been a good listener in the past, make every effort to begin listening...*listening*...to your children today. Overcoming the problem of not listening to your kids is somewhat similar to having a hearing problem before you finally purchase a Belltone hearing aid and suddenly discover that the world of communication somehow seems to just open up. Well, listening to your children can be much the same. After hearing what they have to say, all that wonderful information that is roaming around in their fertile minds and brains is like having the world of entertainment and understanding open up to you. Another thing you will find as you begin listening to your children - they have a whole lot more interesting things to say than television does .

Learn to listen with your eyes as well as with your ears! "Whatta ya mean, with my eyes?!" Believe it or not, your eyes can play a very important part in how well you communicate with your kids.

45

As you sit down to talk with your children, be aware of everything that is taking place around you...the manner in which your son may fidget while he hunts for the right word to say, or the way your daughter waits for your response after she has made what she believes to be an outstanding reply to your comment. Watch with your eyes what your children are saying.

Another thing to look for while communicating with your child has to do with attitude. Does he look sullen and make a long face as he tries to make you feel guilty about something you did that he doesn't agree with? Does your daughter seem overly nervous as she tries to explain why she arrived home later than what was agreed upon before going out on a date? If your kid becomes angry and frustrated during his conversation with you and suddenly stomps out of the room slamming the door behind him, this should be a pretty good clue that something is very wrong. In all these situations, we both *hear* and *see* the emotional response from a child. Both hearing and seeing a conversation are two very necessary elements if we are to have true communication with our children!

We parents must lay the groundwork for good communication with our kids early on in their young lives. It must begin when a child is still a toddler (in fact, there is some evidence that talking and singing to the baby while it is still in the womb has a positive effect on its mental and creative abilities after birth).

Part of the groundwork for good communication with your child is to make every effort to answer his or her questions when asked. Never put off your son or daughter simply by saying, "Not now!" Or, "Go ask your Mom!" "I don't know, go look it up in some book!" And never give them the feeling or impression that what they are asking is dumb or stupid. Always encourage your child by letting him or her know that you appreciate the question...that it is a good question and worth your attention and time.

If you asked someone about something that was very important to you and they responded with some "off the wall" thoughtless comment, how long would it be before you no longer had any desire to be around that person, let alone ask him any more questions?   Remember, if you always put yourself in your child's mind when he or she has come to you with a question, you will invariably know how best to respond and know exactly what to say.

I recall a time when my youngest daughter was in the sixth grade and she came running home from school all excited. It seems she had just met a new boy and was suddenly in love! I'll tell you, she was really excited!

Now, my being much older and wiser, I knew that an eleven-year-old girl would meet many more boys throughout her school years with whom she would certainly think she was in love. I could have very easily told her that she was too young to think about boys (man, that would have gone over like a lead balloon) or tried to reason with her that she would meet more boys later in life with whom she would also think she was in love (this comment would have caused a lot of tears and hurt feelings).   By some careless remark, I could have harmed or destroyed what was beginning to be a very trusting, wonderful, and precious relationship with my daughter.

Instead, I picked her up and sat her on my lap and asked, "Tell me, Honey. What's he like? How did you meet him? Is he in your class at school?" I found out all I could about this boy who had stolen my daughter's heart (for the moment) and who was also very important to her.

I took the time that afternoon to talk with my young daughter about dating, including how her mother and I felt about it. I also carefully kidded her. "Does your friend have a job? Does he have any money? I mean, you know, it takes quite a bit of money for two people to live comfortably?" Well, she just looked straight at me and replied, "Of course not Daddy. After all, he's still in grade school...he's too young to work at a job!"

The issue that day wasn't that I knew my daughter was too young to be in love and that she would have several boyfriends before she ever got serious about one specific fellow. The issue was my daughter's feelings and that she felt the need to talk with me about something very important to her, especially at that particular time in her life.

Do you remember the first person you ever thought you were in love with? I sure do. She was in the third grade and the cutest girl in class. I laugh about it now, but back then it was very serious business! And, it is the same with our children today. When they have something to say, take the time to talk about whatever it is they are so interested in. And you know something? You will also discover some very valuable lessons and gain understanding by sharing this important moment with your young loved one.

One of my sons once caught me off guard when he told me how very much he appreciated the way that I listened to what he had to say, and that I showed real interest when he spoke out about his opinions. He said, "You know, Dad, even when I knew you didn't agree with me, you still listened." He thought for a moment and then added, "Because you listened to me, I'm willing to listen to you. In fact, it helped me want to do whatever it was you wanted me to do. And most of the time, I wanted to do it your way!" After talking for a while, and as we were getting ready to go our separate ways, he off to school and me to work, he concluded, "Thanks, Dad, for listening!" See what I mean about catching me off guard? And it's with a great amount of pleasure that I can also record that because of my son's attitude, there were many times we did whatever we were doing...his way!

When parents work with their children, their children want to please them. When we pay attention to our kids and really listen to what they are saying, they want to talk and tell us about themselves all the more. It's almost like we're saying to them, "You know son, you have some really good ideas. I like what you're saying...it has value and worth!"

Children, just like adults, need encouragement. If you encourage your youngster by listening to him or her, I promise it will improve your relationship and communication not only for the two of you but for the entire family!

There are times when your child comes home really excited about something, and she just can't wait to tell you about it. This is the time to stop whatever it is you are doing, pick her up, sit her on your lap, and listen! Of course, if she is too big to pick up, then sit down together, stand in the kitchen, take a walk, or whatever; But, by all means, listen, listen, listen!

Remember, God gave us the gift of speech for a purpose. It has been referred to as "the mirror of the soul (Publilius Syrus)," "the image of life (Democritus)," "a faculty given to man to conceal his thoughts (Talleyrand)," and "but broken light upon the depth of the unspoken (G. Eliot)." Therefore, speech, especially with our family and children, is of primary importance in living a good life!

There is another problem regarding early communication with our children that I have noticed over the years: when a child is learning to talk, he will most often use improper grammar. As an example, he might say something like, "Daddy, I runned more faster to the store than Jimmy." Believe it or not, I have heard parents reply to their little tot, "Now, if you can't say it properly, don't say it at all!" Wow, what a mistake!

We should never discourage a child from talking to us, no matter what! They love to talk and they need to talk. And besides, I haven't met that many parents who consistently use proper grammar themselves. I don't; do you?!

However, this is not to say that we should speak "goo-goo, gaa-gaa" baby talk to our children when they are old enough to begin learning proper elocution and how to enunciate more difficult words. We should always use words our children understand, otherwise there just isn't going to be a lot of communicating going on between us and our kids; and we might even impair their learning abilities.

A good time to improve family communication is during dinner...and with the TV OFF! No television during dinner! Oh, oh! I can already hear a reader thinking, "Whatta ya mean, talking during dinner?! We don't even eat dinner together! How am I gonna

49

talk to my kids when they are never there?!" Yep, you do have a problem! The best thing might be for you to start setting your priorities straight so that at least several times a week you have dinner, lunch, or breakfast as a family.

You know, unless we make the commitment to change our habits and set up workable and productive communication with family-related priorities, nothing will ever change. We will remain mired in ignorance and our lives will be stalled in a status quo position. Our kids will suffer, our entire family will suffer, and indeed, we, personally, will suffer! And this book, or any other book regarding helpful information for raising our children, will be of little or no benefit!

Okay, now that I've made my "change of habit" and "setting of priorities" speech, it's time to return to "communicating at the dinner table."

You will soon discover, Mom and Dad, as you begin having talks over spaghetti, French bread, cutup veggies, cereal, or a peanut butter sandwich that because you are sitting at the dinner table as a family doesn't mean Junior is prepared to talk about himself or listen to what you have to say. Who knows, Junior may have had a bad day in school, Susie may feel too embarrassed to just sit and talk about what she considers to be nothing worthwhile, or they may surprise you and not stop talking until dinner is over, the dishes are put away, and it's time for bed. The point is, we should set a priority to have time with our children, preferably at the dinner table, to talk and listen. You talk, they listen; they talk, you listen.

I know a lady who has been a first grade teacher for over thirty years. She told me during one of our many conversations that the greatest problem in teaching young people today is that they have never been properly taught to listen. "If the children today had been taught to listen, I wouldn't have any problem teaching them. In fact, those children who have been properly instructed at home about how to listen are the ones who I have watched become successful and prosperous as they grew older."

50

When I asked her how she knew this to be true, she replied, "It's easy. I remember the children in my class. Remember, I've lived and taught in the area for nearly forty years! I know the children and their parents. I know which parents worked with their kids at home and those who didn't." Then she looked me straight in the eye in a coy fashion and added, "Besides, I have an excellent memory!"

This gracious lady who taught school for so many years went on to tell me about how many students she had taught who went on to college, good careers, and successful marriages. She also told me the importance of teaching children how to sit quietly and listen to what others are saying because this one way a child will learn about others, themselves, and about life.

This is how my wife and I taught our children how to sit quietly and listen: when they were very small, we would sit them down on a blanket for a certain length of time and tell them that it was time for them to "sit on the blanket and be quiet. It is not play time!" We started by making them only sit for a short period of time. Then, we slowly increased the amount of time as each child grew to a better understanding of the instruction. At first, it was a little difficult for our children and us. However, with patience and perseverance, we were able to accomplish our teaching goal.

And the result? By the time our children were beginning school, they already understood that there was a time to play, a time to talk, a time to listen, a time to take in, a time to let out, and a time to be quiet.

There is no reasonable apothegm that states that little children have to be uncontrollable wiggle worms in order to have a balanced and sane childhood. However, I suppose some child psychologist somewhere might try to make a point that by teaching small children to be obedient to their parents (as an example, when parents instruct them to sit quietly on a blanket and behave) that this will somehow warp their young minds and that they will probably grow up hating their parents or worse. Well, I have too many years of working with children and parents to buy into that type of notion...nor should you!

The thing is, in order to properly instruct and teach a young child, the parent must be persistent...a loving and attentive parent who is always persistent! I say it again, *Be Persistent! Loving and Persistent!*

How to Communicate with our kids!

There are countless ways we can communicate with our children so that they will learn how to better express themselves, how we might get to know them better, and how the entire family can grow and become much closer as a total loving unit.

Here are a few examples. Let's see how you react to each one.

Example #1: After dinner and a hard day at work, you are sitting on your easy chair watching your favorite television program. In fact, you are completely engrossed as to what is happening to the principal character of the show...is he going to go to the electric chair or will they find out that it was really his brother who committed the crime, because it seems that their mother couldn't pay her rent at the old folks home this month. And now they just discovered that they aren't brothers after all....

Suddenly, your son interrupts your train of thought just as the judge pronounces his verdict. What do you do? What do you say? And, how do you say it? Do you turn off the TV set and patiently talk to him? Do you yell at him to "shut up and go to your room"? Or do you tell him, "ask me about it a little later. Right now, I'd appreciate it if you'd go and play in your room until my program is over. Then we'll talk." You answer the question.

Example #2: You decide that your courage is overflowing so you and your teenage daughter hop in the car to head for the mall...only, today, your daughter is going to drive! Or, a better way to say it; today you are going to teach your daughter how to drive the family car! Suddenly you feel your courage level beginning to fade and you wonder if this was really a very good idea after all.

Well, everything goes without a hitch until she starts the engine and begins backing out of the driveway. Before the car has traveled 100 yards, your wife's daughter has nearly run over a picket fence, two dogs, an old man on crutches, and a stray cat. You immediately question her eyesight because she can't seem to see red lights or oncoming cars. And you think how strange it is that nobody ever told her to stop behind the cross walk when coming to a stop sign. How do you communicate now? Do you holler? Do you put her down? Do you jump in the back seat and hide? Do you take over driving the car? Do you pray for patience? What do you do, and what do you say? You answer the question.

What great opportunities we parents have to teach our children and to show them just how much we love them. And what great opportunities we have to learn tolerance and patience from our children, especially when we take on the responsibility for teaching them how to drive the family car!

Example # 3: It's a lazy afternoon and you decide to do some work around the house. So you wander out into the garage and look for your tool box. But, lo and behold, guess what? It's not there! After hunting for it for some time, you just can't locate it until you remember that your wife gave birth to a son about ten years ago. Suddenly, you know exactly where to look. The problem is, when you finally recover your tools from beneath your son's bed, many are missing. And those tools that are still in the box seem to be covered with a sticky substance that smells a little like chocolate covered peanut butter. Now, what do you do? Hit him when you find him? Curse your wife for having given birth to what you now see as a substandard creature? Go behind the garage and cry? Look in the kitchen for that bottle of Old Granddad? Yell and scream at the ceiling? You answer the question.

Example # 5: You tell your child it's time to go to bed and a little later you notice that nothing has happened. Susie is still lying on the front room floor watching TV. After a few minutes, you think, "I wonder if little Susie heard me tell her to get ready for bed?" So, once again, you tell your daughter to go to bed. And again, nothing happens. In fact, this non-happening repeats itself several times.

You begin to feel a warm crawling sensation slowly moving up your neck and into your brain and all of a sudden it becomes harder to maintain self-control. What do you do? Do you pick her up by the nape of her neck and march her into her bedroom? Do you yell at your husband or wife to take care of this problem so that you can do your thing? Do you question yourself as to why you ever wanted children in the first place? Do you shout at the walls, the family, or the moon? You answer the question.

One thing is for sure with all the examples listed above; if you have gotten angry and lost control of your emotions...your mouth, mind and temper...you might as well go down and hide in the cellar. If you feel that in order to get things done or make others carry out your wishes you need to become angry and domineering, you have not only lost control of yourself, you have failed to communicate and you are failing as a parent!

Proper parental communication is when we tell our children that they have done something wrong, something they should not have done, or something they should be doing. Then with patience, kindness, empathy, control and love, we teach and instruct them as to the right way of accomplishing the task at hand; i.e., going to bed when told to, parking the car without our vocal abuse, using correct manners at the dinner table, taking care of other people's property, and so much more.

Tell them once; tell them twice, and then if they haven't responded in a positive manner, let them know that you are serious in a firm yet loving way. Don't become so upset that you lose control of your temper and say something you will never be able to take back. Why hurt your child with "words of anger" when kind and loving words spoken in a firm and precise manner will get the point across and the job done. "A soft answer turns away wrath" (Proverbs 15:1) Believe me, it works!

While I was working and living in Arkansas, I had the opportunity to visit an elderly lady one day. Well, we got to talking about a number of things when the subject turned to raising children. This lady had a treasure chest full of wonderful experiences with her children, and one of the gems of wisdom she passed on to me was simply, "the problem is that parents and children don't talk to each other like they used to."

I asked her what she meant and so she continued, "when I was raising my youngsters, I would sit them down around the ironing board while I was ironing. I would tell them wonderful stories about our family and about me when I was a little girl. I told them about how we lived and got along. I told them about how they were when they were little babies. My children just loved this time we had together; and, you know, they always had lots of questions."

Answering questions provides the parent with a great opportunity to let the child know more about who his or her parents are, about themselves and others in the family, and it gives the child an opportunity to look to mom or dad for answers.

Today, children seem to find most of their answers from TV, comic books, school friends, or "on the street" because mom and dad are too busy doing their "own thing"...too busy to talk and listen to their children!

I believe the problem so many parents are experiencing today of not having healthy, vibrant communication with their children can be summed up with the following story: One day my older son said to me, "You know, Dad, you and Mom have made it really easy for me to talk with you. For all of us kids to talk with you. You made all of us feel that we could come to you at any time, day or night. You made us feel that you really enjoyed talking and listening to us, especially when we came to you with our problems. You took time to talk with us about what WE thought was important. So I just want you to know that I love you very much for the time you gave to my brothers and sisters and me!"

My experience tells me that listening to, talking with, and then communicating as a family is one of the most, if not THE most, important things a parent can do with their children. What a wonderful feeling it is when a child comes to you and says, "I love you because you listened and talked with me!" I hope each parent reading this book will some day have the opportunity (if they haven't already) to experience that wonderful, stirring emotional feeling that flows from a parent's heart and mind when a child articulates such sound and mature reasoning for truly loving his or her parents! It should certainly bring tears to your eyes!

****

E ducation does not mean teaching young people what they do not know. It means teaching them to behave as they do not behave. It is not teaching the youth the shapes of letters and the tricks of numbers, and then leaving them to turn their arithmetic to roguery, and their literature to lust. It means, on the contrary, training them into the perfect exercise and kingly continence of their bodies and souls. It is a painful, continual and difficult work to be done by kindness, by watching, by warning, by precept, and by praise, but above all...by example!" -John Ruskin

CHAPTER SIX:

PARENTING TODAY:
WHAT WENT WRONG?!

Parents have so many problems today that just making a living and keeping their heads above water make raising children all the more difficult. More so than ever before. Living has never been easy from the time of Adam and Eve. Yet, why is it we find ourselves, as parents and adults, having to face such an enormous onslaught of problems, some of which seem almost insurmountable and very evil? What caused this situation? Why do we seem to have such a growing problem with many of our young people today? Is it simply time, chance and circumstance, or have we been doing something wrong...and are we presently doing something wrong?

First of all, what really is the situation surrounding our very lives today? Is it something that only parents living in the United States are experiencing? Are our Japanese and European friends experiencing the same kind of problems with their children and their families as we are? Is it something we can ever resolve? How did it happen? When did it all begin? And just what is it?

Today, most parents, including younger people and older adults, can no longer hide from the fear and suffering that surrounds them at work, at home, at school, at play, on the street, in the car, at night, during the day, and most of their time awake or asleep! Sounds like I'm a little paranoid, doesn't it?

It's not being paranoid when we see so many people from all walks of life experiencing the devastating *effects* from some very harmful, wasteful and disastrous *causes* that sprouted much like a field full of dry dirty weeds that slowly grew out of control following the end of World War II.

All we need to do is take a moment and look around to see

57

what our neighbors and friends are experiencing almost every day...indeed, what each one of us often experiences on a daily basis! What do you see? I see many educated people no longer reading the news or watching news on television because what they read or view has become so negative...very realistic and very discouraging! The media has come to a place where what they report seems to be a concentration on such fearful and tragic stories that at times it just seems to dull the senses.

I see crimes of every description being committed in large cities and small rural communities, and injustice being meted out at every level of society. Five years ago we might see a story on TV about rape or perhaps a violent murder happening in our city once or twice a week at most; however, today, murder, rape, every type of abuse, robbery, and so many other crimes have become daily occurrences. I see a growing problem regarding illegal aliens including the welfare of their children beginning to affect one and all; I see families experiencing the negative effects from uncontrolled credit spending; I see illegal drugs, alcohol, and tobacco destroying lives including the future of our children; and I see youth gangs controlling sections of cities while expanding their territories at an alarming rate.

I see tremendous unemployment of educated and experienced men and women suffering for lack of work...with no end in sight; I see a great scarcity of concern and love toward family members and neighbors; I see so many government bureaucrats misusing their power - it seems they no longer desire to serve the public, instead they want to be served by the public; and I see federal and municipal bureaucracies totally out of control.

I see the blind leading the blind...not wanting to see or perhaps too fearful to want to see what lies ahead; I see our natural resources rapidly being depleted...our water, minerals, air and soil possibly changing forever, and not for the better; I see our lands being raped, pillaged and plundered by many so-called concerned-citizens (developers) of this country, and large American businesses now headquartering in foreign lands; and I see these same land developers playing off the fears of hard-working people in order to accomplish their greedy desires and goals.

I see a national debt so enormous that it won't be too very long before the interest payable and due on this debt is greater than the total amount of per capita of tax revenue, and it will be our children's children who will be saddled with the responsibility to pay back the tremendous debt our generation incurred; I see too many of our youth graduating from school unable to properly read and write and comprehend...unable to think through many difficult problems...and failing such important courses as math and science, two subjects that are vital to sustaining life; I see AIDS and other terrible diseases having an epidemic effect on our society and taking the lives of so many young people; I see racial bigotry and hatred for people of different backgrounds, religion, race and color destroying the fabric of our society; I see society denying God, His creation, majesty, honor, commandments and omnipotent power; I see fear, greed, overindulgence, materialism, pride, carnality, self-interests, and uncontrolled materialism replacing the commandments of God; and I see a country and its people losing its vision, purpose and resolve.

With all the problems and outside forces attacking the family today, is it any wonder parents are having difficulties just surviving? Is it any wonder our children need assurance from mom and dad that things will be all right? However, who is it that can promise mom and dad that everything will be all right?

Still, someone reading this may ask, "How does all of this affect me as a parent? I mean, how did we arrive at this stage of society anyway? Or, What does this all really have to do with me raising my children?"

Let's take the last question first. The reason we parents must be aware of what is happening to our lives and our global society is simply because everything we do today our children will experience and live with tomorrow! We are bequeathing a very dangerous and destructive legacy to our kids. It's that baby being born today whose life is going to suffer greatly by the time she reaches maturity, and it's that young twelve-year-old boy who, after finishing school, will search for diamonds and be lucky if he finds a small bucket of coal.

59

While we have thoughtlessly provided for ourselves, we have denied our children's children and their children the right to a secure and prosperous livelihood! "How do you know this?", you may ask. Take a trip across this country, read the newspapers and a few well written news magazine articles, look around...it's all there for anyone who is interested to know what is going on in their society!

When did the problems we are experiencing today really begin? How did they evolve?

What I have just described above are the overall effects from causes that began long ago. Hatred toward our fellow man can be traced back to ancient times. It seems that man has always had some score to settle, some debt to be repaid, or some type of vendetta to be fought from the time of Cain. Yet, my question is, "For the most part, are the adults who planted the seeds of discontentment, greed, war, and hatred also children that were once raised by parents...a mom and/or dad?" Some parent, somewhere, sometime, in some place raised a child who became Genghis Khan, Attilla the Hun, or Adolph Hitler. And just as in times past, today, there is a parent someplace who is raising a child who will hate his neighbor, rape some unsuspecting person, or murder a fellow human being. No doubt there will always be that individual child who goes off the deep end no matter how well he was taught in school, provided for at home, or encouraged by others.

However, the point I am trying to make here concerns problems we are facing as a society and not more isolated situations such as an individual who guns down every patron eating at a cafe or working at a job somewhere. I am referring to those adult men and women who have been caught stealing clothes from some department store, committed insider trading scandals, or worked some insurance scam on unsuspecting pensioners or old folks living on a fixed income. The people who committed these crimes all had parents! Perhaps it was a single parent who raised them, it might even have been a relative, friend or foster parent, but someone had the responsibility for raising and caring for them! For teaching them right from wrong, love and honor, truth and purity! Whoever it was, they somehow failed!

Some people might say that there is no way possible we can lay most of the problems we are facing today at the feet of those parents who did not take the time to properly teach and instruct their children. I find that many child psychologists simply want to blame society for what is happening to our children today. Okay. Let's suppose for a minute that Dr. Whatshisname is correct. "It is all society's fault!" But, who or what is society? Isn't society you and me? Doesn't society include working parents who are also teachers, doctors, lawyers, homemakers, and even child psychologists?! There are those within the intellectual community who often speak of society as though it were some inanimate, senseless and mechanical thing! Society is living, breathing, laughing, playing, working and dying. *Society is us!*

We can begin to track much of what we are experiencing today regarding financial woes, social upheaval, white collar crime, and a serious assortment of deadly evils and out-of-control problems starting right before World War II.

Beginning in the 1930's, this country's overriding attitude seemed to be one of "Everything's just Jake! However, it sure looks like the Depression is never going to end, so let's live, love and be merry, for tomorrow we may die!" "By the way, Jimbo, I've just scored some very tasty bootleg whiskey. Com'on over and we'll share a pint!" "Buy an apple for a nickel" "Ten cents for a shine, mister!" "Let's hop a freight to the West Coast and see if we can find a job out there!" "Hoover and the Depression!" Things weren't easy in the 30's!

And in the 1940's, it was "off to war!" "Let's make the world a better place for our kids and stop the Nazi's in their tracks." "By the way, have you seen the latest pin up of Rosie the Riveter?" "Com'on and join the KKK and make America white again!" "All Colored People, Drink out of your own fountain!" "Did you read about the "A" bomb and how it laid waste a couple of cities in Japan?" "Ol' Harry can sure giv'em hell!"

61

During those wonderful and nostalgic days of the 1950's, most people seemed contented as they began to live the good life. "Man, am I glad that war is finally over!" "Hey, Daddy'O, let's cruise on down to the malt shop and dig on the music." "Hey, Mack. Just let me work at rebuilding my life and let's not make any waves, okay? All I want is a good used car, a two bedroom house with a picket fence, and a job that pays me enough so that the wife and kids and I can eat out once in awhile." "Whatta ya mean, credit card?" "Keep the races segregated!" "What's a transistor or an integrated circuit?" "Did you know that little doll down the street had an abortion and a divorce?" "What's an abortion?" "Wow, twenty five cents for a gallon of gasoline, that's highway robbery. I mean, when's it ever gonna end?" "NASA!" "Man, dig that Rock N' Roll!" "Did ya catch Elvis on the Sullivan show last night? He was so cool, and those hips! Wow!"

The 1960's were ushered in with "the American Dream and the Great Society." And, it was a time of great highs and terrible lows for our people, "...ask not what you can do for your country...!" "It's time to integrate!" "James Meredith," "Did you see the Sound of Music or Mary Poppins?" "John, Martin, and Bobby! What a tragedy!" "Buy now, pay later!" "Computers for the home?" "Elvis returns!" "LSD!" "Hell no, I won't go!" "Make love, not war!" "Were you at Woodstock?" "Hey, dude, do your own thing!" "Get high and listen to the sounds of rebellion!" "Turn on and Drop out!" "FM radio and 'Light My Fire'!" "Free sex and social drugs." "Women's Lib" "Burn your bra!" "Viet Nam!" "Haight Ashbury." "The Beatles come to America!" "Space exploration and a trip to the moon!" 1968 had to be one of the most difficult years for both parents and young people in recent times. And, the 60's were the beginning of many changes to come!

A decade passes and a new one begins. The 1970's brought us such wonderful attitudes and experiences as, "Nixon!" "Watergate!" "Looking out for Number One!" "Be aggressive in your work and don't give the next fellow an even break!" "Get your MBA from the best university and I promise that you will be rewarded with a high paying job on Wall Street" "Credit, credit, credit!" "The Cold War heats up!" "Out of the closet!" "The Bar Code enters the marketplace." "Multinationals take over small businesses!" "And the Personal Computer (PC) makes its debut." "Look out, the world is changing faster than ever!"

Then we moved on into the 1980's (who can forget the 80's?). "Good-bye Jimmy, hello Ronald." "Trickle down economics!" "Forget ethics, they can't pay the mortgage!" "Greed is good!" "What does 'Insider Trading' mean?" "Junk bonds and leveraged buyouts!" "Tax shelters" "Did you hear that so and so company had to file for bankruptcy today?" "Yeah, and so did a lot of working people!" "The communist wall is beginning to tumble!" "AIDS, what's that?" "Homosexuals, Lesbians, and Gay rights!" "The ERA" "The 'Crips' and the 'Bloods'" "Columbia, cocaine, and the DEA!" "Read my lips, 'No New Taxes!'"

And so now here we are, having arrived in the 1990's. The Wall did come tumbling down; politicians continue to tell us what they think we want to hear; junk bonds are out and we are now beginning to feel the effect from having been a party to such a disastrous and ill-thought-out scheme; the S&L and banking situation will haunt us for years to come; wars are still being fought on the international front while children and parents are dying of malnutrition and starvation by the tens of thousands; the theory about the warming of the Earth may not be a theory after all; few college graduates are getting well- paying jobs; youth gangs are engaging in car-jacking as an ever increasing crime; millions of children and adults are starving in not-so-far-off countries; drive-by shootings are becoming commonplace; and parents, all over the world, are experiencing much greater anxiety and difficulty with raising their children today, more than any other time in recent history!

Looking back over the past several decades gives us the opportunity to see some of the reasons why we have come to the place where we are now standing. We can see that each new decade inherited a great many unresolved problems and unanswered questions from the previous decades, and that this constant compounding of one decade's problems on top of the next decade's problems has given those in authority more than they are able to cope with.

We also see from the overriding character and attitude of society during the decades just past, how we performed, as parents and adults, in managing our children, our personal affairs, and indeed, our very lives. We are able to see how our lives were affected by so many outside associations, friendships, beliefs, and responsibilities; by geopolitical, geoeconomical, and religious situations and commitments; and finally, by the overall social and political environment at the time.

Understanding the past helps us to realize that for every *cause* there is an *effect.* As an example: If we neglect our children, the effect most likely will be disobedient and unruly children; if we spend more than we make, the effect will probably eventually be bankruptcy; and if we hide from addressing those concerns which greatly affect our lives, i.e., giving our children our time and love, providing for our children's welfare, persevering in the teaching and training of our children on a daily basis, and so many other critical matters that we must not deny, the final effect can only be our failure as parents.

Why is understanding all of this so important? Because your child is going to be greatly affected by everything I have written in this chapter...and so much more. It is your little bundle of joy who is going to become a leader of tomorrow; it is your newborn baby who is going to reap what our generation has sown. It is our children who must heal the wounds we have caused one another; it is our children who must pay the very high price for the damage our and previous generations have inflicted on our land and society; and finally, after overcoming and accomplishing such great feats, it is also our children who must then restore physical, mental, and spiritual attitudes and character to their children if this world is to continue to exist.

If we fail to train, teach and instruct our children properly; if we do not teach them right from wrong, train them in the proper way to manage and direct their lives, and instruct them in the direction they should travel, who will? And, if we don't take the time to help our children learn valuable life supporting principles and business ethics now, beginning today, then how will they ever be able to accomplish the monumental tasks of character renovation and uncompromising attitude adjustments they must achieve if they are to survive tomorrow? You may ask, "Is it really that important for us to acknowledge all the problems we are facing today?" If you want a decent world for your children to live in tomorrow, you bet your very life it is!

The way we have taught our children during the past several decades reminds me of that person who just loves to eat. This person often tells those sitting around the table, "This is the best food I've had all day!" And when the person sitting next to him remarks that the food he is eating is "junk food" and has little or no nutritional value, the one gorging himself simply replies, "Oh, I know it's not really good for me, but I just can't resist its delicious flavor, and besides, I like the way it makes me feel after eating it!" Before long, this person is 100 pounds overweight and suddenly diabetes, heart disease, and the possibility of cancer begin to loom just ahead.

Sometime later, when our gluttonous friend can no longer get into his clothes and every morning he discovers some new ache or pain, he decides to go to the doctor and find out what the trouble is. Well, after the doctor finishes the examination, he looks straight at our friend and with a sober and firm voice he tells his overweight patient to lose weight and begin eating properly or the chances that he will have a stroke, heart attack, contract cancer or even die are very great.

Not liking the prospects he's facing, our overweight and out-of-shape friend decides that it's probably time he loses a few pounds. But how? I mean, it took quite awhile to put all that weight on, and besides, who wants to wait forever to shed a few excess pounds! Right?

So, after meditating for a couple of days about what might be the quickest way to reduce weight, our friend suddenly remembers a new product advertised on television that guarantees weight loss simply by taking a little blue pill before going to bed. "Fantastic!", he yells. "This is just too simple for words. I mean, it should only take a month or so and I'll be back in shape and looking great!" Without hesitation he picks up the phone and dials the 800 number listed on the television screen with his credit card in hand.

Before long, the little blue pills arrive in the mail and our friend immediately begins taking one every night as directed by the manufacturer.

"Now", he reasons, "because I'm faithfully taking these little pills, I'm bound to lose weight. And if I'm going to lose weight anyway, I should still be able to eat some sweets once in awhile...and, I'm sure a soda every now and then won't hurt. Besides, ice cream helps settle my stomach!"

Well, some amount of time passes and one day our friend discovers that the pills aren't working. He also discovers that the company he bought the pills from is no longer in business. At first, he blames the pills not working for all his problems, but slowly it becomes evident that if he is going to lose any weight it's only going to come to pass when he makes a total and devoted commitment. This also means he'll no doubt have to experience some pain and suffering. Will he do it? Does he have the courage and character to overcome suffering and pain in order to get his body back into shape?

Using this analogy let us ask the following questions: Have we taught our children how to overcome and not fear certain types of pain and suffering? Have we instilled in them principles, values and character so that when they see themselves heading for disaster, they can turn it around and stay clear of the evils and temptations just ahead?

Parents, there are no quick fixes when it comes to the proper teaching and training of our children. There just aren't any little blue pills that we can give them in place of our love, trust, care, instruction, and protection.

As a society, we are now beginning to experience the effects from having neglected the proper training and teaching of our children. What has happened to our families and society during the past several decades reminds me of that poor ol' frog who finds himself in a slow burning kettle of water. At first the water is cool and refreshing and as the water becomes warm, the frog only senses pleasure and security. But as the water slowly begins to heat, the frog begins to tire. After a short period of time, he can no longer hold his eyes open so he falls asleep. Soon, he is being carried out of the kitchen on a fine sterling silver platter, under glass, prepared to satisfy a patron's appetite in a fine French restaurant.

How did we get into the mess we see all around us today? We parents, as many of our parents before us, neglected teaching our children some very important lessons. We have failed to properly instruct, teach and discipline those little ones who have been given into our care. We forgot or didn't really understand that it takes time, perseverance, patience and a whole lot of giving on our part if a child is going to learn and mature and succeed. And, like the frog, we felt comfortable and relaxed and we soon fell asleep!

I realize that there are many wonderful parents doing the best they can to properly raise their children today in a society that has become extremely difficult at times, and that much of what I have written in this chapter may be viewed by some as somewhat simplistic and negative...much of the truth is often simplistic and negative! However, our society, indeed every society worldwide, is now beginning to reap what we have sown over the past several decades. Is it too late to make those changes needed if we are to turn our society around? Is it too late for our kids? Not if we study to become better prepared and more knowledgeable about our world and our place in it; not if we ask God for His help and guidance in directing our daily lives and the lives of our children; not if we decide to return to the basics and set our priorities in proper order; not if we begin, one person, one family at a time, to do what is needed to be done; and not if we spend QUALITY TIME WITH OUR KIDS, no matter what their ages, so that we can properly direct them in the *way that they should go!*

"LISTEN
TO THE
CHILDREN"

by
Thelma Evelyn Jones

Listen to the Children
Hear the things They say,
Be careful for these Little Ones
Someday, They will lead the way!

Hear the Little Children
Let them talk with you,
Try to learn to understand Them
For Children are people, too!

When They have a problem
Take in every word,
For they need love and understanding
And, Children should also be heard.

Jesus said, "Forbid Them not!"
For They are not defiled,
And, no one ever stands so tall
As when he stoops to help a Child!

♥♥♥♥♥♥♥♥♥♥

CHAPTER SEVEN:

GRANDPARENTING TODAY!

THE JOY AND THE FEARS
of being a
GRANDPARENT
in the
21st CENTURY!

Old isn't in anymore!" The spokeswoman being interviewed by a network news anchor was very emphatic during her disputation on a major television news program regarding how the old ways in child rearing just were not "valid" anymore. "No," she continued, "the old way of teaching children much the same way our grandparents taught our parents just isn't applicable to the manner in which young children are to be taught today. You see, old isn't in anymore!"

She then went on to expound the virtues of why children today must be taught differently from the past. "After all", she explained, "today, nearly 1 out of 8 children are born out of wedlock; 25% will be raised from birth by a single mother; and, 50% of our children will, at some time during their youth, be raised in a single family dwelling. You see, this is a much different time and place than when our grandparents were raising their children!"

I cannot help but feel that her indoctrination seemed more like treating the *effect* than addressing the *cause*. This spokeswoman believes that it is a foregone conclusion that the breakdown of the family unit and children being raised by a single parent will remain the same throughout the foreseeable future; therefore, she preaches that it is now time to get on with a more modern method for raising children.

While listening to this lady speak, I just couldn't help but recall how in the past so many other "expert" baby doctors and professional "social service" spokespersons tried to promote (and some were very successful) their own brand of "modern methods for raising children". It took a while for these people to succeed at what they started to proclaim, but succeed they did! The consequences on our children, parents, and society from having accepted such academic, child-rearing theories as truth and then applying these "modern-day" assumptions into the family management program has proven to be an important principal cause for many of the most debilitating and damaging effects being perpetrated on the family today.

Still, her words, "old isn't in anymore," kept bouncing around in my head for some time after the broadcast. Then I suddenly realized that this lady hit the nail on the head! In just four short words, sixteen English letters, she was able to vividly illustrate one of the major reasons why we are having so many problems with our young people today.

Because so many teachers and spokespeople believe that "old isn't in anymore," we have gotten too far away from the type of teaching, training, and instruction that can only come from knowledge and understanding handed down from generation to generation; the type of wisdom our parents and grandparents were taught, not from some modern-day child psychology theoretician, but rather from hands-on experience, considerable time, and a whole lot of tests and trials; and above all, from the spiritual guidance and direction our parents, and those before them, gained from having studied the teachings of the Holy Scriptures...the Bible.

Without a doubt there are certain distinctive characteristics a parent today must be aware of regarding proper instruction for training their children that our parents and grandparents knew nothing about. Today, as never before, we have very definite concerns we must address while teaching our children and preparing them for their future, i.e., computer science, television, modern medicine, high technology, bioengineering, drugs, sex and so much more. Our grandparents knew little or nothing about what most parents are experiencing today during this modern day technical and social revolution.

Today, we are able to find physical cures for such diseases as polio, chicken pox, heart failure, liver transplants, certain cancers and other types of sickness that can often lead to death. However, in this modern day we are also able to annihilate every living being on Earth; every human, animal, fish, fowl and plant one hundred and fifty times over using more than two hundred scientific methods! Grandpa Jones would probably turn over in his grave if he could see the type of destructive capabilities we mortals have under our control.

This is just one more reason why it is so necessary to raise our children not only with the physical and mental knowledge they receive at school, play, and in the home; but, with the spiritual wisdom and understanding they can only inherit from their parents, family, pastor, church, and grandparents. Grandparents have a sizable physical, mental and spiritual treasure chest from which they can supply their grandchildren with, so many resources filled with priceless gems of experience, knowledge, understanding, wisdom, time, patience, devotion and love!

Grandparents have the ability to help balance a child's life. Take a moment and consider: your child gets up in the morning (usually running a little late), eats a fast bowl of cereal, grabs his books and heads for school. During the next 5-6 hours Junior's mind is being inundated with great words of wisdom and tremendous volumes of overflowing enlightenment. The instruction and physical dimensions for learning often seem more than his mind can accept (or so he says when he brings home his report card!).

After school, Junior hangs around with his friends for awhile (doing what you hope to be something of value and certainly not illegal or harmful), then later returns home. After dinner he might study his homework (if he has any...so often it doesn't seem he ever has any school work to be completed at home), watch some TV, then go to bed (if it's the weekend, he will probably be out somewhere with his friends). So, with each day's academic training and social activity constantly penetrating his young, fertile mind, where does the spiritual teaching he requires, in order to help balance his life, come from? Who, other than his often overworked and tired parents, can provide this vital information for his mind...indeed, for his entire life? Probably, only his grandparents!

Before continuing on, let's understand just what the word "spiritual" really means. Webster's New World Dictionary defines "Spiritual" as 1. *of the spirit or soul as distinguished from the body or material matters.* 2. *of, from, or concerned with the intellect; intellectual.* 3. *of or consisting of spirit; not corporeal.* 4. *characterized by the ascendancy of the spirit; showing much refinement of thought and feeling.* 5. *of religion or the church; sacred, devotional, or ecclesiastical; not lay or temporal.* Sometimes we parents may not truly understand what certain words actually mean. "Spiritual" is probably one of these words.

So, when taken at its true meaning, we can see that having "spiritual" input is something we want our children to have. However, where they get this "spiritual" awareness and who gives it to them should be of major concern to every parent.

Spiritual understanding is an element of intelligence and reasoning that must accompany the mental and physical senses if any human being, young or old, is to be exceptionally balanced in all aspects of life.

Where do our children learn about the spiritual perspective of life? And who gives it to them? Do they gain this deeper understanding at school? Not hardly! Especially when most schools mandate that teachers steer clear from anything that even comes close to spirituality...that is with the possible exception of teaching children about the world of ESP, magic, levitation, UFO's, or the fantasized darker side of the spiritual world. Too many modern day educators believe that true spirituality can only be related to a specific religious interpretation. Yet, we read in Webster's dictionary that "spiritual" means intellect, intelligence, and the *"ascendancy of the spirit; showing much refinement of thought and feeling."*

How about films and the media? Do these forms of education and entertainment provide spiritual instruction and input into a child's youthful mind? Of course they do! Some of the most successful films ever made deal with the spiritual world as seen by a Hollywood writer, producer or director, i.e., "ET", "Fantasia", "Star Wars", "The Exorcist!", and practically every Steven King story. Music can also be included when looking at forms of entertainment which include the "spiritual" world in the body of the creative work. Here, almost every Heavy Metal band has at one time or another included the darker side of the spiritual world in the lyrics of their recorded songs.

The "soul" is the human "spirit!" It is through this "spirit" that we learn and are taught; it is this "spirit" that provides our ability to reason and grow in knowledge and understanding; and it is this "spirit' that separates us from the wild beasts in the fields and the tamed animals in the home. It is also this "spirit" that can be very susceptible to outside influences, whether good or bad. This "spirit" takes time and patience to mature. And it's this same "spirit" in our grandparents which enables them to pass on such wonderful knowledge, experience, and wisdom to us and to our children.

If we acknowledge that intelligence and the *ascendancy of the spirit; showing much refinement of thought and feeling* can only come from a person with years of valuable experience and refinement, and from one who has achieved a priceless maturity of sound reasoning, controlled emotions, patience, understanding, and a perspicacious wisdom, who then, other than mom or dad, is best qualified to instruct and help train our children? Why, of course, it's our childrens *grandparents!*

Who or what is a "grandparent"? What does it mean to be a grandparent? Well, why don't we go once again to Mr. Daniel Webster for his help in our defining just what constitutes being a grandparent.

First of all, let's determine what "grand" really means. 1. *higher in rank, status or dignity... 2. most important; chief; main; principal. 3. SYN. grand is applied to that which makes a strong impression because of its greatness and dignity... .* "Higher Status, Chief, Greatness, and Dignity"!

Okay, now how about the meaning of "parent"? Here Mr. Webster lets us down a little. 1. *a father or mother.* 2. *a progenitor or ancestor.* He sure didn't take us into a very deep or philosophical explanation of what a parent is, did he?

Anyway, we know that "grand" means higher status, chief, and one who makes a very strong impression because of...(his or her)...greatness and dignity. And, "parent" means father or mother. So, a "grandparent" must then mean a *father or mother, higher in status and dignity*, a *most important chief*, and someone who *makes a strong impression because of (his or her) greatness and dignity* ! Are you this type of grandparent?

With such great unemployment and welfare today, many grandparents are once again strapped with the responsibility of raising children. Only this time, it's not their own children, it's their children's children!

After working for so many years and finally getting to the place where they can relax a little and begin to take life somewhat more on their own terms, many grandparents are now finding themselves washing diapers (or tossing disposable diapers in the trash), buying expensive baby food by the case, preparing the baby's formula for their two A.M. feeding, spending much of their retirement pension or Social Security check to help keep the baby warm and secure, and, finally, teaching their little grandchild about so many important things in life, such as what to eat, how to eat, what clothes to wear, how to behave, why he should not tell a lie, how she must carefully cross the street or ride a bike, and much, much more. Just when they thought they had finally finished raising their own kids, along came the second batch!

Can being a grandparent today be difficult at times? It certainly can!

Not long ago, I had the opportunity to meet an older couple who live on an island in the Pacific Northwest. He is a retired police officer from the Seattle Police Department, and she is a retired executive.

Well, we got to talking about raising children and I soon discovered that even though this husband and wife team are living comfortable lives as older adults in this modern age of child rearing, they are also two very aware grandparents who are quite concerned with the way the age group of their children are raising their children...their grandchildren.

I asked the wife if she would be so kind as to write out her thoughts regarding her views as to how she feels about being a grandmother in the '90's. Here is what she wrote:

"In the mid-seventies, life was going along merrily for my husband and me, and we had no desire to have our family enlarged. Our children had moved away from home and were living independent lives, and my husband and I were finally free to do our own choices (or as much as business would allow).

"Our first grandchild did not affect our daily routine because his parents lived too far away. So, we only got together on birthdays and holidays. Also, our number two son wanted to control his child's environment and he stated, "Grandparents don't know much about child rearing!" This same son and his wife had another child and the scenario was also as strict, although they did welcome a little more loving contact between us and our grandchildren. I was careful as to how much "unasked for" advice I gave; however, if I felt strongly about something regarding my grandchildren, I would speak to my son about it when we were alone.

"Our first daughter produced the next grandchild, and our relationship was very different. Her desire to control her environment included both grandparents (whether they wanted to be included or not!) One of the first things she said was if I didn't visit her and her children, she would bring my grandchild to see me. Even though the business demanded most of my waking hours, I was determined that my grandson was going to know his grandmother!

"Many times he was brought to my office where he

75

would nap. Sometimes I was too busy for my grandson, still his parents welcomed any advice or any help they received from me.

"When my second daughter had her child, she was determined that we should bond. And bond we did, especially when they moved in with us. It was impossible for me not to love this little miniature person, because I helped take care of her most nights and during the weekends. And my daughter accepted any and all help in rearing her baby girl, because she did not have enough confidence in her own ability as a mother.

"Within eight months two more little girls joined our family. It was truly overwhelming to have our family increase by six grandchildren in less than seven years! Just when we thought we were going to be free of some of the many demands parents experience, new demands were suddenly being heaped upon us. And this was on top of some serious business decisions. I know that at times I resented these dramatic changes and accompanying requests upon my time. I am a private person, and I feel time for myself is important because so much of it has been given to others.

"As a critical observer of our children and their spouses and the way they have (and are) rearing their children (our grandchildren), I think they have been too lenient regarding the discipline of their children and too lax in teaching them moral issues, personal hygiene, and cleanliness.

"Still, my children want their children to be well educated, and even though they are going about providing this for their children in different ways, I am confident my grandchildren will become well-rounded and successful adults."

JF
Freeland, Washington

Certainly, raising young children, especially when one has grown tired and a little weary, can be somewhat overwhelming at times! Yet, at the same time, it can be very rewarding and fulfilling! It really depends on the attitude and character of the grandparent!

For those grandparents who only want to see their grandkids when it best serves their own selfish desire, helping raise a child today will probably be very difficult at best. However, for those grandparents who have empathy and compassion for their own children and the day-to-day problems they are facing (realizing that their kids would rather be spending time with their own children instead of working at two different jobs sixteen hours a day), life while helping raise their grandchildren can be very enjoyable, refreshing, and rewarding!

Through the years, along with experience gained by others, I have discovered that the one sure way grandparents will succeed in helping to rear their grandchildren is for the parents to give the grand-parents full autonomy to teach, discipline, and instruct each child especially when the grandparent has the responsibility of helping to raise him or her. Believe me grandparents, this is not an easy thing for a parent to give up!

How many adults do you know who believe their parents made a lot of crucial mistakes in the way they were raised? I can't count the times I've heard grown children arguing with their parents about the manner in which they were brought up, or about how different they are going to raise their children as opposed to the way they were raised.

Where do you think this problem regarding the difference in how to raise children, between parents and their parents, originated? How much of it, do you suppose, came from books and articles written by authors who perhaps didn't have the best of childhood's and then went on to foster their own misguided beliefs and theories on college students, newlyweds, and naive young parents having just given birth to their first baby girl or boy?

There appears to be a proclivity for us human beings to want to read what some new author or professor writes regarding whatever subject we are interested in. It seems to matter not that if ten so-called experts were to write a thesis on any one particular subject, we would no doubt have ten very different attitudes and approaches to digest on this subject. Why do you suppose we find it so difficult to believe tried and proven instruction from a parent, family member, pastor, or some close relative rather than just accept what they say as valuable information or cherished admonition?

Do we actually take the time to scrutinize what we read or investigate the credentials of the author who writes what we read? Do we thoroughly examine the content of whatever it is we are studying or reading before we pronounce it to be believable and of value? I'm afraid we don't, nor have we for some time!

As an example, take the theory of evolution: here we discover a hypothesis written by a scientist while visiting some islands in the South Pacific that has greatly altered the course of history. It has changed much of how society views life, life's purpose, death, religion, and much more. Yet, in fact, it is only a theory...an unproved academic assumption! It is a theory that has provided those who do not believe in a creator God with a supposed answer as to where they came from and who they are. To many young people at the time, this theory of evolution replaced a recorded history of mankind that had first been written over four thousand years ago! So, along with the "Big Bang" theory, these professed scholars now have all the answers they seem to need for such meaningful questions as to why was I born? Is there a God? What is my purpose on Earth? Is there life after death? Is the Bible fact or fiction? And so many other important issues that stimulate our intellect.

There are many other examples that support my claim regarding how we all too often fail to fully examine and deeply scrutinize those physical programs or academic theories which we later accept to be factual, i.e., the Communist Manifesto, Nazism, fascism, an insurance scam, healthcare fraud, junk bond leverage buyouts, etc. Did our grandparents ever buy into some of these unfounded theories or programs? Absolutely! However, we now come to the place where we can prove that wisdom comes only from time, experience, and maturity.

It takes time for a new theory or assumption to develop. And, during this time, a person who may have subscribed to a particular theory in the beginning may, once the theory begins to evolve, have the opportunity to examine it more thoroughly. Most often this examination is the result of having experienced the theory's effect in one's personal environment. And, sooner or later, this person begins to see the theory or program more clearly. Much of life is based on theory, and grandparents have experienced more theories (life) than anyone else. If this is true, then why don't we pay more attention and heed their caution and words of wisdom? Why don't we accept their instruction and teaching as something very precious and to be valued? After all, there is so much more than just gray hair and wrinkled skin regarding the hoary head of a grandparent! Now, can you, as a parent, begin to see why it's so important to have your children spend time with their grandparents...your parents? It is!

Can children really learn anything from their grandparents? They can learn more than one can imagine! Some of my most vivid and favorite recollections of my youth are the times when I spent so many precious moments with my grandmother. Boy, she was some lady!

The things I learned from my Grandmo (I called her that until the day she died at age eighty-one) were some of the most valuable teachings and instructions a child could ever discover or experience. She taught me about love, devotion, trust, honesty, hard work, and the value of one's name. She taught me about friendship, kindness, neatness, politeness...she taught me about life!

My Grandmother was a very strong woman. Not long after the turn of the century, her husband died when she was still young and left her with five children to raise on a farm in southern Colorado. And, she did just that. She never remarried ("Once you have found the best, who else is there?"), and although none of her children lived perfect lives, she raised them the best she knew how. And she gave each child a very large portion of love, caring, compassion, time, discipline, training, and hope.

My grandmother also helped raise me. Often, after a hard day of work at the downtown Goodwill store, she would come home (my grandmother lived with us right after WWII) and after settling down in her favorite rocking chair, she would hold me on her lap (she held me even after I left home and on into my twenties) and tell me about those things in life that she knew about...farming, raising cattle, raising her children without a husband, what it was like during the "great" depression, working at difficult jobs in the "big city," losing material possessions when things got tough, having to discipline my mom and uncle when they did something wrong (I liked those stories the best!), and much, much more.

"Can we get some ice cream, Grandma? Okay, Grandpa?"

She sang to me; rubbed my back when it was sore; scolded me when I did wrong (and even meted out stronger punishment when the offense warranted it); told me about Jesus Christ and His great love for us; fed me whenever I was hungry (and like most kids, I always seemed to be hungry!); dried my eyes when I cried; provided me with much needed used clothing that she purchased at the Goodwill store and then brought it home gift wrapped; and she always showered me with her love. She was indeed some lady! And, to this day, I miss her very much! Did she make an impression on me? You bet she did! Did I learn anything from her? Without a doubt!

Those of you who are grandparents, take a moment and think about your life with your children. Think about your love for them and how much you miss seeing them on a regular basis. If you live some distance away, speculate as to what they might be doing at this very moment. Hey, who knows, after a little thought and reminiscencing about the past, you might even pick up the phone and give them a call! Stop for a moment to think about your young grandchildren. Is there something you might do to help them grow and learn that maybe you're not already doing? Don't you have some small bit of advice, some tidbit of information, that you can pass on to them so their lives might be just a little easier now and on into the future? Are you giving them enough quality time...your special time? If you're helping your children by helping to raise their children, are you giving this opportunity and responsibility the very best you have to offer?

Do you ever become so weary you sometimes regret the time or material things you may be giving up in order to provide some type of necessity for your grandchild? Are you so involved with your own selfish needs, including the staggering responsibilities you have just to get by each day, that you fail to see clearly the positive effect you have on your grandchildren? Do you realize that any positive effect you might have on children can only result from your having personally been involved in their lives? Do you ever take the trust and love your grandchild has given you for granted? Ask yourself again, "is there anything else I can give? Is there anything at all that I may be holding back that could help my grandchild grow up and succeed in life? How about proper training? Unconditional Love? Mercy? Patience? Discipline? Instruction? Attention? Quality time? MY time?!"

I received a letter from a woman who with her husband raised three really great kids. She is now the proud grandmother of seven. Here's what she wrote.

What is a grandparent?

Webster defines grandparent as a parent of one's father or mother, and a parent is one that begets or brings forth offspring. Webster has as much trouble as the rest of us deciding the meaning of being a grandparent. My description reflects the memories I have of my maternal grandmother. The only grandparent I ever knew. Now that I am a grandparent of seven, I wonder how I might be described.

I find that being a grandmother or "Nana" as I am called, to be one of God's most enjoyable blessings. It is a second chance to sharpen our parenting skills. It is still exciting, challenging and a lot more fun, and not nearly as scary. I can truly enjoy being with my grandchildren. I think maybe not having the total responsibility for their character development and not having expectations of perfection is the reason. As I watch my children reflect back to me my parenting skills, I see the strengths and weaknesses and I am thankful to be a part of a new improved generation.

It is so fascinating to see family traits demonstrated and to know DNA is in action from the very beginning. This special little person that is a composite of their family genes. I see the familiar smile...and abilities...and hear the sound of a recognizable laugh and feel connected.

My grandmother was very special to me as I was growing up even though we lived in different parts of the country. She was able to make me feel loved and valuable. I knew she was, and would be, my supporter, and would listen to and encourage me. Our relationship was special and different from the relationship she had with her children, or that I had with my mother.

My goal as a grandparent is to instill love and the awareness of their worth as a person to each of my grandchildren.

I am able to spend time with each of them, one to one. It is a special treat to be able to see, hear (most of the time) and touch them as we talk. Their hugs make the world a much friendlier place to live. We live fast paced lives and we have to choose how we use our time and energy. It is easy to forget my goal, but God blesses me with loving, energetic and attention demanding grandchildren and I love to be with them.

As I think of the future and wonder what the family unit will look like, I am convinced we will need grandparents tomorrow even more than we do today. Grandparents that will choose to give their time and energy to supporting, listening and loving their grandchildren...grandparents that will live as an example and teacher of truth. Grandparents that will recognize their grandchildren as precious, living treasures.Grandchildren are very rare and precious treasures.

Yours truly,
Jan King
Bellevue, Washington

There is nothing you can do to help your grandchildren grow up and succeed in life that is more important or meaningful than to make sure they know how much you love them; how much you care for them; how much you support them; and how dearly you hold them close to your heart!

Finally, I received the following letter that illustrates how so many grandparents feel about being a grandparent today:

What Does It Mean to be a Grandparent Today?

Times sure have changed since I was growing up in the 1930's and 40's. For instance, family values are different from when I was a child. There was much more respect for authority in the past compared to nowadays. I learned early in life that respect begins at home. If there's little or no respect in the home, this type of attitude will be carried over into the rest of a young person's life. It will affect both thinking and actions.

The Ten Commandments were a big factor in my youth. Not that I kept them perfectly for I broke every one either in the letter or spirit of the law. Nevertheless, I was conscience of them to the point where I knew when I had done something wrong.

My parents were not overly religious. In fact, my father seldom darkened the door of a church. However, he always stressed that I should obey the law...both God's and man's. And he assured me that there was always going to be some type of punishment as a result of breaking the law (sometimes, the punishment didn't happen right away, but it did happen!). So, there was a healthy fear of doing wrong instilled in me (and most of the other children in the neighborhood) when I was growing up.

Today, it seems that if a child disobeys in school and is punished for it, instead of the parents backing the school authorities, they want to sue the school system for mistreating their juvenile delinquent. What I find so interesting is, the parents are the ones who must take responsibility because it is they who trained (or mistrained) their kids in the first place. There is a Proverb that goes, "Train up a child in the way that he should go: and when he is old he will not depart from it." You know, the opposite to this proverb also holds true.

Certainly, I was not always the most obedient child when I was growing up. I got my share of spankings and deservedly so. Today, if a parent spanks a child it is called "child abuse". What a shame! I had an older cousin who once told me that if he had taken the time to discipline his children the way my father disciplined my brother and me, he just knew that his kids would have had different lives. As it was, due to his overly indulgence and permissiveness, his children experienced drugs, had illegitimate children of their own and finally spent time in jail.

The world has changed drastically from bad to worse: I can remember when Crack was a broken line in a sidewalk; one got married first and then lived together; closets were for clothes, not something to "come out of"; grass was something to mow, not smoke; Coke was a soft drink; pot was something a person cooked a stew in; rock music was grandma's lullaby; AIDS were helpers in the Principals office; and, having a meaningful relationship meant getting along with one's friends.

No wonder there is so much confusion and such a generation gap today!

After my wife and I were married, we became proud parents of five children...three boys and two girls. Needless to say, we were not permissive parents. We disciplined our children whenever they needed to be disciplined. And, we did it with love. It is very unfortunate that parents don't seem to realize that the definition of the word "discipline" also means to "teach". Because we dearly loved our children and wanted only the best for them, we taught them to fear God and to love their neighbors.

I believe it is because of the way my wife and I loved our children to the point where we were not afraid to discipline and teach them right from wrong, none of our kids ever tried drugs nor were they promiscuous. All of them went to college (and I might add, each one of my children helped pay his or her own tuition and school costs) and they all have successful careers and are happily married.And the thing that I cherish the most is, every one of my kids attend church regularly and are Christians both in name and in deeds...they all live what they have been taught and believe.

Now, my wife and I are grandparents and have four grandsons to help our children rear...and what a great pleasure and joy it is!

It's not difficult to look around and think how much the world seems to be coming apart at the seams. Even so, I am convinced that just as my father and his father before him used a formula of love, discipline and teaching in order to raise their children properly; and just as my wife and I used this same formula in the way we reared our kids with very positive results, this same formula...love, discipline and teaching...will work for our children and their children tomorrow. It just takes love, time, compassion, understanding, discipline and teaching. It takes a lot of time and love but it's worth every effort given and minute spent!

Your friend,
Bill Vernich
Nashville, Tennessee

Indeed, Grandparenting is

worth every effort given
and
minute spent!

P arents must give good example and reverent deportment in the face of their children. And all these instances of charity which endear each other - sweetness of conversation, affability, frequent admonition - all signification's of love and tenderness, care and watchfulness, must be expressed toward children; that they may look upon their parents as their friends and patrons, their defense and sanctuary, their treasure and their guide. -L'Estrange

CHAPTER EIGHT

RAISING CHILDREN
AS A
SINGLE PARENT!

During the past several decades, our democratic society has encountered some very interesting social movements, for both the good of mankind and the not so good. One of these movements has been the change in attitude by a growing group of women who are determined to raise children alone. It seems they have little or no desire in having a husband help with this responsibility.

Another change in attitude, definitely in the not-so-good-for-society category, is the way more and more fathers no longer have the desire or inclination to help support their kids. This usually happens after a bitter divorce where he loses custody rights, or when he discovers a new love interest which leaves little or no room in his life for anyone else. At this point, his selfish motivation leads him to the pit of disaster, where he now abandons his children and betrays his wife. A very complex and destructive situation!

In some cases, the wife may have made it clear to one and all that she wants nothing to do with her ex-husband. She does not want his financial help and as far as she is concerned, he has forfeited all rights to his children. Also, what seems to be the growing trend today is for the father (and sometimes even the mother) to simply move out of the house and vanish...thus neglecting any type of child support payment or association with his or her kids. The result? An increase in the number of single parents who have the very difficult job and responsibility of raising their children alone! And the result of raising children by a single parent today? A much different and possibly more negative type of society tomorrow!

We have just read in the previous chapter that most statistics regarding raising children in the 1990's and on into the 21st century indicate that one out of every two children will be reared by a single parent. And this single parent will more likely be the mother rather than the father. There is more than just the child involved in this type of situation, and the overall ramifications for both the family and society will be overwhelming at best. The results will include, but not be limited to, higher taxes, loss of jobs, higher illiteracy, increased financial ruin, and a bulging crime rate.

Very few children are being raised in a single parent home by a financially independent mother who has little or no need for government support, such as Aid for Dependent Children, food stamps, etc. Nor are the vast majority of these kids raised in a home where they are able to increase their knowledge and attend school without requiring physical and/or financial assistance from an outside source. Most single mothers have a very difficult time in making both ends meet, and without welfare and government aid, she and her children would more than likely not survive...or, at best, remain in health both physically and mentally.

I realize there are women reading this chapter who will not agree with what I have written. However, the facts reveal without a doubt that during the past ten to twenty years, the amount of welfare compensation paid out in this country has risen sharply in a direct parallel to the birth rate of single mothers. And, I firmly believe that if one were to ask single mothers in any state, city or township this question: "Are your children in need of material things such as financial help, food, shelter, clothes and/or toys?"; the vast majority of them would reply with a resounding, "Indeed they are!"

Certainly, there are single professional women who have succeeded in business and can well afford to raise a child on their own. However, just because one can afford something, doesn't make it right. Aren't there more valuable considerations to be addressed in raising a successful child other than having enough money to buy his clothes, her prom dress, a Nintendo game, or a room full of toys and dolls? What about promoting the concept of having a two-parent family? Or is this simply an outdated idea that no longer has any relevance? What about obeying the Word of God and keeping His commandments regarding raising children and managing a complete family? Or is God really dead and therefore His message and commandments no longer valid?

Having a spouse become ill and die, leaving the surviving parent to care for the children alone, is one thing. In this case, a *"family"* consists in reality of the surviving parent and his or her children. And they will continue to be a single-parent family unit until mom or dad either remarries or the children leave home. Death of a parent is certainly a natural cause for creating a single-parent household.

However, in the context of what I am writing regarding most

single parenting today, I mainly refer to those single parents who are either not married and have no intention of doing so; are still in their teens and have given birth to a child simply because of an accident that happened in the back seat of a car; are older, single women who have never had a child and look forward to caring for an infant much the same way they did when they were young and played with a favorite doll; or, are single individuals who adopt a child in the same manner as though they were passing by a pet store and suddenly,

"How was your work today, Mom?"

without thought or malice, decide to purchase a puppy.

Still, no matter what your motive might be for your becoming a single parent; no matter what your circumstance or why you find yourself raising a child as a single parent, realize that your child really needs you and that he or she loves you unconditionally. As a single parent, you have an awesome responsibility to properly raise your child. So, by all means, take the time and spend the energy to understand how best you might give your little one those certain accouterments that help support a child's life which only a spouse of a different gender can provide.

I realize it isn't easy to be both mom and dad to a little boy or girl; however, our makeup as human beings requires that we have both male and female role models to help form our lives. Little boys and girls need male as well as female influence if they are to mature into bright, caring, thoughtful and balanced young people. If a little boy has no female influence in his life, how will he ever be able to express how he feels regarding the hurt and pain of a disabled friend? Without a male influence in her life, how will a little girl ever learn to appreciate the more bold and exciting things in life? God simply made human beings to need both male and female influences in their lives to assure that we might grow to become well-rounded and mature adults. I realize that some will fault what I have just written and say, "I can give my kid everything he or she needs, emotionally and physically." I don't agree. And the type of family violence and parental problems we are experiencing in today's society supports my disagreement.

Why is it so important that children have both male and female role models in their youth? To answer this question, let's take a look at our present society. Television, music and movies have had a major impact on the way our children have become so desensitized to much of what they experience in society today. A large number of kids no longer seem able to express deep, emotional feelings toward sick friends, hurt animals, elderly people, and other problem situations each one of us faces on a daily basis. Yet, how can we expect our young ones to grow up and become caring and loving adults when so much of what they see and hear through the media and on the street is so violent and negative. How can we expect them to understand the importance of life and death when they see so many films and television programs where violent death, murder, rape, drug deals, prostitution, and other crimes and evil acts are depicted as something not out of the ordinary. "It's just the way it is!", they are told.

"Hey, it's no big deal!", a group of youngsters answer a TV interviewer when asked about drive-by shootings and gang related killings. "It's just the way things are!" Wow! Do you realize that when you were a child there was no such thing as a "drive-by shooting?"

My point is this: if we don't teach our children how to be sensitive toward a fellow human being's situation or problem, who will? If we continue to allow our children to grow up without someone helping them to understand the value and great worth of everything God created, what kind of world will we be living in within the next few short years? This is why it is so important that children have both a male and female influence involved in their lives - especially during their formative years. Think about it. Remember, what you teach or don't teach your child is exactly what you and all of society will reap in the near future! So, the question remains, "In a single-parent household, is it important that a little boy or girl have interaction, communication, and companionship with a loving and caring adult of the opposite sex?" You bet it is! More so today than ever before!

If you are a single parent raising a young son or daughter alone, who is there from the opposite sex that might help you and your child have this interaction and communication that is so important? You might look to a family member, grandparent, friend, pastor, Big Brother or Big Sister. Someone you know and care for, and who you can completely trust with the life of your child. It takes time and thought to locate this person or persons, but in the long run, it will be well worth it!

For those reading this who consider themselves to be true Christians, ask yourself, "What is a true Christian and what do I do to be one?" The Bible tells us that true Christianity is, "To look after the fatherless and widows in their distress and to keep oneself from being polluted by the world." (James 1:27 NIV). If you know of a child who doesn't have a father or mother, why not take the time and get to know him or her - take a moment out of your busy life and look after this fatherless child, while also helping the widow. Don't just be a talker, be a doer!

Let's stop for a moment and think about how many abortions are performed each year here in the United States alone. Now consider: instead of terminating the lives of these unborn children, let them complete their birthing cycle and come to full term. The question that will be asked is, "What will be the overall effect on our government and social welfare system when so many children are born without family or financial support?" The answer is, "It will have a negative effect, and it will have tremendous consequences!"

A life-style of licentious living and unrestrained sexual activity by young, unmarried partners, resulting in unwanted births, will have a devastating effect on our society (if not controlled soon)! Look around and you cannot help but see some of the effects already! Yet, will destroying an unborn fetus solve the problem? And where does accountability come to play in this scenario? Is it too late to alter the onrushing tide of sexual immorality we are experiencing today? And, if not, then how do we change this decadent attitude that has been manifesting itself during the past several decades? It is plainly evident that it can't be controlled by abortion!

Just because our elected lawmakers pass law after law which supposedly protect the rights of pregnant women (including social and financial benefits regarding those involved with the pregnancy) over the rights of the unborn child, does this make everything okay? A more important question is: as man continues to establish his own physical laws which often invalidate those great spiritual laws that formed the basic foundation for our national constitution, as well as the constitutions for other countries, how then does Almighty God view the way man is now destroying himself, his neighbor, and his or her unborn child?

Again, let me repeat: single parenting in the 90's and on into the 21st century will be anything but easy! If you want proof, look around at what we are now witnessing on a daily basis throughout our surrounding environment. How many friends do you have who are unemployed? How many are divorced? How many have children on drugs? Are any of your single female friends pregnant? How many people do you know who are seriously ill? Do you know of anyone who has AIDS? Cancer? TB? Heart disease? Is the air you breathe and the water you drink as pure as it was a generation ago? Do you feel safe when you travel out at night? Is the money in your pocket worth what it was twenty years ago? Ten years ago? Five years ago? Last year? Yesterday?!

What about the cost of raising a child? Is it less expensive to feed and clothe a little tot today than it was when you were a kid? Will you be able to afford to send your child to school or college during the next five to ten years? And, if not, what will happen to our country? Where will our future leaders come from? What type of person will he or she be that ends up directing your future and mine...indeed, the future for all mankind? And, what type of attitude, character, knowledge, or abilities will our kids be taught along the way to adulthood? What will they really learn? And who will teach them? So the question is: will raising a child now and on into the future be more difficult? Without a doubt!

How do we overcome this overwhelming problem of raising children in a single parent household, while living in an environment where resources are strained and life is becoming more difficult? How do we raise our kids to become worthwhile citizens and pillars in the community when there is only mom or dad attempting to carry out the awesome task of teaching, training, and disciplining a child, especially when it really takes two parents to manage this tremendous responsibility?

It ain't easy, but with a lot of perseverance, patience, and unconditional love it can be done!

I hope that I am not so naive to actually believe we will suddenly begin considering the consequence of our actions to the point where the vast majority of men and women will marry, *commit to one another their very own lives...for life,* accept full responsibility for their actions - both for the good or bad - and raise their children in a loving home with both a father and a mother to guide and direct them. I realize I'm writing about a utopian future with these suggestions; however, the day is coming when this will take place, but probably not for a while.

In the meantime, if we parents, single or married, take the time to properly instruct our offspring as to what sex is all about, why marriage is so important, why raising children in a home filled with love, hope, and desire is consequential to having a safe and prosperous society; if we explain what AIDS is and what it means, how to abstain from contracting sexual transmitted diseases; and, what the word "love" actually means, as opposed to what Hollywood and television portray it to be, our children will then raise their children in such a way that hopefully their children will put a screeching halt to the decadence, immorality, and evil we are experiencing today. And in doing so, they will also be responsible for altering the course of a society heading for the doldrums or worse! If change is to come soon, it will take time and energy; however, it all must begin in the home by teaching, praising and loving our kids!

This is not to say that our children's children will not divorce or raise their children as a single parent...this most likely will continue for decades into the future. However, if properly taught now, during their youth, the likelihood of our grandkids surviving and prospering in a safer and more pleasant world will greatly increase.

If you are a single parent, I am not suggesting you run out and find the first available person to marry to help raise your kids. I am suggesting, however, that you consider the need each of your children has for a role model, from both their own gender as well as from the opposite sex. I am strongly suggesting that little boys need a male influence in their lives just as little girls need a female influence in theirs. And they both need to be influenced by mature adults of the opposite sex.

I know a man who, after going through a rather nasty divorce, won the custody of his daughter while losing custody of his son. It was a devastating trial and experience for both the children as well as the father and mother.

Knowing the father so well, I can recall there were many times when he thought he had more than he could handle with raising his young daughter alone. One rather amusing time in particular happened while on a business trip away from home. Late one night in his motel room the phone rang and while still half asleep he heard the frantic caller on the other end shriek, "When your daughter came home from school today, she had a note from the teacher explaining that during recess she had experienced some bleeding while going to the toilet! I guess it really scared her!"

By now, the concerned father was completely awake and pacing the floor. "What do you mean, she was bleeding?", he asked the lady caring for his daughter during his absence. "Is she hurt? Did she get into a fight with some one? Is she okay?"

"Don't worry," came the reply. "Your daughter has just started her menstrual period."

"Her what?!" He exclaimed. "What do I do now?!" The moment his plane landed, the father headed for the local library to research every book and article written regarding the menstrual cycle and everything else this feminine phenomena entails. He made a marvelous attempt at helping his daughter through a very important time in her life. Nevertheless, it was not the same as it might have been if it were the mother instructing and helping her daughter understand what was beginning to take place in her body. Only a mother, or another woman, could really talk about all the necessary information and patient understanding his young girl now needed as she began to change and grow. Without a doubt, it was another test and trial for both the father and his daughter!

During this same time, the father and his son began to let distance and difference separate them. Certainly it was difficult for both of them because the father felt he was imposing on both his ex-wife's and son's new life. And, it seemed to him that most of the men his ex-wife was now dating or living with were completely different from who he was; and more important, they handled their approach to his son far differently from the way he taught and instructed his boy.

When the son was with his father he had to do what he was

told. He could not run loose, talk back in a nasty way, nor be disobedient. Even though the father constantly worked to reinforce a very positive attitude of love and support toward his son, including letting him know the divorce was not the little boy's fault; nevertheless, he felt he could not buy his son's love and respect with candy, toys or other goodies, as so often is the case when a child tries to make a parent feel guilty for having left him.

The son's life away from his mom was as different as night is from day, up is from down, liberal is from conservative, or black is from white. It's not difficult to see why the young boy wanted only to be with his mother. It was a most confusing and perplexing time for both the father and son. And considerable damage was inflicted on both!

So far, this true story has had a rather sad ending, yet it is not unlike many stories we hear about today regarding children and parents involved in divorce. The daughter, in this case, became so entangled with sex and drugs, and had such a disobedient attitude toward her dad and his new wife, that after some time of attempting to make things right, with little or no positive results, she was put out of the home. This was, without a doubt, the most difficult thing the father ever had to do, and I'm sure he hopes and prays he and his daughter will one day be close again.

The father and son hardly speak to each other now. Although the son, now in his twenties, cares deeply for his father, he believes his dad is too "religious" and far too conservative for his tastes; the father wanting only the best for his youngest son, feels his boy has abandoned certain values and principles which he was taught early in life, in order that he might achieve an earthly desire for physical success and material gain! And the ironic thing about this is that the son is acting much like the father did in his youth!

Although both the parents and children love one another, their polarization began a long time ago when the parents, out of selfish desire and greed, failed to fulfill the commitment they had made to each other and to their kids...*to make sure their children's best interests were always the priority!* It was not the children's fault that things

96

resulted the way they did, it was the fault of the parents!

What is that wonderful adage we were taught when we were kids? Something about how we reap what we sow. Do we reap what we sow? At some point in time, we do! I imagine that every reader knows a story similar to the one I have just related. Sad, isn't it?

If you are a single mom, make sure your son spends time with the men in the family. Let him be involved with his dad, your dad, your brothers, cousins, or any other male family members. Or, have him become involved with a Big Brother through the organization by the same name. Participate with him during his youth, especially when he goes out for team sports, the drama club, spelling bees, etc. Teach him about the legacy of his family and the importance of knowing his relatives; explain why he has freckles, red hair, brown eyes, dark skin, or speaks with a drawl. *And never put your ex-spouse down in front of him!* Of course, what I have written holds true for daughters. Also (this is very important), always make sure you know what kind of seed the person you are dating is planting in your child's fertile mind! Always remain in complete charge of the situation! Your little boy or girl is your responsibility, not the person's you are dating!

Always be aware of what your young daughter is thinking about, what she dreams about, what she cares about. Be sure that you take her to school functions. Participate in the PTA or any other social activity that might help her in some way. Talk to her about boys in a positive way; yet, tell her why boys do what they do and that there is a difference between how little girls think about little boys and how little boys often overreact to little girls! Let her know you truly care. And protect her by giving her sound advice, even though there are times when she will not want to accept it. The same goes for boys.

Never degrade or put down the opposite sex in front of your child. Help them to grow and mature with a healthy respect for both their peers and those of the opposite sex. Constantly reassure your child that just because he or she is being raised by a single parent

97

doesn't mean that marriage is negative or bad. Help them understand that marriage is something to be honored and cherished, fathers are to be valued, and motherhood is something very precious and of great worth; that the mother is *the* person a daughter should want to emulate just as the father is *the* person a son should want to emulate.

Help your children understand that even though you know very little about some certain sport or ballet dance, you will always support their interest by helping them discover the fundamentals of the sport or dance if only by introducing them to that certain person who does understand...a teacher, friend, business associate, family member, professional ball player, dancer...

The bottom line is this: it matters not if you are happily married to your childhood sweetheart, divorced and now traveling life's highway alone, or single and just starting out in life, if you have a child to support, do it with all your might!

Certainly being happily married and raising kids is what our great Creator God had in mind when He created us. Yet, when circumstances prevail that change the course we are on, no matter who is at fault, if a child is involved it is the responsibility of the *parents* to make sure their little one is cared for, nurtured, protected, disciplined, trained, and educated in the *right way,* so that he or she will grow up and live a decent and productive life!

Raising a child, no matter what your circumstance, should be the most joyful and fulfilling experience you will ever encounter during your time living on this Earth!

CHAPTER NINE

HOW TO HELP YOUR KIDS
MAKE WISE DECISIONS!

As I travel throughout this country talking with parents and counseling kids from all walks of life, I notice a major area of child development sorely missing: many young people today lack the ability to make right and proper decisions. Parents want their children to be able to make good decisions, but somehow they have failed to properly teach them how to do so.

Every parent, who has ever watched his or her child go before a judge to be sentenced for having committed a crime, or spent time pacing the floor of a hospital waiting room while their teenage son was being operated on for a wound inflicted by a rival gang member, knows exactly how it feels to have failed in some way to properly teach his or her child about how to make wise decisions.

After a mother can no longer dry her eyes from having cried so long and so often since the death of her first born child, while a father attempts to numb the pain of his son's death by alcohol or drugs, realization soon begins to set in that it is now too late to teach the difference between right and wrong; it is now too late to explain why making the right decision is so very important; it is now too late to teach their child anything!

There is, however, good news regarding teaching a child about how to make wise and proper decisions. Good news that can help increase the chance that your child will never end up before a judge, on an operating table, or on a cold slab in a morgue because of some stupid thing they may have done. To achieve this good news means that you as a parent must make every opportunity to teach your children the principles of proper decision making while they are young...while their young sensitive minds are fertile and susceptible to your instruction. You can never begin teaching your children too early!

First of all, we must realize that every decision, good or bad, is a decision that we will have to live with, probably for the rest of our lives. And just as we adult parents must live by those decisions we make, so will our children live by the decisions they make. And what makes this so interesting is that each decision has a cause and effect element which determines how some decisions lead to opportunity and success while other decisions lead to failure and even death. How we make each decision is the thing that is so very important!

What type of decisions will our children be called upon to make? The same ones we had to make as we were growing up! As examples: how to properly cross a street, why we should not touch the hot stove, why we should trust our parents, why we should study and complete our school work, how we should properly drive the car, whom we should date, and later, whom we should marry, how we should behave around the opposite sex, why we should not smoke, use illegal drugs, speak profanities, or engage in illicit sex, what type of music to listen to, television to watch, or movies to go see.

And other questions like, what kind of friends to hang out with, how to say "No!", when is it time to leave a party, plus many other consequential decisions kids have to make today, just as we parents did yesterday!

Decision making never ends. We have a responsibility to live life to its full potential, and doing so means having to make decisions. It all begins when we are very small and can't decide which rattle to toss out of the crib, which class to take in school, which career will be the most rewarding, whom to marry, and how many kids to have. And it all ends the moment we take our last breath. The way we can truly measure success has everything to do with the decisions we make between the crib and our last breath. It's not how many "toys" we have when we die that decides if we succeeded or not, it's how many wise decisions we made; what kind of person we were, what kind of character we had.

The question is: If you had been taught when you were young how to make wise decisions, would you have done anything different as you were growing up? Of course you would! We all would. I certainly would like to relive some of the decisions I made in my youth. But, sad to say, just like you, I am also reaping the effects of the decisions, both good and bad, I made yesterday and the day before.

The nice thing about the aging process is, with experience we gain wisdom, and with wisdom we have a better understanding as to how we can best make proper and right decisions. Needless to say, this doesn't always work out the way many of the so-called experts reported in the textbooks we read as young students; however, as we grow older, we do have a semblance of discernment which should provide us with a somewhat easier exercise during our decision-making process.

To demonstrate how we gain knowledge and wisdom as we grow and mature, I am including something interesting a friend of mine wrote regarding his views about youth, aging, the fallacy of having a secular education, and the desire for wisdom. It goes something like this:

"In my teens and early twenties, I studied whatever academic material I was told to, or that which I thought would benefit me in some marvelous way. And, in my youthful zeal to gain recognition, succeed in studies, and just get ahead of the rest of the pack, I often resorted to using whatever material tools were available at the time to help in this endeavor.

"I was also governed by what I considered at that time to be great maturity on my part. I relied on many of the more viscid theories being taught at that moment, most of which I no longer remember, to direct and counsel me, for I considered these theories to be very relevant and most useful in the building of my career. And during that time in my youth, I just knew that I knew it all!

"In my thirties and on into my forties,
I traveled much of the world, directed more
than a few companies and the lives of those
who worked for me, and, basically, gained an
understanding, wisdom and knowledge from my
daily endeavors, difficult studies, hard work,
and the accepted responsibilities I so
eagerly undertook.

"As I became more involved with the mental and
spiritual aspects of life, based on the
statutes and commandments of God, I slowly
began to realize that I didn't know nearly as
much as I thought I knew!

"Now, as I trace my life back across so many
calendar years, I see that this was the
beginning of my great awakening. As with
most adversity and growth, I also experienced
stress and pain, for there was still much to
learn and overcome!

"So, by the grace of God, I have arrived into
my fifties. And, as I look back over the life
I have lived thus far, I see many of the things
I experienced those difficult yet very reward
ing lessons I learned in my twenties, thirties
and forties provided a firmly entrenched foun
dation enabling me to proceed forward toward my
desires and goals.

"It also provides me with the courage, will and
determination to accept new ideas, theories,
objectives and responsibilities so that I might
continue to grow, learn and mature; while at
the same time, providing me the opportunity to
give back to society some of what I have so
graciously been given!"

> Larry Ray,
> Alamosa, Colorado

"Okay," you might say after reading the above, "I see the point. But, what about my children? How can they make wise decisions when they don't have experience or maturity to fall back on? How can I help prevent future emotional scars from ripping my children's lives apart because of some stupid mistake they will make in their youth?" Well, I could probably come up with hundred dollar-an-hour answers, but if we take a moment and look at these questions without trying to make them more complicated than necessary, the answer is very simple: you begin training your children now, while they are still young, how to make the right decisions! You take the time now to give them the information and instruction they need, in order for them to live a life that is right and proper! And you teach them that there are right and wrong decisions...there are absolutes! It's as simple as that!

However, putting my answer into practice might not be so simple. It will take time, energy, patience, devotion, perseverance, and unconditional love!

Here are a few examples of how we can help our children make wise decisions. However, before we commence with this, let's remember that if we are to succeed in teaching our kids how to make wise decisions, we must start just as soon as they begin recognizing certain elements within their own surrounding environment, i.e., daddy, mommy, toes, food, toys, bed, sky, birds, etc.

If we are to properly teach our children to do anything, we must first show them *how* to accomplish what we are asking them to do. We must demonstrate what it is we want them to do by our doing the chore first.

Let's take toys as an example: the decision your child must make is this: "Should I pick up my toys or should I let them lie where they are so I can watch daddy slip and fall on them as he comes out of the bathroom?" Of course, if your child is still crawling you will no doubt be the one who reaches over and picks them up . However, if she is old enough to think about whether or not she should be the one to pick up her toys, it means that someone at some time has demonstrated the proper way to carry out this chore, and in this case, she should definitely be required to pick up her toys! And praised for doing so.

But how do you get her to do so? Yell at her over and over to "pick 'em up or else?!" Threaten to spank her if she doesn't obey you? Call out for help from your spouse who is in the shower and can't hear you anyway? No, you say? Well, then how about a little parent-to-child reasoning with solid enforcement to back up what you say? Something like this, "Susie, I am only going to tell you once that I would like you to pick up your toys now. And if you don't pick them up immediately, then you are telling me that you don't want to play with them for the next couple of days. So it's *your decision* as to whether or not *you decide* to pick them up. Think about it, but not too long. Okay?"

What do you think will happen? Nothing of course! You will be tested! But now it becomes your decision as to how many times you will be tested!

If your little girl decides to test you and doesn't pick up her toys, it is your decision to either pick them up or exercise your enforcement back up system. So let's say she just isn't going to pick up her toys. Okay, you do. You quietly walk over, reach down and pick them up. Then you put them away so your little girl cannot have them for as long as you told her they would be confined to your care. The nice thing about this is you won't have to pick them up tomorrow, because she won't have them to play with. However, this approach will only work if you abide by what you tell your daughter will be the result of her action or inaction. You must always do exactly what you say you will do, no matter what!

It is most important that you explain to your child the consequences of her action or inaction...in this case, the consequence of her decision not to pick up her toys. If you expect to succeed with this training, don't let this be just an occasional punishment. Be consistent! Be very patient and always be consistent!

This type of training will help your child begin to learn how to think and how to reason. And even though a child's level of responsibility and punishment must be applicable to his or her age, including the ability to understand and reason, nevertheless, before long, little Susie or baby Junior will begin realizing that they are indeed responsible for their actions. And, just as each one of us continues to learn throughout our lives that there is a cause for every effect, our children will also come to understand that there are rewards for doing things correctly and punishments when things are done incorrectly. The idea is to lean on the reward side and be consistent with the punishment side...accentuate the positive!

Once again, to really help children understand and appreciate the value of principles and the importance of instruction, it is necessary that we begin the teaching and training process early on.

Another example in helping children learn how to make proper decisions is overcoming the age-old problem of making a bed. After showing my sons exactly how to properly make their beds, I can't recall the number of times when I would have to remind them that making their beds was their responsibility. Of course, they were now a little older and this was an assignment I felt they were old enough to handle.

I must confess that my girls were a lot better at making their beds than my boys. I suppose girls simply like things a little neater than boys do, and most young boys think making a bed is girls' work. Sounds a little chauvinistic? Perhaps. But not in my family! We all had chores to do, and it mattered not that some of the chores the boys had to complete might have been thought of as being "girls" work!" Actually, with the possible exception of weight loads, we really didn't recognize a difference between "girls' work" and "boys' work" in the home. Our boys slept in their own beds, and it was their responsibility to make sure each bed was clean and made up each morning.

Whenever one of my younger sons (not yet attending school) would become a little lazy with his bed making chores, I would take him aside, look directly at him, and say, "Son, I want you to make your bed. But first, I am going to give you an opportunity to make a decision. It seems to me that by you not making your bed, you are telling me that you would rather get back in it. Is this correct?" While he was studying the question, I continued, "Your decision is either you make your bed now or you get back into your bed for the rest of the day."

When my sons were older and attending grade school, I took a different approach. "By not making your bed you are telling me that instead of playing ball when you get home from school, you want to go back to bed. It's your decision."

By helping my sons understand that it was their decision as to whether or not they would spend the day in bed or go out and play with their friends, I was able to start the teaching process whereby they could begin to realize in a very basic and elementary way that from that time on they will have to live with the results from the decisions they will make throughout their lives.

The important thing for me, as the parent, was to make sure that I always followed through with my part in administering either the reward or the punishment side of the lesson; and that I did so in patience, understanding, and love. I always tried to support my children's decisions while making sure I never harmed their spirit of their will; and that each decision made by one of them was something they could fully understand and relate to. It makes little sense to punish or reward a child if he or she has no idea why they are receiving the punishment or the reward, or even what it's all about.

I can just hear one of you parents thinking to yourself, "This might work for you; but my kids would love to spend all day in bed!" Well, maybe so. However, my experience tells me that after a day or two in bed with nothing to do...no books to read, TV to watch, or music to listen to..a child, any child, isn't going to look forward to this type of experience very often. If you patiently and consistently carry out this type of child decision-making and instruction whenever needed, you will have made your point. And I believe you will be amazed at how easy it will be the next time when you ask your child to do his or her chore!

As parents, we should make every effort to teach our children the lesson that for every decision we make for the good or bad, in return, the result will also be for the good or bad. If we fulfill our responsibility in this matter, hopefully later in life, when our kids begin to make those important adult day-to-day decisions, which can affect their very lives to the point of either gaining prosperity or experiencing personal defeat, odds are they will end up making, for the most part, right and proper decisions.

However, if we fail to do our part in teaching (showing and demonstrating the proper way or method) and training (following through with the teaching in a consistent manner) our children how to manage and accomplish the smaller things in life while they are young, chances are, as they grow older, they will fail to make the best possible decisions regarding the more important issues, and the result might end up to be sorrow and failure. We parents will be held responsible for having failed to carry out our responsibility for properly *teaching* and *training* our children!

Wouldn't you really rather correct your kids in their youth for not picking up toys, making beds, taking out the garbage, or any number of other lessons and chores to be learned, than to see him or her suffer the consequences for having made a poor judgment...like using drugs, driving recklessly, engaging in illicit sex, carrying a gun to school, or any number of other wrong decisions that can ruin a life?

How about using dating as an example? We will discuss this parental anxiety teaser in chapter 15, but for now, let's examine one of the more difficult problems a parent must confront when allowing children to date - what time they should be home!

Before your daughter (or son) leaves for her (his) date, you might decide to have a conversation that goes something like this: "Honey, I would like you to be home by eleven o'clock."

"But, Daddy!", she whines. "The school dance isn't even over until eleven!"

"Okay. I wouldn't want you to have to leave the dance early, so instead of eleven, let's make it eleven thirty."

"But, it takes that long to drive home from school!"

"I know."

"But..."

"No if's, and's or but's. You have an opportunity now to make a decision. If you're not home by eleven thirty, and I don't mean eleven thirty-one, you're telling me you don't want to go out for the next two to three weeks! Is this right?"

"Well, I..."

"Right?"

"Yeah, okay Dad. I hear what you're sayin'". Of course I deflated her balloon somewhat, and she felt let down and sad for a moment. I mean, what kid wouldn't? But this is the point: by fulfilling my responsibility to properly teach my daughter, I helped her begin to understand that throughout life every human being experiences the necessity for commitment, *restriction*, obedience, and decision making. Without acknowledging and practicing these fundamentals, which continually help guide and direct our lives, we, as individuals living in a society, would most assuredly experience anarchy, confusion, societal breakdown, or worse.

Finally, another way to help a child learn to make wise decisions can come from having to learn to pick up his or her clothes. And parents, if you are the type of person who doesn't pick up after yourself, you're going to have a very difficult time teaching your children the value of picking up their clothes!

We had six kids who needed to be dressed and groomed every day. If my wife and I hadn't taught them about neatness and how to tidy up their rooms and pick up their clothes, this problem could have easily gotten out of hand. Even so, there were times when things did become pretty wild!

"Hey, gang. Guess what? I'm going to give you another chance to make an important decision." I could just see how excited they all were by the expressions written all over their faces. Nevertheless, I decided then and there that I would prevail. "If you don't put away your clothes and I have to pick them up for you, I will keep them for the next couple of weeks, and you won't be getting any new clothes!"

"You mean you're even including our new team uniforms

and school jackets?"

"You got it. Remember, I'm only trying to help you learn how to make a wise decision."

For some families today whose kids have drawers stuffed full of expensive shirts and sweaters, this may not sound like such a big deal. But with six children to dress with only my salary to buy new clothes, our kids didn't have a lot of extra clothing to fall back on. By the time I collected a couple pair of pants and a skirt or two, they soon began to feel the pinch.

There were a few times when I had to pick up some clothes and put them away. Then later, when the owner of said clothing would ask me for his or her favorite shirt or dress, I would simply reply, "It was your decision to leave your clothes on the floor. I'm only carrying out your decision. You can have them back next Monday." It took a while, but it worked. In fact, you might be very surprised how effective this method is for keeping your childrens clothes picked up and their rooms in order.

One father I know would remind his children that their closets were so untidy that they were beginning to bulge (and the odor wasn't so great either!). Because he was somewhat fearful that the closet walls might break down under such extreme pressure from so many crumbled up socks, wrinkled denims, T shirts, skirts, and blouses, after some warning and still nothing was done to alleviate the problem, his kids would come home from school one day and discover a pile of clothes in the middle of their rooms ready to be ironed, sorted, and placed on hangers in the closet or folded neatly in dresser drawers. This also worked!

The point to all this: prepare your children so they won't travel through life without knowing the proper way to make wise decisions. Teach them while they are still young how to think, how to use their minds. Support them as they work to make correct decisions, and then show them the way to put that decision into action. When they stumble and fall and do something you might consider stupid or dumb, pick them up, hold them, praise their effort and the fact that they tried.

Remember, our children experience throughout life the effects from the types of decisions they will learn to make in their youth...and the final result will either be one of happiness or one of sorrow!

Finally, as my grandmo use to say, teach them to *"use their heads for something more than a place to lay their hats!"* She did and I hope you will.

"All wish to be learned,
BUT FEW
are willing to pay the price!"
Juvenal

"PRECEPTS and AIMS"
of a
YOUNG HIGHLANDER!

A close friend of mine attended military school as a child. And while in this school, he was required to learn the meaning and principles of the following Precepts and Aims. I thought it might be of help to the parents reading this book to include these Precepts and Aims between Chapter Nine, "How to Help Your Kids Make Wise Decisions" and Chapter Ten, "Youth & Leadership". Take a moment after reading each Precept and Aim and think about what the words mean, and how you might apply this knowledge into your childrearing program.

BE KIND
LIVE PURE
SPEAK TRUTH
RIGHT a WRONG
DEFEND THE WEAK
PLAY THE GAME SQUARE
BE PROMPT
OBEY ORDERS
BE NEAT
AVOID SLANG
BE POLITE
BE POSITIVE

HIGHLANDER BOYS
Denver, Colorado

The Loving Parent

vs.

The Nihilistic Parent.

Is it possible to be a loving and caring parent and yet possess a nihilistic as well as narcissistic attitude at the same time? Not hardly!

How can any mother or father who subscribes to philosophical principles that reject authority and tradition and view morality and truth with skepticism, while at the same time living his or her life only for selfish pleasure and greed, raise a child to become a loving, caring, law abiding, truthful, thoughtful and giving citizen? The truth is: it is nearly impossible.

In a world today where so many parents seem to desire carefree, nihilistic and narcissistic lifestyles, desiring the materialistic over the spiritual, the physical over the mental, is it really any wonder so many of our children are failing so early in life?

CHAPTER TEN

YOUTH & LEADERSHIP!
The QUALITIES of HAVING BOTH!

"Let's take a break over by that hot dog stand, Okay?"

Leadership is certainly one of the most important characteristics we can ever help our children to achieve and develop. However, to accomplish this task, we must first know something about the subject. The fact is, true leadership is something we are definitely missing throughout our society today, worldwide. And why do we have such a void regarding this important attribute which is so desperately needed to support society and man? Because we were probably never taught how to be real leaders in our youth, and our children are being taught even less today about this subject at home or in school!

Leadership is not something we are born with, it must be taught, nurtured and developed. And for it to be developed properly, parents must first understand what it means, then apply it into the fabric of their very lives, and finally, set an example for their children to follow. It works much the same way as so many other examples which we, as parents, must provide our kids, if we are going to properly teach and train them.

When we teach our kids not to lie, we must not lie. When we teach them not to steal or cheat, we must never steal or cheat. And when we teach our children how to become leaders, we parents must also be leaders. In almost every situation, our children learn from our example...good or bad!

It can be a little scary today, looking at the world around us and seeing such a lack of leadership, not only with our youth, but with those to whom we have given the responsibility of leading our people and our countries. Certainly not all men and women who have taken on the responsibility for leadership today are inept and poor leaders. However, it seems that somehow, someone forgot to explain and instruct a large number of adult men and women, when they were young and eager to learn, how to become dedicated, honest, and responsible leaders. Either their parents missed the mark or their teachers failed to properly instruct them. Whatever the reason, it sure seems something very important got lost in the while they were growing up!

Just how do we know that many of the problems we are facing today are the result of decisions having been made by poorly qualified leaders? Hey, look around at your immediate environment; watch television, read a newspaper, or pay more attention to how much you spend, where your money goes, how your taxes are spent, why your real estate property is becoming less valuable, how special interest groups persuade local and national officials to do their selfish and greedy bidding, how your surrounding environment is deteriorating, how healthcare has climbed out of sight, and, finally, how your elected leaders manage the affairs of your government!

What is the definition of being a "leader?" Mr. Webster tells us it is, 1- "a person or thing that leads (shows the way; directs the course; to guide or cause one to follow; to guide or direct, as by persuasion or influence, to a course of action or thought; a guiding force)"; 2- "directing, commanding, or guiding head, as of a group or activity." And what about the word leadership? 1- "the position or guidance of a leader". 2. "the ability to lead". 3. "the leaders of a group". *"A Guiding Force!"*

Now just because a person has authority or even responsibility doesn't mean that he or she is a leader, a guiding force! As an example: when a person is placed in the role as a leader, he or she is in a position to guide and direct the lives of other people. How they carry out this responsibility is what is important. And, if they have not been properly taught and instructed as to how to be a real leader, an ethical and honorable leader, how then will they ever lead?

As parents, let's take a moment to ask ourselves, "How do I guide (lead) and direct my children? I mean, just because I have the authority, do I direct my kids and their lives in the best possible manner? Do I lead and instruct them with love and compassion, or do I shove and push them a little too much?" If we shove and push them a little too much, it is only a matter of time before our kids begin to shove and push back. And this is something every parent should want to avoid!

Here is an axiom to ponder for a moment: *real leaders are always willing to give of themselves.* Their main purpose in life is to give to their fellowman whatever it is they have to offer, instead of hoping to receive monetary gain or personal adulation in return. In this context, ask yourself, "How do most of my government leaders measure up to the test of "giving of themselves" as opposed to receiving whatever they can get?" "What about my children's teachers? Do they really provide my kids with the best education possible, or are they simply carrying out their duties because they are being paid to do so?" "What about my fellow employees? Do they give quality time to help make life a little better for those who they work with or the customers who buy our products or services. Or, are they only giving the least amount of effort because they want to receive a pay check and not lose their jobs?" "And what about me? How do I lead my family and my children? Do I give them all that I have to give - quality time, experience, help, guidance, instruction, patience - or, am I more interested in providing myself the pleasures of this life...just wanting to get ahead?!" So, what type of leader are you?

Proverbs 11:14 (The Living Bible) warns each one of us that "without wise leadership, a nation is in trouble..." This refers to every nation no matter its size, racial make up, military might, or the nature of its financial substance and ability. It also takes into account a smaller nation (or people) such as a "family."

If we parents lack leadership qualities, how then will we ever be able to truly develop and support our very own family...our children in particular?

If we parents fail to be honest, dedicated, and sincere leaders for our children, who then will teach them how to lead? The kid down the street? The drug dealer hanging around their school? The idol on television or at the movies? One of your children's peers who is left alone to learn by himself? Let's be honest; if we parents fail to become conscientious and effective leaders today, so that we can direct and maintain the paths we walk and the foundation which supports our family, and if we fail to teach our children now how to become the leaders of tomorrow, tomorrow will only bring forth a very great profusion of sorrow and trouble for both our children and their children! No doubt about it!

One test we can use to see if we are growing and becoming wise leaders for our family, home, and nation is to ask ourselves whether or not we have the ability and character to help solve problems before they become emergencies. In order to do so, we must be very aware of our personal surroundings; who we are, including our strengths and weaknesses, and, most important, we must understand our priorities and the focus of our daily lives.

What a blessing it is for children to have parents who take the time to instruct them in proper leadership. Not only is this a blessing for our kids and family, it is also a blessing for our nation and society as a whole. If our kids are ever going to be able to fully accept the responsibility of becoming successful leaders and fulfill this responsibility in a magnanimous and thoughtful manner, they must first understand how to solve problems before they become emergencies; how to prevent troublesome situations which might have an negative impact on themselves, the family, or their country.

A strong leader never has to raise his or her voice to those under authority in order to get the job done. Nor does one need to insult another person by calling him or her an offensive name, thinking that this is the best way to coax and prod that person into action. It just doesn't work! It never did, and it surely doesn't work today! Yet, how many times have you heard a parent use some type of verbal abuse on their children? Ask yourself if you have ever been guilty of such a major infraction in your child rearing...of such lack of proper leadership!

Throughout my experience as a husband, minister and counselor, I have noticed that whenever a father or mother displays true parental leadership with patience and devotion in a thoughtful manner toward their children, including proper respect and love toward each other, the question of one's authority over the family and children almost never comes up.

However, I have also witnessed that when a wife is pushed and shoved either physically or verbally by her husband and is never given credit for having intelligence and abilities of her own, or is never listened to; and if children are subsequently yelled at and browbeaten by either the father or mother, parental authority and leadership has indeed become an issue. The longer this type of abuse continues, the deeper the seed of resentment and bitterness is planted by all concerned, and the chances of the children growing up to become trusting, caring, and capable leaders greatly diminishes. And who suffers? We all suffer!

True leadership also must be willing to meet sacrifice with sacrifice. If we expect others to sacrifice on our behalf, we must be willing to do the same. We must also be willing to set an example for our children, family, friends and society when called upon.

As an example: How can a parent tell his or her kid not to smoke when he or she puffs away on cigarette after cigarette? How can we admonish our children about the evils of alcohol abuse if parents are alcoholics? How can we ask our kids to pick up after themselves if our home looks like a pigsty? How do we explain to our kids why they should not use foul or vulgar language if we cuss out a neighbor while at the same time losing control over our emotions and temper? The truth is we can't! Not if we don't want to become hypocritical!

As parents and adults, we must learn to sacrifice our own desires and overcome our many weaknesses if we are ever to become wise and proper leaders in our home, to our family, and for our nation. And especially if we want to reach a healthy level of parenthood which we hope our children will want to emulate. I once heard a saying that has stayed with me all during the time I was raising my kids. It goes something like this: "If you are going to talk the talk, then be willing to walk the walk!" Sounds simple enough, but what it is really saying is that we must be willing to make the necessary sacrifices in order to become a real leader. Real sacrifice is a basic substance for true leadership! And children love to follow parents who fully understand what it is to be a leader!

A real leader must meet patience with patience! It is true that the head of a household can demand from his or her children that certain things be done or carried out. But this is not leadership. It is no more than exhibiting a lack of character or being an impatient bully! I thank God for teaching me many years ago the simple truth that I would never be able to lead my family or instruct my children if I lacked patience!

I remember one time when I arrived home and my wife didn't have some report I needed typed , waiting on the table and ready for my signature. Well, I got hot under the collar and began to show my anger. I didn't take the time to stop and realize that with six children to care for and a house to manage, she had more to do than simply watch over me and take care of my needs. In truth, I was only thinking about myself.

My wife knew I was upset, and after a moment of looking straight at me with concern written all over her face, she said, "Before you get too angry, let me tell you about my day. Let me tell you about what happened to me and our kids today. Then after listening to what I have to say, if you still feel you've been wronged and you want to be angry, you have my permission to get as mad as you think you must. But just be patient for a minute and listen." She then went on to tell me about her day which was not uneventful. Kids down with the flu, bills to be paid, washing to do, trying to iron clothes with a broken iron, clogged sink, et cetera. And you know what? There was no way I could stay angry. In fact, I felt very foolish!

Later, I told this story to a marriage class I was conducting, and a lady attending my class wrote a poem explaining my sorry plight much better than I could. It goes like this:

TRIBUTE to a GOOD WIFE!

I CAME HOME AS CROSS AS A BEAR.
    I COMPLAINED TO MY WIFE, "IT'S A JUNGLE OUT THERE!
I'M TIRED AND I WANT YOU TO KNOW I'M MAD
    BECAUSE YOU'LL NEVER BELIEVE WHAT A DAY I'VE HAD!"

MY WIFE CALMLY SAID, "NOW WAIT A JIFF.
    AND SEE IF YOU REALLY NEED TO BE IN SUCH A TIFF.
JUST SIT DOWN AND WE'LL TALK IT OUT
    AND LET'S FIND OUT JUST WHAT IT'S ALL ABOUT.

YOU CAN STILL BE MAD IF YOU WISH TO BE
    BUT FIRST LET ME TELL YOU WHAT HAPPENED TO ME!
THE KIDS BROUGHT HOME A SCROUNGY PUP
    THEY OVERFED IT AND THEN IT THREW UP!

ONE OF THE BOYS FELL OUT OF A TREE
    I BANDAGED HIS ARM AND KISSED HIS KNEE.
TWO OF THE BOYS GOT INTO A FIGHT
    I HAD TO STOP THEM AND SET THINGS RIGHT.

I STARTED TO WASH, THEN THE WASHER BROKE
    SO I WASHED BY HAND AND THAT'S NO JOKE!
WHEN WASHING FOR A FAMILY OF EIGHT
    YOU SOON DISCOVER EVERYTHING RUNS LATE.

DIAPERS TO CHANGE AND BABIES TO ROCK
    WITHOUT MUCH TIME TO WATCH THE CLOCK.
I BURNED THE LUNCH AND SERVED IT RAW
    THE FIRE WENT OUT AND THEN I SAW

THE PUP HAD DUMPED THE GARBAGE OVER
    SO, YOU SEE, MY DAY WASN'T A BED OF CLOVER!
IN SPITE OF ALL THIS, LET ME TELL YOU WHY
    YOU SHOULDN'T GET MAD (AND THIS I'LL BUY),

WE'LL COMPARE OUR DAY AND STAY IN TOUCH
    SO I CAN LOVE THE MAN, I LOVE SO MUCH!"
THEN I SMILED KNOWING THINGS AREN'T SO BAD
    IT'S GREAT HAVING A WIFE
WHO WON'T LET ME GET TOO VERY MAD!

Thelma Evelyn Jones

A leader must meet fairness with fairness! A father who works at being fair in his decisions toward his wife and children stands ten feet tall in his family's eyes. But, for him to be fair means that he must first strip off the "self" and regard those around him as being more important than his job, his interests, his hobbies, his self.

    Parents who desire fairness and justice in their family structure must become *just, as impartial, unbiased, dispassionate, and objective* in the way they manage their children's lives, including the way they direct their own affairs. And until such time as parents forego their own selfish interests and desires and become more *just* and *objective* in their dealings with their children, there is little hope they will ever be able to achieve a real level of fairness. And, fairness and leadership walk hand-in-hand!

    A leader must demonstrate compassion with compassion! And, *love with love!* First Corinthians thirteen, commonly referred to as the "Love Chapter", tells us that even though we might have faith enough to move mountains, and yet, if we do not have love or compassion toward others, we have nothing. Zero!

In order to be a successful leader of a family, home, school, or nation a parent, president, or professor must above all else let *love* become the basis for every decision, direction, discipline, or doctrine which he or she will make.

Unless children experience love in the home, how will they ever be able to express love in their own lives? How can they teach their children about love unless their parents have not only taught them about it, but have also demonstrated through their actions and deeds just what it means and what it is? Keep in mind that we want our children to be smarter, wiser, more caring, and have more character and a much better positive attitude than we did or than did our parents! So, how do our children achieve this? By our giving them our time, energy, devotion, patience, and love. And, by being fair!

For nearly the past two decades, I have been a summer camp director working with youth from all walks of life. I have counseled and taught young people, ages eight to eighteen. And I have heard of individuals who believe it is impossible to manage a successful summer camp made up of kids in this age group.

Well, the success I have experienced working at such a wonderful and rewarding endeavor dictates that it is indeed possible to accomplish such a task, especially when we start building proper leadership qualities in our children at an early age.

Over the years, I have watched young people on my staff at summer camp become real leaders. Through their training and experience working with small children, they gained a knowledge and understanding which forms a basis for the type of solid character one needs to become a real leader. What makes this even more exciting is that the lessons and understanding these young staff members gained while working with the kids under their care now enables them to take this valuable experience and apply it throughout their lives.

I know without a doubt that if we apply the principles I have set forth in this book toward the raising of our kids, the end result

121

will be our having produced children who have the ability and talent to become successful adult leaders tomorrow!

I have used these same principles over and over again with my staff at summer camp. I tried to teach them the importance of being patient with their young charges; that what seems easy to them might be very difficult for a young person, especially if that person is handicapped or disabled in some way. I taught how important it is for the older person to explain and demonstrate what he or she is asking the younger person to do, exactly what is being said, what is being communicated, and, that we should never belittle another person, especially if the other person has difficulty accomplishing something that might seem very simple to us.

I believe by teaching these principles to my camp staff members (as well as to thousands of parents across this nation), I have helped them find the road to become better leaders and, hopefully, better parents when the time comes.

Let's take a moment and look at the reality our children face every morning as they head off to school. You know, very few kids today live on some isolated island where the Beaver, the Nelson family or Father Knows Best resides. Most kids live in a very dangerous environment, and their environment is becoming more dangerous and life threatening every day. The streets of most cities and towns are not what you and I grew up in - evil has become the dominant force, and our naive and trusting children are very impressionable and susceptible to the pull of this force.

The other day I watched a television program where several young people were being interviewed. The objective regarding this particular program was most interesting and had every thing to do with how each one of these children had either been shot by someone in a drive-by shooting, or they knew someone who had been shot and killed. Each heartrendering interview was filled with sorrow and pain! Where we might once have remarked that the locale where so many of these injured and slain children lived was far away in some other city, today this violence is happening in our own backyards!

One of the adult experts on this program talked about how television and movies add to the violence our children are experiencing. How true. I felt a deep sense of sadness when I considered the large amount of negative and tragic material pertaining to child violence here in America, which we compiled while writing this book. It's painful to realize how so many children harm or kill other children today, how more than a few kids are growing up with little or no real values or principles, how more and more boys and girls are experiencing tremendous voids in their lives where there should be a family relationship, and how large numbers of youngsters are traveling self-destructive paths because of little or no direction, correction and love...because their parents don't seem to care!

Violent films, suggestive television shows, and rebellious music would not be the cause for so much of the violence in the streets if parents took the responsibility for leading their children away from such influences. The sad part is that most of what our kids are experiencing today has everything to do with the way they have been taught and/or neglected at home! It makes the two writers of this book want to sit down and weep!

If nothing else comes from your having read this book, if you begin spending more time with your children, teaching them about the more positive and wonderful aspects of life, while at the same time leading them onto the right path in which they should travel, then the time and effort we have given to writing this book will be well worth it!

How do we teach our children the way to become successful leaders? What type of experience can we fall back on to help us accomplish such a worthwhile and important task? Well, we can start by my telling you about a favorite uncle of mine. I worked for this particular uncle when I was a young lad. He was a butcher and he owned his own shop. He was a very patient and kind man, and he never belittled me or put me down and was always supportive of whatever it was I tried to do.

Whenever I would make a mistake, he never yelled at me or

made fun of me in front of others. Instead, he would take the time to help me see just how I had made my mistake, how best to correct it, and how not to make the same mistake again.

During much of the time I spent with my uncle, my job was to learn how to clean and cut up chickens. Believe it or not, it was pretty interesting work but it was also very messy. Some of the chickens were to be cut up as fryers, while others were to be prepared and left whole for roasting. On any good night, I cut up and cleaned as many as one hundred and fifty chickens.

"Ah. Huh?!"

Of course, come Friday night, I wanted to be where the action was and the action certainly wasn't in my uncle's shop cleaning and cutting up so many stupid ol' dead hens. On this night, I tried to get my work finished as fast as possible!

Well, in my zeal to do my job well, while at the same time getting it done with as quick as I could, I would often cut off the leg of some ol' hen that should have been left whole. Can you imagine this young boy holding the body of the chicken in one hand and its right leg in the other hand and all the while wondering if it were possible to sew the leg back on! It wasn't! And in no time, I came to realize that once I cut off any part of a hen, it was too late to do anything about it. Whenever this would happen (which was more often than I really wanted), I would begin feeling very insecure because I thought I was in big trouble!

However, instead of scolding me or putting me to shame, my uncle always took the time to explain what I had done wrong. He would look at me, shake his head, and say, "You need a little less speed and a lot more efficiency if you plan to get home sooner!" He always displayed a quiet type of patience as he demonstrated how I should do something better or overcome something I was doing wrong. And to this day, I am very thankful he took the time to teach me the value of being patient.

Looking back, I can see that my uncle was a real leader. He

didn't command a battalion of soldiers or direct a mammoth corporation, but he knew how to lead others so they might accomplish substantial quality work, and he did so with patience and in fairness. And all the while during the time I was raising my six children, I relied on these same principles of patience and fairness that my uncle taught me many times over.

I remember a time when, once again, my uncle had worked twelve hours straight (which he did quite often). This particular evening we were just about to close shop and head for home when I heard somebody beginning to knock on the front door of the store. Now it was pretty late and I really wanted to get home, but my uncle asked me to see who it was so I unbolted the door.

As I opened the door, I looked down on a small boy holding his two-wheeler bike close to him. He wanted to know if my uncle would fix his bike for him. "No way!," I said. "It's too late. Come back tomorrow!"

Well, my uncle heard me yelling at the boy and came out to see what was going on. After listening to the boy tell his story about how his prize bicycle had broken down and he had no one to fix it for him, my uncle told him to take his bike to the rear of the store where he had his workshop and he would fix it right then and there. Needless to say, the boy was elated.

I thought it was a little stupid that after working twelve hours while standing on his feet and lifting heavy carcasses of meat all day long instead of going home to eat and get some badly needed sleep, he decided to fix some kid's broken bike. It just didn't make sense!. It seemed crazy to me. But you know what? Not only did my uncle fix the boy's bike, he also taught him how to fix it himself the next time it broke down. It took almost an hour of this tired man's time, but he didn't seem to care at all.

Later, my uncle told me that the young boy's father had recently been killed in the war (WWII) while fighting a battle somewhere in Europe. I was very proud of my uncle that night. Not only did he display great patience, he also demonstrated his conviction

125

to serve his fellowman by showing this young boy his deep concern and love for him. What a lesson! It was this type of lesson that I never forgot. In fact, many times I used what I learned that night while raising my kids or teaching parents how to raise theirs.

The point of this lesson, aside from taking the time to help another person, was that if we take the time to help another person by showing them *how* to properly take care or *fix something themselves,* they will become more valuable to themselves, their family, and to society. This is leadership!

My experience has taught me that if we, as parents, do everything for our children today, we will end up doing most everything for our children tomorrow. However, if we teach our kids how to do for themselves whatever it is they want to accomplish, and we show them how to do it properly and with a good attitude, who knows, later on they might just be helping us do what we have set our minds to accomplish! What goes around, comes around!

Later, I met the young boy my uncle had helped, after he became a teenager. At the time, he was helping another kid fix a broken bike! I couldn't believe it! All because one old butcher had taken the time to patiently show a little boy how to repair his bike.

Today, we could sure use more of the type of character and attitude my uncle possessed!

From that experience with my uncle, I adopted his principles when I started raising children. I always tried to make sure I gave each child enough of my time so that I could help teach them how to do different things and how to do them properly. As an example: I taught all of my kids how to wash the family car, paint the house, plant a garden, and fix their own bikes. As a result, today my children are looked upon by their peers as being able to understand how best to accomplish a myriad of tasks. My kids understand what they are doing as they are doing it! This is what I call leadership!

Before we go any further, in fairness to you, the reader, I'd best stop for a moment and explain that there are some pitfalls parents will no doubt experience when they begin to teach their children how to fix things.

This is what happened to me: My children had a mini-bike and finally they wore the engine out. Of course, not wanting to have to walk where they were going, they spent days trying to get the engine fixed. But, it just didn't seem to want to run.

Then one of my sons got the bright idea that my lawnmower engine and their bike's engine might be compatible. So, without further delay, my boys began stripping the lawnmower engine to use its parts on the broken bike engine.

Later that night when I arrived home, I saw that the bike was running, and I told my kids how happy I was that they had found the problem and fixed it. I also commented on how much I appreciated their display of determination and leadership. All the while during my adulation and praise for my very gifted children, no one mentioned a word about my lawnmower lying behind the garage stripped clean!

A few days later, I got up early one morning and looked out at the lawn and noticed it was getting high enough to need cutting. So, at breakfast, I told my kids I would appreciate it if they would mow the lawn. "We can't, Dad. The lawnmower doesn't work!", they said in unison.

"It was working this time last week. Why isn't it working now?", I asked, almost fearful of the answer.

"We used the parts off the mower so we could fix our mini-bike," they proudly replied.

Needless to say, I almost lost it when they told me why my lawnmower had died and gone to lawnmower heaven. I thought about getting angry, but I couldn't! I mean, after all, I had earlier congratulated my kids because they had taken the initiative and fixed their bike. Besides, the most important piece of equipment in their minds had been the one they had repaired. Still, it did take some patience on my part that morning for me to not blow up and destroy some of the relationship I was building with my children. However, I did go out and purchase a push mower so that my kids could mow the lawn, even if it was by hand!

One final story about my uncle comes to mind. During my

teenage years, he taught me something else about patience and leadership. You see, I stuttered badly. So badly that I couldn't even talk to girls. Especially to girls!

My uncle thought about my problem for awhile, then one day he made a suggestion. "I want you to slow down when you are talking and think about what you are trying to say." He wanted me to think before I spoke. As a teenager, I had never heard of such a thing!

Soon, he had me talking in front of the mirror fifteen minutes a day. I spoke slowly while at the same time thinking about what I was saying. And in time, I got much better with my speech. So much so, and to my delight, I discovered that I had no problem when it came to talking to the girls. And after all, wasn't this what I lived my life for?!

I had no idea at the time that one day I would speak in front of thousands of people! And mostly, this was made possible because one man took a little time to help this young boy overcome a speech handicap. How very thankful I am that he did!

Whenever we stop to help another person, a child, an elderly man or woman, we cannot possibly understand the importance of our action at that very moment. But later, whatever we were able to give to that person will have an effect, good or bad. And in a small way, this can make a very big difference in the world around us.

Rest assured when you take the time to show your children how to become leaders, when you teach them how to accept and carry out responsibility, the chance that they will become leaders and successful adults greatly increases. I've watched it happen to so many young people, and I've experienced it in my own life!

Earlier, I mentioned the subject of fairness. Here is something I try to drill into the young minds of my summer camp staff members: If we are ever to be truly successful, we must first of all be fair! It's a simple saying but not necessarily simple to put into action. And parents, this especially applies to you.

I remember a little game we played at camp which I often used with my own family. The object of this game is to find a way to produce a fair method for determining who would wash the dishes or who would get the last piece of pie (or any number of other difficult decisions a parent or camp director has to make in the course of an evening).

The game is called, "Horse Ma-gagle". A crazy name, but a great way to teach a child how to be fair.

It goes like this: Line up all the children in no particular order (or it can be done while sitting at the table) and begin from the left. When the leader yells, "Horse Ma-gagle!", the children all together hold up both hands with their fingers indicating any number from one to ten. A single count per finger. The leader then totals the number of fingers displayed by counting from the child on his left and continues to the last child on his right.

Now, as a hypothetical, say the final count of fingers being held up totals 27. The leader now begins counting each child from left to right until he or she comes to number 27. The twenty-seven fingers that were held up equals the multiple counting of every child until the number 27 is reached. And the child who ends up number 27 is either the winner or loser. He or she gets the pie or does the dishes! This game is always fair and entertaining. And, best of all, it prevents arguments!

Leaders must have a sense of humor! Something else I constantly tried to teach my camp staff was that a good leader always needs to have a great sense of humor!

All too often the only laughter we hear today seems to be related to a dirty joke or some type of racial or religious slur against another person. Put downs and ethnic witticisms are really no laughing matter!

The sad thing is so many families and people on the street have little or no humor today. Look around. How many people do you see walking down the street smiling or whistling? How many do you see laughing and joking with one another? Not many. And when you do, it's so unusual that it makes quite an impression.

This reminds me of what a friend told me recently that he

tells his kids. When he was a young boy, the bad guy in the black hat stood out like a sore thumb. Today, the good guy stands out like a sore thumb. And, the same analogy works regarding humor. A person who really has a good time and demonstrates a sense of humor stands out like a sore thumb today. However, I would much prefer to think of this person as the good guy wearing a white hat and not a sore thumb!

If we or our children are ever to be considered leaders, we must be able to see the humorous side of life and not take ourselves too seriously!

My wife Nancy had a great sense of humor. When she laughed we could hear her throughout the house. She had that kind of laughter which is very infectious.

Late one night on the way home from a trip I had taken the family on, we were rounding a bend in the road when suddenly our small utility trailer broke free and didn't make the turn with us. In an instant, it slammed into a large sand bank and rolled several times tossing its contents all over the side of the road before finally coming to a stop.

To put it mildly, I was upset! Without any warning, my wife suddenly began to hoot and holler. Before long, we were all sitting there staring out of the car at our wrecked trailer with tears rolling down our faces, laughing our fool heads off. The people slowing down as they drove by must have thought we were crazy! And maybe we were! Because someone had a sense of humor, and took control of the situation by using her humor to lead us out of what could have been disastrous, everything remained under control, including my temper and emotions!

When my first born son got married it was a very formal wedding. His wife-to-be, a sweetheart from Arkansas, had two brothers who were in their late teens or early twenties. And unbeknownst to every one at the wedding, these two characters decided to create the illusion that their sister's wedding was really some kind of a "shot gun wedding". And guess who was performing the wedding ceremony that fateful afternoon. Me! And I had no idea what was about to happen.

Now, as the music began to play and all three hundred people in attendance stood to honor the bride as she passed by, everyone suddenly noticed that the bride's brothers were following her and her father down the aisle dressed as "hillbillies"! They were wearing boots, big floppy hats, flannel shirts, and blue jeans. And, of course, each lad was carrying a shot gun!

For a moment, the entire gathering stood silent - totally silent - and then suddenly the room filled with loud, joyful laughter. And you know what? Those two boys never cracked a smile! Their mother could have strangled them, and I know their sister couldn't wait to get her hands on them!

A little while later, we finished the wedding ceremony, the bride and groom kissed and soon left on their honeymoon. But you know something? That was one wedding I will never forget. And part of the reason it has such wonderful memories for everyone involved has everything to do with the fact that two young men had the courage to share their humor with a family with whom they felt close enough to be themselves. It was great!

Again, let me reiterate. To become a leader we must have a sense of humor. We must be able to laugh when life may not be all that humorous, or at least smile when things don't always go our way (or the way we hope they will). There is a time for laughter and a time for seriousness, but let it be known that laughter must become an important part of our character if we or our kids are to ever become leaders!

Leaders must also have self control! Proverbs 15:1 (NKJV) teaches us a very important principle, "A soft answer turns away wrath, but a harsh word stirs up anger."

At times, achieving self control seems very difficult if not down right impossible. However, it is those times when we begin to lose faith, when we think we cannot possibly overcome temptation

131

and we begin to lose control of our emotions, when we strike out at someone or something that has angered us, that we need to remember, "For with God nothing will be impossible!" Luke 1:37 (NKJV)

Believe me, I know from where I speak. I raised six children and there were many times when I just knew I was going to explode - that I was going to lose it altogether. But because of the help I had from my wife and my faith in Christ Jesus, I realized that true leadership can only become part of our mind and character when self control is established by our actions and deeds. We all make mistakes, we err and sin, and this is something we can forgive and be forgiven. However, it is impossible to teach a child, have a good marriage, be successful at living life, or praise the name of God when we are not in control of our emotions, especially our temper and anger!

How much more of a positive view will kids have of their parents if parents remain calm and in control during difficult situations, if parents refrain from anger or loss of temper? The view they will have will be very positive, very rewarding! From our example as parents, our children will gladly follow our direction, guidance, and advice!

Finally, *imagination is an important characteristic we must develop if we or our kids are to ever become true leaders!* We often used imagination when we would think about doing something as a family, such as camping out, roasting weenies in the back yard, conducting group sing-along's, and even when we found ourselves alone.

Many is the time we had little or no money to spend on entertainment so we would tell our kids stories, and in turn they would tell us their stories. It was a great time for mom and dad AND the kids! Let your imagination pave the way for having interesting discussions with your children; let it also be payment for fun times when you can see the bottom of your piggy bank and you don't have the money to go to a movie or eat out. It's amazing what a little imagination can do.

The point to this chapter regarding leadership is this: we parents must always think of ways to help our children become tomorrow's leaders. It may be that the only thing they will ever lead is themselves or their family. But, no matter how big or small the responsibility, leadership will always be a very vitally important part of their lives. So, we must be willing to pitch in and help teach them how to become real leaders.

If parents are going to be successful in teaching their children how to become leaders, a couple of "do not's" seem to be important enough to mention at this point. First, *don't manipulate your children.* Always be up front and honest with them, and never threaten or make them do something out of fear or anxiety. Second, *don't demand from your kids what you are unwilling to give or do yourself.* Try never to be hypocritical when you are training your children.

I promise if you follow what I have written and train your kids in the proper way to live their lives, they will follow you to the ends of the earth. They will emulate your every move, and by your example and leadership, they will indeed be on their way to becoming the leaders of tomorrow!

Dear Reader:

I realize that as parents and/or grandparents, you are reading this book in part because you want to be the best mom, dad, or grandparent possible.

So, please, stop whatever you are doing and take a moment to honestly ask yourself:

"Am I giving my child everything I have to offer
– *all that I am able* –
so that I can fulfill the awesome obligation
and often overwhelming responsibility
I have as both a parent to my child
and as a child to my God?"

CHAPTER ELEVEN

Something to Consider
about the
Mind of a Child!

Our brain is a fabulous physical and spiritual *creation*! The brain, made up of physical material matter, converts into a spiritual, electrified-mental substance once information is applied and stored. The brain, which houses this spiritual human mind, is constantly at work applying, storing, and recalling bits and pieces of information throughout the day and night...awake and while asleep.

In reality, it is our incredible brain and the way it works in harmony with our entire physical body, i.e., the nervous system, respiratory system, emotions, etc. that makes every man-made computer, no matter the size, style, make or model, look like a kindergarten plaything!

The fantastic and awesome brain (mind center) sitting on our shoulders was given to us freely at birth. True, there are cases at birth when the brain doesn't fully mature or function properly; however, the great majority of babies born all over the world come into this world with minds that are very active and ready for exposure to all kinds of information and physical engagements. The mind (brain) in synthesis with the heart is a key central element for sustaining life.

It is also interesting how our minds begin to slow down and skip a beat as we grow older. Like any muscle in our body, the brain also becomes tired and worn. I can tell you from experience that at times this can be downright confusing and very exhausting! And, to some people, even frightening!

135

Stop for a moment and consider how the mind works: a thought begins and is translated inside the brain before working its way to the voice, where once again it is translated into a physical sound that floats through the air to the ears of another person where it now reverses itself, going from sound back into a thought pattern inside the other person's brain. It is more than a little complex! It's a wonder!

For example: you are now reading what I have written. When I began to write the first words of this book, my mind went through several phases of transference where I was able to recall past experiences, academic knowledge, and so much more. All this various information was stored in my brain, but I didn't realize it until my work began. Not only did my mind have to think back over past experiences, contemplate what is presently going on in the world, and see as far into the future as possible, it had to direct my thoughts, which in turn guided my fingers so that they would hit the proper letter keys on my computer keyboard. A fantastic operation to say the least!

Where did my thoughts originate? What inspired me to consider the problems between parents and children to the point that I felt the need to write this book? Where did my information come from? What did it look like inside my head? Or, is it even possible to see anything except gray matter inside our brain or a few electrical brain waves on a scope in some lab? How was this information stored and kept intact until its time of release? How is it that we can recall past experiences which may have happened years ago?

Is our brain different from an animal's brain? There are animals with larger sized brains, so why is it that only man is able to reason, plan, set goals and create? Is there a spiritual element inside our mind that produces reasoning and creativity that few individuals understand or can relate to? Why aren't we taught more in school about how this marvelous brain really works and functions? After all, isn't the human brain phenomenal proof that we humans were indeed created? Why do we pay so little attention to the one tool that provides our ability to create material objects, understand a lovely poem, appreciate a beautiful sunset, feel the pain of sorrow, and so much more? Finally, how does our mind accept what we see through our eyes (which is another marvelous piece of creation) and then faster than a nanosecond transfer this data or information into our brain which in turn begins the thought-to-physical action process?

For the sake of argument, say that we are now beginning to understand a little more about how our brain actually works. Okay. Now the question is: here you are reading this book (or any book) and suddenly you read a passage that triggers something inside your mind which begins to motivate your thinking process with deeper understanding. Suddenly, you begin to sense, from what you are reading, that you need to change something regarding the way you are managing your home, your kids, or yourself. What causes you to think about this? And, even more importantly, what causes you to want to make a change in your life? We understand that there is something in the human mind that causes an electronic impulse or thought pattern to change into a physical action or deed. We think it and then we do it. Why?!

And, what about dreams? Do you dream? If so, why? What do you dream about? What do your dreams mean? Where do they come from? Are dreams spiritual or just some physical manifestation caused by something we ate before going to bed? Why do we sometimes dream in color and other times in black and white? Why are some dreams beautiful and warm when others might be violent and cold? Why do little children and not just adults dream? What is a nightmare? Have you ever awakened from a dream crying or laughing? If so, again, why?

I don't think anyone will ever be able to answer every one of these questions; however, we do know that dreams take place in the mind. We may be asleep, but our mind is still active and working. And, we know that there is also a spirit at work in man, a spirit of reason and creation.

Can we now begin to see what a marvelous, powerful and magnificent creation our mind really is? Can we begin to understand that it is this magnificent human mind we have been given that provides each of us with the ability to create such marvelous physical wonders as a light bulb, fire, telephone, automobile, television, airplane, space shuttle, integrated circuit chip, films, virtual realization, and much more? Can we also now begin to understand that just as our mind has the ability to create and perform for the good of mankind, it is also capable of creating and performing for evil, i.e., making war, taking human life, lying, cheating, stealing, child abuse, spouse abuse, parent abuse, divorce, jealously and anger.

And can we now begin to see why it is important that we nurture, protect and cultivate our mind so that we might be able to use it to its full potential to serve others and to serve ourselves? Do we really understand why it is particularly important that we take special care regarding what we allow to enter into our mind? Especially what we view as entertainment, what we experience on the job, what we listen to on the radio, and what we read.

And, finally, once we begin to understand just how important our mind really is, once we realize how it works and what a marvelous creation it is, once we acknowledge the reality that God has provided us with this powerful tool we call a brain to help us overcome and succeed in life, we suddenly begin to recognize and appreciate the importance of why it is so essential that we parents unconditionally accept and embrace the tremendous responsibility to protect, guide and direct the minds of our children! The magnitude of this challenge is so very great that applying this responsibility is perhaps the most important thing we parents will ever achieve in the rearing of our children!

QUIET MINDS
can not be
perplexed or frightened,
but go on in
fortune or misfortune
at their own private pace,
like a clock during a thunderstorm.

Robert Louis Stevenson

CHAPTER TWELVE

WHAT
IN THE
WORLD IS
SUCCESS?!

A while back, I decided to stop by our local municipal court to see if anything was going on that might provide the type of research information I was seeking, and to authenticate material I was using for counseling work which I was doing with some parents and their children. As a minister of God and a man who wants to help young people whenever the opportunity arises, I make every effort possible to understand the various problems that our young people are facing today. And believe me, our kids are experiencing a wide range of some pretty difficult problems!

As I took my seat in the crowded court room, I noticed several young men sitting in the front row with their backs to me facing the judge. One young man, probably in his late teens, stood handcuffed before the judge with his attorney at his side.

After the judge finished reading what seemed to be a very long list of serious charges against this young man, he slowly looked down at the boy and with a firmness to his voice said, "I just read in your indictment and conviction that you robbed a grocery store using a sawed-off shot gun. And, about three weeks before this, you did the same thing at another store using the same gun!" The boy just stood there as the judge continued. "It seems, you just casually walked into that convenience store and threatened the sales clerk that you were going to kill her if she didn't give you the money!" The judge paused for a moment, slowly shaking his head as he stared at the defendant who was nonchalantly standing in front of him. "Do you fully

139

understand the charges being brought against you today?"

"Yes," the young fellow said, his eyes focused on the floor.

"Do you realize I have the authority to send you away to a very nasty and lonely prison for a very long time?," the judge asked as he leaned forward in his chair. "Do you understand what I'm saying?"

The young man just nodded. Then the judge passed sentence.

Looking back, I can't imagine for a moment that this young man had even a smidgen of an idea what thirty years out of his life, behind bars in prison, really meant.

Also in court that morning was another young man standing trial for allegedly having raped two girls, assaulting an older lady, and stealing a purse from another woman. This fellow appeared to me to be in his early twenties.

Once again, after reading the complaint to the young defendant, the judge told him almost the exact same thing he had said to the earlier defendant, "Do you realize I have the power to send you to prison? Do you understand that you could spend the next forty to fifty years behind bars? Do you understand what I'm telling you?"

The defendant shrugged his shoulders, showing little or no concern or remorse.

The judge then asked the young man, "Can you read or write?"

"Of course I can read and write!," the man replied sarcastically, staring directly at the judge.

Shaking his head the judge slowly looked away from the defendant, saying, "I want to make sure you understand what I am telling you this day, because you're going to stand trial and face a jury for allegedly having committed some very serious crimes! Take him away!"

I couldn't help but think what a loss both of those young men were to society, their families, and themselves. Each man had pled not guilty; however, the judge had more than sufficient evidence to try and convict them both. As I sat there listening to several other cases which were all very similar in scope and magnitude as the first two, I was suddenly faced with the realization that there is indeed a major problem of violent crimes being committed by youth in our society today...more than ever before. (And that morning, I also realized that our system of justice seems to be bordering on complete lack of authority, discipline, control and respect.)

Also in the court room were some of the parents and friends of the young defendants. As I studied each parent, I saw great sorrow and a lot of pain written on their faces. I saw tears streaming down the cheeks of many brokenhearted mothers, and witnessed the sober expression of each parent as a verdict of guilty was pronounced. I felt deep and painful emotions - bitterness, resentment, sorrow and numbness - emanate from parents, friends and loved ones as the judge pronounced his sentences that often included time in jail. It was nothing less than heart breaking for me and, most likely, everyone else sitting in that court room!

I wondered to myself just what could have gone wrong in the lives of these young people which caused them to stand before a judge this very day, allegedly involved in some very serious crimes and felonies.

I found myself staring at one particular mother in the court room, sitting on a hard bench directly behind her convicted son. Her head hung low and tears rolled down two elderly weathered cheeks on a face that revealed signs of sleepless nights and more than a little mental anxiety and sorrow.

My heart went out to her as I sat there thinking about how she must have felt as she watched her son being lead off to some cold, crowded prison cell where he would be confined until the day of his sentencing.

I thought about how she might be remembering the times when her little boy eagerly sat on her lap, laughed and played in the living room, got caught raiding the cookie jar, or any number of other wonderful experiences from her past...from the joy of the youth of her son. And sad to say, I also thought how each remembrance must now only increase her pain and sorrow.

I wondered how she must have felt if, upon closer

examination, she realized that perhaps there were too many times when she wasn't at home to take care of her young son; times when he needed someone to come to for help and guidance, but no one was there for him; or perhaps the time he got into his first skirmish with the law and she couldn't be there, or when she couldn't take the time or didn't have the money to help him overcome his anger, greed, drug habit, or whatever it was that caused him to take the wrong direction. Perhaps this was a big part of the reason her heart was breaking that morning!

Whatever the reasons those young defendants had for standing before the judge, one thing is for sure, no one had taken the time to teach them how to succeed in life. Someone, somehow, somewhere had failed to properly teach and instruct these young men while they were still children. They failed to teach them about how to overcome adversity, stay clear of bad influences, do well in school, and live a clean life with respect toward others. Chances are, if the parents sitting in that court room were given the opportunity to start over again, knowing what they now know, they would do a lot of things differently. We all would!

The problem is, when we parents finally come to realize some of the crucial errors and mistakes we've made in raising our kids, it's often too late. And for the most part, we are never able to relive our lives or completely undo the damage we have done. Therefore, if we are to ever escape the sorrow and pain of having to go through an ordeal such as watching one of our children be sentenced to prison, or have his very future restricted to the demands of a parole officer, or possibly even lose his life because of some horrible act of violence, we must teach and instruct our kids early in life about what success is and how to obtain it!

What comes to mind when you hear the word "success"? Do you think of fame, fortune, a career, happy children, a perfect marriage, retirement, or what? What do you think the word "success" meant to those parents sitting in court that morning? Do you think it even crossed their minds? I believe it did! If not then, certainly later!

142

Daniel Webster tells us that to "succeed" implies the "favorable outcome of an undertaking.. or the attainment of a desired goal; prosper; flourish; thrive." He goes on to tell us that "success" means (1) "result or outcome, (2a) a favorable or satisfactory outcome or result, (2b) something having such an outcome, (3) the gaining of wealth, fame, rank, etc., and (4) a successful person."

Okay, let's say success means having gained a favorable outcome or satisfactory result. This can mean one having gained wealth, fame, power, rank, etc. But isn't there something more to success than gaining wealth, fame, rank, etc. Absolutely!

How do we measure success in child rearing? If we raise our kids to become wealthy tycoons, does this mean they are successful, or that we are successful as parents? Not necessarily! What if we raise our kids with the best education, superb cultural instruction, and every advantage money can buy; does this mean they will end up successful? What if Susie or Junior grow up to become the President of the United States, Chairman of Megabucks, Inc., or Senator Blowhard; does this mean they have achieved success? Not really! So then, what is "success"?

Every minute or two someone in the United States tries to take his or her own life. Worldwide, hundreds, even thousands, of human beings succeed in carrying out this dastardly deed on a daily basis. They "succeed" in committing suicide; in killing themselves. They "gained a favorable outcome" (as far as they were concerned) in taking their own lives. They may have "succeeded," but I'm sure no one reading this book will agree that to "succeed" in killing oneself is even remotely related to the meaning of what "success" is. Even though the person committing suicide "succeeded," the deed itself is not success; it's just the opposite, it's *total failure!*

Recently, we have all read about several men and women who intentionally bilked a large number of investors, and an even greater number of taxpayers, out of millions, even billions, of dollars. They "succeeded" in bringing about a "favorable outcome of an undertaking," insofar as they were concerned; but again, is this real "success"? It seems that Ol' Daniel Webster missed the deeper

143

meaning of the words "succeed" and "success!"

Parents who truly love their children have high hopes and lofty ideals which they expect each child to attain. We want our kids to succeed in life. However, in today's world, there are more than just a few ideas and notions about what success really means. Chances are if you met with your local PTA and asked each member to write on a piece of paper what they considered "success" to mean, you would receive a myriad of answers and definitions. And the majority of these answers and definitions would probably miss the point altogether!

Stop for a moment. Ask your children to come and sit down near you, each one take a pencil and sheet of paper, and then complete the following self-evaluating test regarding what the word "success" means to you and your children. Answer each question in 25 words or less and be honest with yourself. You answer the first 7 questions (part 1) and then have your kids answer the final 3 questions (part 2).

Remember, if you nonchalantly ask your kid about what success means, more often that not, he or she will answer that having won the last football game or dating that special someone in class is success. Some parents might feel that having received a new promotion at work or being able to purchase the latest luxury car is the thing that makes them successful. What matters in this test is, when you and your children take it, you are honest with yourself and you ask your children to be honest with their answers.

First of all, answer the following: What is my definition of "success"? Now using your definition of what you believe the word "success" means, answer the following questions:

1- How successful am I as a parent?

2- What can I do to be a better parent?
   A more successful parent?

3- How successful are my kids?

4- What can I do to help my kids become

more successful?

5- How successful am I as a spouse?
How can I become a better husband
or wife?

6- How successful is my spouse?
What can he or she do to be a better spouse?

7- How successful am I as a Christian?
Do I follow in the footsteps of my Lord
and Savior?
Am I overcoming and setting the right
example for my kids to follow?

Finally, if you have teenage (or grown) children or grandchildren, ask them the following questions:

1- How do you define "success"?

2- Are you successful as a person?

3- Am I successful as your parent?
If not, what can I do to be successful?

You may be surprised at the answers you and your children jot down. If you really think about what you are asking yourself, if you meditate on your response before you reply, and if you take the time to complete this test, even if it takes more than a day or two to finish, you will soon discover that you have gained a deeper understanding of what success really means. You will better understand who you are, what your children think about you, what they think about themselves, and what you may need to do in order to grow and become more successful as a parent, grandparent, spouse, human being. Important stuff, right?

An example of what success is not: The late oilman, super billionaire J. Paul Getty, wrote that he would have gladly given away millions of dollars for one happy marriage (he was married six times!).

Now to look at Mr. Getty's life, especially for those men and women in the business world of high finance, corporate buyouts, and stock manipulation, most would probably say that Mr. Getty was a great success. Just like Ford, Trump, Forbes, and many other wealthy men and women, Mr. Getty had more than his share of palatial estates, luxury automobiles, and bulging bank accounts. But was Mr. Getty successful? Was he or any other tycoon, movie star, king, or knight, who having gained great fame and fortune, yet all the while failing with their kids and their marriages, successful?

What is real "success"? There is a wonderful Christian principle that goes something like this, "One has achieved success who has lived well, laughed often, and who has shown much love." In this allegory we see that success, real success, has very little or nothing to do with careers, material playthings, or large bank accounts. It has everything to do with happiness, giving of oneself, and love.

How do we achieve success? Where does it come from? "Blessed is the man/woman who does not walk in the counsel of the wicked or stand in the way of sinners or sit in the seat of mockers. But his/her delight is in the law of the Lord, and on His law he/she meditates day and night. He/she is like a tree planted by streams of water, which yields its fruit in season and whose leaf does not wither. *Whatever he/she does prospers.*" Ps 1:1-3 (NIV).

From what we have just read, we understand that if we live our lives according to the way of God, to His purpose, we are bound to prosper both spiritually and physically!

As a parent, ask yourself, "Have I taught my children about these Godly principles which lead to true success?" "Have I applied the laws of God in the way I have instructed my kids, and, if so, are they aware these laws play an important part in how each of us, man, woman, or child, achieves real success?" "Am I living my life as an example to my children, by what I do and not by what I say?"

Through His mercy and love, God offers every one of us parents the opportunity to teach our children how to live their lives to the fullest, how to overcome the trials and tests they will face throughout their lives, and how to become successful adults. And, you know what? The best way our children can learn this is from the example we set and the way we live our lives! That is the secret!

If we parents are to ever achieve real success; if we are to teach our children about what love is, what hope is, what true success is; if we are to help guide them through their youth in such a manner that they will surely have the opportunity to fulfill their goals and dreams and achieve the joy of real success in their lives, we must first come to the understanding and conclusion that it is only God who provides the physical and spiritual substance, which in turn brings about real success in life. Everything we do, say or think must first of all be measured by His standard and under His subjection!

As a diversified people living in relative freedom for over two hundred years, we have raised children who have become great leaders, creative inventors, intelligent business executives, notable thespians, prominent scientists, academic scholars, line workers, poets and writers, and educators. Yet with all this scholarly and physical success, man has nevertheless progressed to the point where he can now destroy all living matter from the face of the Earth many times over and by hundreds of methods.

When we consider the computer, electricity, space exploration, and the telephone, we truly marvel at such accomplishments, and we refer to those who created these wonders as having great minds and intellect. We see them as individuals who reached their goals and achieved great success. But does this type of physical success last forever? Is there anything of greater value?

Consider a mother who remains at home with her children so that they might have support, love, and an opportunity to grow up and succeed at living life. Her children do not become a burden to the state, don't end up in prison or in a hospital due to a drug overdose, or dead in some darkened street because of a senseless gang-related drive-by shooting. Do we think of this mother as being successful? If so, will her success last from generation to generation? And if not. Why not?

What about the high school teacher who could have gone

147

into private industry after graduating from college and made a fortune creating hi-tech widgets. Instead he or she chose to use their talents instructing young, fertile minds and teaching the leaders of tomorrow, today. Do we regard this individual as someone who is truly successful, someone to admire?

Is that lonely soldier standing guard in some far off country - protecting the lives of people all around the world - considered, by most of the people he or she is protecting, to be successful? If not, why not?

It seems that one of the more negative aspects of living in a materialistic world, such as we have experienced over the past several decades, is the way we have come to simply take for granted those things in life which are precious and worthwhile: love, joy, faith, patience, children's laughter, a warm bed, a nutritious meal, companionship, friends, loyalty, health, wisdom, regard for the welfare of our neighbors, and respect for God. These undeniably significant life supporting components, when framed together, form the basis for our being able to live a truly successful life!

I once had the privilege to hear a famous college basketball coach speak about how he prepared his team to win each game. The reason I wanted to hear this man had everything to do with the fact that he was one of the most successful coaches in college level basketball. His teams won more national championships than any other college in the history of the game.

During his long career, this coach not only directed his teams to victory on the basketball floor, he also helped prepare his players for their roles in life.

Just as almost every coach in any sport, this man really enjoyed winning the game. However, his approach was very simple: he never told his players to win no matter the cost. Instead, he instructed his team to always play the game with honor and respect for the players on the opposing team. He wanted his players (or students) to succeed in every aspect of their lives, not only at the game of basketball. This coach was John Woodin, Head Coach for the University of California at Los Angeles...the U.C.L.A. Bruins.

I have often quoted Coach Woodin's approach to the way in which he inspired his players. And by doing so, I have found his words to be very helpful in my teaching and counseling of younger kids. Coach Woodin often explained, "Success is peace of mind, which is a direct result of the self-satisfaction of knowing you did your very best to become the very best at what you are able to be!" Read this quote one more time. When we stop for a moment and think about what this very simple yet profound statement means, we soon discover a highly edifying and uplifting message for anyone who will listen. And, hopefully, we will apply it to our daily lives.

There are times when some of what we have been told in the past may no longer be relevant today. In fact, it may not have been so relevant even at the time it was told to us. An example is a saying I heard many times during my youth, "If it was good enough for Granddad, it's good enough for me!" Really?

Our great Father in heaven wants each of us to succeed at whatever it is we undertake. If we are working at building a home, raising a child, serving a customer, studying in school, writing a book, being a parent, or simply living our lives, God wants us to succeed, to move forward, and to do so with respect and honor toward Him and our neighbors.

What was good enough for our grandparents doesn't necessarily mean that it is good enough for us or for our children. Some grandparents never listened to their children. Should we not listen to our children? Some grandparents never took a chance in life nor did they work to provide a better livelihood for their family. Should we always play it safe and deny certain opportunities when they come our way? Of course there are many grandparents who have done the very best they knew how when raising their children and living their lives. But to say that just because it was "good enough for Granddad" or anyone else doesn't necessarily mean it's right for you or for me...or for our kids.

On the other side of the coin and for whatever reason, we

The JOY of Raising Our Kids...

have denied a great many sayings and pearls of wisdom handed down to us from generation to generation. And by denying such wonderful pieces of tested knowledge and wisdom - "we reap what we sow," "what goes around comes around," "better to be safe than sorry" - we have all but lost their true meaning. Shame on the generation who thought these truly meaningful proverbs were foolish and old fashioned! Shame on us for denying the value of these wonderful principles.

I have tried to apply the following principle, regarding what was good enough for someone in the past being good enough for those living in the present, in the work I do with young people. The principle simply stated is, I have come to realize that just because something didn't work for me in the past doesn't mean it won't work for a young person today. After all, it is a different time, a different place, and a different individual involved.

God has given us many wonderful principles and laws which will support and guide mankind as long as there is human life. Once we accept these laws and principles and begin to live by them, our lives will become enriched and more complete. Nevertheless, we will still have moments when it will be necessary to make decisions that relate to the present, yet, at the same time, require wisdom and understanding that only faith and experience can provide.

How would granddad respond to our world of high technology today? Would he understand it? If he had an open mind he would. But if his mind only allowed him to cling to the theory that "if it was good enough for Granddad, it is good enough for me", then given what we are experiencing today, which is completely monitored and managed by high technology, he would definitely find himself in serious trouble.

We cannot, and should not, remain in a status quo situation, if at the same time we expect to grow and succeed. However, the manner in which we grow and succeed is what is really important. *How we live our lives is what will in effect determine whether or not we succeed in life!* And it is this piece of understanding and knowledge that we must teach our children!

Remember the uncle I wrote about in an earlier chapter? Well, you may think you weren't going to read any more about him, but I have another story regarding this wise old man.

When I was a kid, I really hated school. Because I felt the way I did about having to attend school, I never did as well as I should have. I had the smarts, but I lacked the drive and inclination. I suppose many of you will be able to relate to how I felt. My uncle did. After a while, he began to see just how bad things were between his nephew and the public school I was attending. He could see I was groping along getting very little done and not growing as I should. So, he decided to take me aside and give me some fatherly advice (my dad had left our home so my uncle took on the responsibility to help me as much as he could).

"Boy," he began, looking me straight in the eyes, "as long as you have such a negative view of school and you aren't going to buckle down and study like you should, you need to learn how to work with your hands and become the best you can be at whatever you do." It's interesting how many years later I would hear Coach Woodin tell his players almost the exact same words my uncle told me.

"The thing is," he continued, "you've got to do your very best and never let anyone else be better than you at what you do. Ride your success on the shoulders of giants. Find out who the biggest giant is in whatever field you want to go into...whether it's becoming a baker, a butcher, a businessman, or a plumber, it doesn't matter. Just find out who the best and biggest giant is in that industry and then ride to your success on his shoulders!" Ride to my success on some giant's shoulders! This sounded kind of heavy for a young lad who wasn't doing too well in school. However, I later came to understand my uncle was telling me that I must learn from the best if I was ever going to become the best.

In the years following the advice given to me by my uncle, I applied what he taught me. And with a lot of hard work, deep abiding faith, and considerable perseverance, I did succeed. As a young man

I had always wanted to be a baker and a baker I became. In fact, I worked for one of the largest bakeries associated with a giant grocery chain. And later, I even became manager of that bakery. Now I realize this may sound like a slogan for the U.S. Army, but nevertheless, I was determined to learn from the best and become "the best I could be."

Today as I look back to the time I spent with my uncle, I am very thankful for his advice and the time he spent with me. I am sure that if I had not spent quality time with such a kind and caring man who felt the need to instruct and teach me - often denying his own pleasures and desires - I would have just gone along with the crowd, doing little or nothing with my life.

God admonishes each one of us that whatever it is we put our hand to do, "do it with all your might!" He encourages every child of His to strive for true success, for He is not pleased with failure, nor should we be.

God also expects us parents to teach our children how to be the best they can be. At times this may be difficult; however, it is a very important part of being a true Christian parent. And something we must learn to do.

How does laziness affect a person's progression toward achieving success? Everyone has a proclivity toward becoming a little lazy from time to time. It is true that we all need rest and sleep, but laziness has very little to do with rest or sleep. It has everything to do with poor attitude and lack of character.

Let's stay with the sport of basketball for an analogy to demonstrate why overcoming laziness is so important.

If your child were to try out for the high school basketball team and he or she had an attitude of wanting to lay around on a bench while the rest of the team ran their laps and practiced layouts, do you suppose your kid would play very many games or even make the team? Not hardly!

However, if your kid is not the best player on the team - being somewhat uncoordinated and clumsy - yet he or she gives a total effort during practice and scrimmages with the other players, chances are your pride and joy will get to play in a game soon. The more he plays, the better he'll become, and as he or she improves, success will come a knockin'...getting to play on the school's basketball team!

Some time ago, during a visit with my son, I decided to play a game of one-on-one with my grandson. He was only four years old, but this little guy could sure dribble a ball! My son and daughter-in-law worked at teaching him, while he was still young enough to accept their instruction, certain principles and values that will help him in school and later as an adult.

Our kids want their kids to be successful. And if their kids are ever going to achieve success, it is very important their parents teach them early in life how to reach certain goals by using the abilities and talents they discover that they have while still in their youth. Accomplishing this will enable each child to be better prepared to accept and manage greater successes later in life. I cannot over emphasize the importance of parents beginning to teach their children at an early age. Give them the opportunity and share your experiences with them now, while they are still young!

I had a conversation a while back with a young lad who was interested in playing basketball with our church team. I want to share this conversation with you. I hope it might provide a deeper under-standing about how we can help our kids learn more about what real success means.

"Com'on, Coach. I'm just not a very good basketball player. I mean, you know, like I have a hard enough time gettin' the ball down court let alone making a basket Besides, everybody laughs cause I have all I can do to hit the back board! I'm sure no Larry Bird or Magic Johnson!"

"Do you ever make any points?" I asked.

"Yeah. I usually make a few points." He replied.

"In every game?"

"I guess so." He seemed embarrassed to admit

his being able to make points with a basketball.

"So what's the problem?"

"I wanna make more points. I wanna do better!"

"Well, then, that's up to you. You can become the best basketball player you want to become, but you're going to have to work for it." I didn't want to lose him by using the term "work for it", so I immediately continued. "If you are satisfied with three points a game, fine, that's exactly what you'll make."

"But you told us we were not to try to win the game at all costs."

"That's right. I don't want you or anyone else on the team trying to win each game no matter what the cost. However, I did tell you and the other boys that I wanted you to develop your game so that in your mind you would know that you played the very best you could. You never want to hurt the opposing player or run over somebody else just so you can make a basket or get your own way."

"Okay, but what if the other guys win?!"

"If you've done your best, you've succeeded. And when the other fellow does a better job than you, no matter what the circumstances, go over and shake his hand and give him a pat on the back and tell him what a great game he played. Learn to honor the other person's performance in whatever it is they do."

"Man, that sounds like something that's gonna be pretty hard to do!" He said shaking his head.

"You're right. It is hard, but it becomes easier the more you do it. And, believe me, this is what the game of life is all about!"

Some time ago, I had the opportunity to hear an Olympic gymnast speak about her gymnastic experiences during the Olympics a few summers ago. She told us, "I never won a gold medal in my life. Never! However, the last time I went to the Olympics I was a success! I was a success because I knew I did my very best and I was satisfied with my performance. On the day of my competition another gymnast was better than I was and she won the gold medal. But in my mind, I won because I did the best I could. I succeeded!"

Whenever a child does better than what he or she did before, this is *real* success!

Tom Sullivan is an actor, musician and athlete who is also blind. His blindness could have become an obstacle if he had let it, only he refused. Was it difficult? Certainly. Was it a barrier? Absolutely not!

Mr. Sullivan is a success today because he used his blindness to his advantage. He not only succeeded in music, he also succeeded in sports. He was a wrestler on the US Olympic team, and one of the things I find so interesting about his story is he never saw one of his opponents. He was never intimidated by the other fellow's size or demeanor, and he was able to hold his own on the mat because he was determined to do the best he could with what he had. And the satisfaction he has experienced throughout his musical and acting career, indeed his very life, has given him a deep sense of pleasure and accomplishment. Tom Sullivan is a wonderful example of what real success is all about!

We parents need to consider just what we are teaching our children and what they are being taught in school, if we are to help them succeed in life. So far, we have looked at such issues as teaching our kids how to persevere, overcome laziness, deny the need for selfish pleasures, practice good health, not allow a handicap to become a barrier, make every effort to drive oneself toward the goal, and always put God in the picture.

If our children are going to overcome this world and its tremendous pulls and temptations, if they are ever going to reach their goals and live successful lives, parents need to establish the following foundation for each child to build upon: first of all, we must "train up a child in the way he should go." Let all decisions, instructions, and discipline be under subjection to Jesus Christ and there won't be child abuse, family quarrels, or divorce. Then begin teaching each child by personal instruction and participation, using the principles of academics, athletics, citizenship, cultural awareness, career and vocational training, and spiritual understanding for guidance.

Following is an overview of what I am suggesting:

Academics: if children are going to succeed in supporting themselves and a family when they grow up and leave home, it is important that they at least get a good education. If they intend to advance within their chosen vocation, they will need to complete additional studies and postgraduate work. It is a fact of life that higher education is a must today if a young person is going to succeed in his or her career.

Athletics: sports build character. Not all sports are character building nor should our children participate in every sport. A parent should really consider the dangers and potential hazards before allowing a young boy to go out for football. So many young boys are getting injured, some very seriously, playing this contact sport. Still, most sports build team spirit, and team spirit is something a kid will need to understand when he or she goes out into the business world, no matter what their profession.

Citizenship: this is an area where modern society, especially parents and teachers, has really dropped the ball. Why is it that our children lack the courage, grace, and desire to help their community by volunteering their time and effort for the support and welfare of others? How can a child learn what it is like to be disadvantaged and in need until he helps someone who is disadvantaged and in need? How can a child understand the problem of aging unless she has helped an older person mow a lawn, climb the stairs, or cross a street? Unless we begin to teach our children the importance of community service, we may lose our communities as we know them to be today, in the not-so-distant future.

Cultural Awareness: schools are cutting back on every type of expense possible. It seems they have to, if they are going to keep their doors open. So, if schools can't afford it, then who is going to teach our kids about the beauty of literature, music, art, and dance? How will they experience the feeling and power of a well written story, the beauty of a poem, or the grace of a ballet? The answer is they won't unless we parents teach them, unless we take them to the art gallery, a music recital, an opera, or a ballet.

Career and Vocational Training: what does your child want to be when he or she grows up? Do you know? I know a gentleman who was very gifted as a writer when he was in the ninth grade. That is until his English teacher gave him a writing assignment to write a poem. For the next week, every night after school this young boy worked very hard trying to make words fit a meaning while at the same time structuring the poem so that it would rhyme. It wasn't easy.

Finally as he handed in his poem, he felt elated because he had been able to write the poem exactly the way he wanted. He was proud that day, until he was called to the principal's office. His teacher said that the poem was so well written that no ninth grader could have possibly written such a creative piece of work. And it wasn't until the boy brought his mother to school to verify his having written the poem that he could return to class. The sad thing is, even though his mother confirmed he had written the poem without any help or plagiarism, his teacher never really believed him and the parents never picked up on the magnitude and scope of their son's talent. He received no support, guidance or direction from either his school or at home regarding his talent, which could have greatly influenced his career choice, his very life .

So, be sure to know your kids. Understand their talents and abilities as well as their needs and fears. And then, help them nurture and cultivate their talents so they will have a better opportunity to choose the right career when the time comes...so they will also have the opportunity for success.

Spiritual Understanding: in our society today, children have the opportunity to come to know about God only if we teach and instruct them at home or at church. Most schools (other than private or religious) do not have the proper education and understanding to teach our kids about God, His way, and His Son.

What most schools do teach today is the theory of evolution, alternative life-styles, atheism, competition, the darker side of the spiritual world, and other such ideas, theories, and philosophies.

The most important thing we parents will ever give to our children is an understanding that there is a power and majesty far greater than any human being; that we live in a world created by the great Creator God and we must obey His commandments and follow the teachings given to His Son, if we are to live happy and successful lives; and that He loves each and every human being on the face of this earth. Unless we instruct our children with care and concern, how will they ever understand the meaning of brotherly love? And how will our society continue to exist and prosper unless we teach our child the principles and laws of the One who created us and all things? The answer is they won't and we won't!

During my experience as a businessman, counselor and pastor, I have discovered that to achieve real success means succeeding at what we do one step at a time. This step is often difficult, but taking the step is what's important.

For the most part, we humans casually run along life's pathway hoping to advance our intellect, wanting to create something worthwhile, desiring growth in spiritual faith, and living the good life until suddenly one day we hit what I call, the "Pain Threshold!" This "Pain Threshold" is the one thing that stops people of all ages from succeeding in attaining their goals more than any other factor of life. It includes mental pain, fear, anxiety, insecurity, loss of faith, worry, depression, and many other negative feelings and emotions.

To succeed means having the will, courage, hope, desire, perseverance, and faith to complete what we have set out to do. And for whatever reason, there is always someone or something that tries to prevent us from accomplishing our goals - especially if our goals have value and purpose. And it is often these same people or things that set up a myriad of "pain thresholds" in order to try to stop or deter us.

So, how do we go through this "Pain Threshold"? Well, after we identify just what our "Pain Threshold" is (i.e., self-doubt, fear of being put down by some of our peers, insecurities, doubts about what we are trying to do and questioning if it has real value and purpose, etc.), we then move forward with our minds completely focused on achieving success. Through prayer and faith and with determination, tenacity, and the help and generosity of others we overcome the obstacles in our path. And this holds true especially for our children. If they are to be successful at whatever it is they choose to do in life, we must make every effort to teach and instruct them on how to overcome adversity, tests, and trials; how to make it through their own personal "Pain Thresholds"!

What is success? Remember what Coach Woodin told his basketball team, "When they beat us, they beat us. But, they will never beat us if we do our best!" Success is peace of mind knowing we did our very best to become the very best we are able to be! And the very best way to be the very best parent is to go before God and ask Him for His help, direction, guidance, and mercy and then take the time and give the energy to begin teaching and training our children today!

*"Discipline your son,
for in that
there is hope..."*

(Proverbs 19:18 NKJV)

159

Here's a little something to help
PROD YOU
to become more involved with your children or grandchildren:

Whenever you find yourself not taking the time to spend with your children, stop whatever it is you are doing and think about all the great shifts in our society that we have experienced during the past ten years. It's very interesting how fast things change, how little control we have over this change, and how much of this lifestyle modification isn't necessarily a change for the better.

Yesterday our children were little tots playing in the back yard, today they are attending school and spending more time with their peers, and before we know it, they are grown and living away from home. What they will experience later in their lives we have no way of knowing; however, we can help them now to live life to the fullest and overcome much of the tests and trials they will face tomorrow...only if we spend time with them today!

CHAPTER THIRTEEN

"DISCIPLINE!"
A Very Controversial Subject!

"Sometimes mere words are not enough -
Discipline is needed.
For the words may not be heeded"
(Proverbs 29:19 The Living Bible)

R eady or not, here comes the big "D" word! What is the big "D" word? The word is "Discipline"! Every parent, every adult, at one time or another has experienced the receiving end of being disciplined. In the military service, on the job, at play, and in the home, we all experience to one degree or another the effects of discipline when we do something wrong. And, when we err in life and sin, God most assuredly will discipline those whom He loves ("My son, do not despise the Lord's discipline and do not resent His rebuke, because the Lord disciplines those He loves, as a father the son he delights in." Proverbs 3:11-12 NIV)

Discipline of children is one of the most talked about, controversial and misunderstood subjects in child rearing today. The library is stacked full of books, pamphlets, and papers advising parents why they should or should not discipline their children. It seems so many so-called child experts have much to say regarding this subject, yet very few truly understand what discipline is or how to properly correct and discipline a child.

DISCIPLINE MUST ALWAYS BEGIN WITH LOVE!

"OK. Troops! LISTEN UP!!"

This is a subject where caution must be carefully considered if we parents are going to properly instruct and correct our children without harming their self esteem or causing them to become resentful and bitter; thus creating an overall attitude of intolerance and rebellion. It is important that we parents never become negligent or guilty of mistreatment and abuse when we discipline our kids. Certainly discipline is one of the most difficult aspects of childrearing, and it can cause both the parent and child considerable pain and anguish if it is not handled correctly.

So, where do we begin? Let's see what Mr. Webster has to say about the word "discipline" and then let's go to the word of God to seek His instructions and answers.

"Discipline," so says Daniel Webster, is "1- a branch of knowledge or learning. 2a- training that develops self control, character, or orderliness and efficiency. 2b- strict control to enforce obedience. 3- the result of such training or control; specif., a) self control or orderly conduct b) acceptance of or submission to authority and control. 4- a system of rules. and, 5- treatment that corrects or punishes.

Okay, we can see from what Mr. Daniel Webster tells us that "discipline" is a part of knowledge and training to help develop character, efficiency, and obedience.

Now what does God tell us about discipline (especially in the context of teaching and training our children)? As you read the following instructions, please keep in mind that these are the words of the One who inspired those who wrote the Bible:

"He who spares the rod hates his son (daughter), but *he who loves him (her) is careful to discipline him (her)"* (Proverbs 13:24 NIV).

"Discipline your son (or daughter), for in that there is hope; do not be a willing party to his (her) death." (Proverbs 19:18 NIV).

"Folly is bound up in the heart of a child, but the rod of discipline will drive it far from him." (Proverbs 22:15 NIV).

"Do not hold discipline from a child; if you punish him (or her) with the rod, he (she) will not die." (Proverbs 23:13 NIV).

"Fathers, do not exasperate your children; instead, *bring them up in the training and instruction of the Lord."* (Colossians 3:21 NIV).

"Only be careful, and watch yourselves closely so that you do not forget the things your eyes have seen or let them slip from your heart as long as you live. Teach them to your children and to their children after them". (Deuteronomy 4:9 NIV).

"Train a child in the way he (she) should go, and when he (she) is old he (she) will not turn from it!" (Proverbs 22:6 NIV).

What wonderful instructions regarding how to properly raise the children that we parents have been given by our great Creator God. Nowhere in His word does God tell us to beat or abuse a child. He tells us, "And now a word for you parents. Don't keep on scolding and nagging your children, making them angry and resentful. Rather, bring them up with the loving discipline the Lord himself approves, with suggestions and godly advice." (Ephesians 6:4 The Living Bible). We are admonished, as parents, to properly discipline and correct

163

our children while still in their youth. And we are to do so with unconditional love and in control of our emotions, attitudes, and tempers!

As we begin to seek additional understanding regarding the discipline and correction of our kids, let's first take a moment to answer the following questions: "Where did you learn (as you became an adult and parent) about how to discipline your children?" "Who taught you about this very important and often misused and abused child rearing principle?" "Did you just assume that once you reached adulthood you would automatically understand everything about how to raise your kids, how to love them, and how to correct and discipline them?"

Ask yourself if you are the type of parent who, when your little boy disobeys or becomes stubborn or perhaps bad-tempered, immediately begins spanking his behind before you talk to him about what he has done wrong, or before you exercise patience and emotional control. Proper and effective punishment is not abusive or ill-thought out and it never neglects that special element of love needed by a parent prior to the discipline.

On the other side of the coin, perhaps you have recently read a child rearing book which strongly suggests that parents should by no means resort to spanking their children, nor should they be firm and resolute in their child's correction. Believe me, this is not wise advice. Not only is this contrary to the way our Lord admonishes us to teach and correct our children; my experience tells me it is also one of the most, if not the most, important reasons why so many young people are running wild today. Some examples include: (1) disobeying their parents, (2) getting strung out on drugs, (3) ending up standing before a judge (such as the story I wrote about in the last chapter), and (4) tragically dying very young.

Many children today are running away from home, smoking dope and shooting smack, robbing stores, raping both young boys and girls, killing adults (including their parents), and committing all sorts of evil crimes, partly because they were never corrected nor properly disciplined in the home.

I realize I'm taking the chance of being ridiculed and criticized by some of you reading this book because of your opposition to my advice regarding correction and discipline in child rearing. However, my experience with counseling a great number of parents and children for the past twenty-five years dictates that I write the truth, and the truth, according to the Bible, ordains that discipline and correction, which are major elements for proper child rearing, are vital if parents are to be successful in teaching and training their children.

–If we fail to properly correct and train our children, the type of social failure and family decline we are witnessing in almost every country, state, and region dictates that our future, instead of being effectual and a growing civilization, will instead be something far less than desirable!

What do I mean when I write about *proper* correction and discipline? If we misuse the authority and power we have over our children and become harsh and abusive in our discipline and correction, we will certainly "provoke our children to wrath and anger." (See chapter 15, "How NOT to Provoke your Child to Wrath!"). And by doing so, we become the *cause* for many of their mistakes and sins! This is why we must never allow anger to control our emotions whenever we correct our children. Anger and lack of self control is probably the greatest cause leading to child abuse. And child abuse is something no loving parent ever wants to commit. God is not pleased with an adult who mistreats or abuses his or her children!

The other day I witnessed a women in a store become so angry and upset with her little boy that she lost all control and hit him hard enough that he fell out of the shopping cart onto the floor. She could have seriously injured her son. And even though he did not seem to be physically hurt by the fall, he will no doubt have some type of mental wound from that incident as he grows older. And, unless his mother seeks immediate help and begins to control her emotions, there is a strong possibility that her son may not live to grow older. Far too many children today are dying because of child abuse.

Not long ago, I was in a grocery store pushing my cart around looking for the best buys. When I wandered over to the bulk food section, I noticed a small child playing with the candy in one of the food bins. This cute little tot was probably no more than two or three years old. The interesting thing about this little girl is that she was left alone to fend for herself in the store. Because there was no one nearby, I immediately wondered where her mother or father was.

I began to think about what we read and hear regarding little girls and boys who have been left alone, like this child. Often they fall prey to some demented pervert who kidnaps them and causes them bodily harm, or worse. It happens all the time. So, I stood there for a moment watching her, making sure she was safe and hoping all the while that mom or dad would show up.

The thing that caught my eye was how she was putting her not-so-clean little hands all over the unwrapped bulk candy. I also wondered if the amount of candy she had just eaten might not send her into sugar shock at any moment!

After awhile, seeing that no one was going to help her, I walked over and kneeled down and as lovingly and kindly as I hoped I could be said to her, "Honey, what you're doing is a 'no-no'". I then asked her where her mommy was. All of a sudden this little darling threw herself on the floor and began screaming and kicking her feet, carrying on and having quite a temper tantrum. I tried to console her, but nothing seemed to help.

After what seemed too long, a woman appeared from nowhere. I asked her if she was the little girl's mother. She replied, "Yeah" as she looked down at her out-of-control kid. While her little darling laid on the floor kicking and screaming, I told her what happened, and after I finished my explanation, she simply shrugged her shoulders, picked up her daughter and headed for the cashier.

The point is, so many parents today fail to tell their children "no". They fail to properly teach and discipline them because of some strange idea or theory they may have read or heard somewhere along the way - warning them that if they discipline or correct their kids, they will cause their children to become immature, emotionally wrecked and bound to fail in life. And all I can reply to this kind of nonsense is "hogwash!"

You have read in previous chapters that there is a cause for every effect. When we begin to understand many of the discouraging and threatening *effects* our children are experiencing today in school, at home, or at play with their friends, then we begin to realize that many of these *effects* culminate into more than a few of our children having to stand before a judge, spend time in a hospital, or end their lives at an early age. We parents need to ask ourselves, "What was the cause?" "What caused my child to behave as he or she did?" "Why did this happen to my kid?" "What could I have done to help prevent it from happening?" "What will the long term effect be?" and "Did I ever say "no" and really mean it?!" The trouble is, by the time a parent asks these questions, it's usually too late!

Parents are only human, and as human beings, we all have a particular breaking point where we lose control. Some might say it's where common sense ends and emotions take over. However, as parents trying to teach and train our children the best we can, we must always strive to correct and discipline our kids before we reach the point where we lose control. Hopefully as we mature and grow deeper in understanding and wisdom, we will finally come to a place in our lives where we maintain complete control of our emotions and temper. But until that time comes, we must *never* punish our children when we are not in total control of our emotions...in control of our very minds!

When is the proper time to correct and discipline a child? When we are relaxed and thinking logically and rational. Before we ever begin to correct or discipline our kids, we must first of all understand *how* to discipline and *what type* of discipline to employ. Just as every child is different and every reason for correction is also different, so, too, the type of discipline or correction for the transgression is different. And this is one reason why it is so very important to know and understand each individual child so that when

167

we have to discipline and correct him or her, we will do so in a way befitting the child and the offense.

Every one of my six children is different from his or her siblings. And even though I tried hard to treat each child the same as I treated the other five, there were times when I found it necessary to correct one of my kids in a manner different from the others.

One of my sons could become so obstinate in seeking to have his own way that only when I firmly punished him with a paddling on his buttocks so that he could feel it, would he begin to turn around and head the right direction. On the other hand, one of my daughters was so impressionable and sensitive that all I had to do was to look at her in a threatening manner and tears of sorrow would suddenly begin rolling down her cheeks while real remorse and repentance took over. If I spoke with a firm voice to another daughter, it just tore her apart and she would immediately begin seeking ways to overcome whatever it was she was doing wrong. One son got the message whenever I took away his most important privileges. When they were young, our kids were no different than your kids. Each one had his or her own particular (and sometimes most peculiar) personality and character traits and, almost always, each child had to be corrected in a different manner and method from their siblings.

I didn't have to punish my children often, but there were times when it did become necessary. And like almost every parent I know, I hated it when the time came where I had to stop and punish my kids for their own good. It was very hard, but I knew I had to do it for the sake of those little ones who I so dearly love.

I remember the time when I was in a room toward the rear of our house doing some work when all of a sudden I heard a loud crashing sound come from the living room area. As I ran to the front of the house, I suddenly felt my blood beginning to drain from my head while at the same time I began stepping on a lot of small pieces of broken glass lying all over the living room floor. Nearby lay a smooth rock about the size of a small child's hand. As I looked at the broken pane in the window overlooking the front yard, I saw a gaping hole, shattered glass, and kids scattering in every direction.

"OK, which one of you little angels broke the window?!"

I had taught my children that they were never to throw rocks or stones except when I was present (and this was only when we tossed them out of the garden or skipped rocks across the lake).

I immediately called all my kids together and with a tone in my voice that only a father can emit, I looked each kid in the eye and asked, "Okay, you guys. Who broke the window?!" Now, I used special emphasis on each word just so they would be sure to understand exactly what the question was!

What I got in return was six blank stares and a short two-word reply spoken by each kid in unison, "What window?"

I don't know how it is with other large families, but my kids always stuck together like glue (especially in a time of crisis, which, of course, this was).

I waited for a minute, then asked, "Is the guilty party going to

169

step forward?" Nobody moved. "Okay, if you won't tell me who broke the window, then each of you bend over." Each child turned around and bent over exposing their cute little rear ends for punishment.

I gave each one a swat and then I asked again, "Who broke the window?" Still, no response.

After I got up to five swats with a short rod, I laid it down and decided I had to think this situation out! I couldn't allow myself to become angry or frustrated and in doing so lose control. Nor could I allow the misdeed of one of my children to go unpunished. What was I to do?!

I thought for a few moments, then said to them, "I will give you five minutes to talk it over among yourselves. If the one who broke the window doesn't speak up and admit what he or she did, you will force me to initiate some very heavy restrictions for **all** of you! And so you'll know I mean what I'm saying, I will add one swat to each of you until the one who broke the window 'fesses up." I added, "By the way, I know which one of you did it!" I knew each of my kids like the back of my hand, so I had a pretty good idea who the culprit was. I left the room so they could be alone to consider what I had said.

When the five minutes were up, I returned and after lining them up in a straight line by age, I asked each one individually, "Did you break the window?"

"No, Daddy," the first three replied.

When I came to the son who I felt was the one who had thrown the rock, I looked him in the eye and said, "Son, I know who did it." He looked down at the floor for a moment (probably seemed like an eternity to him) and then quietly said, "You're right, Dad. I did it."

"Why did you break the window?"

"Well, Dad," he began. "I threw a rock at a bird and I guess I just didn't realize the window was going to be in the way." He was very matter-of-fact and honest in his answer and I appreciated it.

I told him I was proud of the way he told the truth (although it did take some coaxing), and then I asked the rest of my kids if they wanted to give their swats back to their brother. One by one they all replied "no," that they would keep them. And so, after nearly an hour of pretty intense emotions, fear, and sensitivity, we worked it out. My son would pay for the window from the money he earned doing odd jobs around the house. Later, when he had finally saved enough money for a new window, we went down to the hardware store and bought a piece of glass and the two of us repaired the broken pane together.

We all learned some important lessons that day, and we can laugh about it now. But, you know what? None of my kids allow any of my twenty grandchildren to throw rocks or stones! And whenever their kids do something wrong, my kids aren't afraid to punish them.

Is spanking a child wrong? Not if we obey the teachings of the Bible. Yet, it can be wrong if it is not carried out in love, tenderness, and patience. It is also wrong if it ever becomes a form of abuse!

"Spare the rod and spoil the child," the saying goes. My experience, after working with so many parents and children throughout the years, tells me that when we spare the rod (fail to discipline), we indeed spoil (damage, injure, or destroy) the child! God tells us that, "He who spares the rod hates his son; but he who loves him is careful to discipline him" (Proverbs 13:24 NIV). Paraphrased, this verse tells us, "If we refuse to discipline our children, it proves we do not love them; for if we love them, we will be prompt to punish them."

A problem I see with a number of families is what I call, "just you wait...". I hear so many mothers tell their children, "Just you wait until your father gets home. He's going to punish you for what you did!" We should never put off punishment or neglect our responsibility for disciplining a child by simply waiting for our spouse to carry out the punishment. Both parents need to show their children that they have the authority to rule their young lives and that by doing so they are demonstrating their deep and abiding love for each of them.

We parents need to understand that when God created us he

gave us His manual or book of instruction for the purpose of helping us live our lives in a righteous and Godly manner, and His instruction manual does teach and instruct us how to be parents. Proverbs 19:18 (paraphrased) tells us, "Discipline your son in his early years while there is still hope. If you don't, you will ruin his life." Did you get that last part? "If you don't, you will ruin his life!" Such wisdom comes only from God. It is not something man has made up and believes to be true.

In fact, man says just the opposite from what God tells us in His word. God admonishes us parents to discipline and correct our children, and if we fail to do so, we will be the cause that will later ruin their lives. But, man comes along with his "super" intellect and theoretical wisdom and loudly proclaims that if we parents discipline and correct our children, we will surely retard their minds and destroy their future livelihoods. The question is: who should we believe? Personally, I'll follow the instructions of my Lord.

"Foolishness is bound in the heart of a child; but the rod of correction shall drive it far from him!" (Proverbs 22:15 KJV). And to repeat a verse already quoted, "Do not hold discipline from a child; if you punish him with the rod he will not die." (Proverbs 23:13 NIV) and continuing with verse 14, "Punish him with the rod and save his soul from death!" (Proverbs 23:14 NIV).

"Save his (my child's, your child's) soul from death" is pretty heavy admonishment. But, just what is the "rod"?

To understand what a "rod" is and how it is used, let's once again go to the Bible for instruction. "...your rod and your staff they comfort me." (Psalms 23:4 NIV). Here the psalmist tells us that there is comfort in the use of the rod if it is used properly. Still what is a "rod"?

One of the Hebrew words for "rod" is "shebet", meaning "a stick for punishment". A rod can also be used figuratively as a rod or staff such as a shepherd's staff. However, when God admonishes parents to "...not spare the rod...", He is referring to a rod ("shebet") or "stick for punishment."

When King David used his rod to protect his sheep from the dangers of this world, he did so in a way as not to harm his sheep but rather in a way to protect them. And just as with King David's sheep, our children live in a very evil and dangerous world, and it is by our faithful and loving use of a physical rod ("shebet") that we can help protect and comfort them...saving them from harm and possible death.

The "rod" in King David's time was also used as a weapon. In the past, we have even used the term "rod" to mean gun or weapon. In Moses' day he carried a rod to show his authority. And today, God commands every parent to be on alert in order to protect our children, our little flock - much the same way as David and Moses and others throughout history had to protect their sheep (their flocks) - not allowing them to wander off to dangerous areas where they might be harmed or worse! How did King David protect his flock? By carefully using his rod.

If we truly desire to follow the instruction of our Lord and serve our children as best we can, we must keep our rod and staff close at hand. We must always remain watchful and protective of our children. There are times when this may mean having to punish (discipline and correct) our little ones so that they will not fall into dangerous pits, i.e., being hit by a car, falling off a high ledge, being burned by a hot stove, talking to strangers or accepting rides from those they don't know, running with the wrong crowd, doing illegal drugs, committing crimes, doing other wrong things.

I feel certain that King David never beat or abused his sheep; but, he did discipline them and he took great care to see that they remained unharmed and safe. King David used his rod to help keep his sheep from straying onto the wrong path and away from the safe road...away from his watchful care and protection.

I have a very close friend who is also a fellow minister. Awhile back he told a story to his congregation regarding a time when he was forced to discipline his son.

It seems my friend had told his little boy not to go into the street. Although they lived on a quiet culdesac, still, all streets were off limits. After making sure his son knew what he meant about not going in the street, my friend went inside his house to do some paper work. From his desk he could watch his son playing, making sure he was safe and secure.

Only a few minutes had gone by when my friend noticed that his little boy was beginning to slowly edge toward the street. Without letting his son know he was watching his every move, he stopped what he was doing and went to the door to see if his son was going to mind or if he was going to disobey and step into the street.

Well, the little guy slowly looked around and when he saw that no one was watching him, he casually wandered over to the curb and stopped. Again, he looked around and when he couldn't see his father watching him from the house, he lifted his little foot and stepped just one foot in the street, but that was all his father needed to see. Like an arrow shot from a bow, my friend rushed out of his house, picked up his little boy and, without a word, rushed back into the house.

My friend told his congregation that his little boy knew immediately that he was in big trouble. And, you know what? His little boy was right! After explaining to his son why he was going to be spanked, he dealt out the punishment. And he did so with love, patience, firmness, and resolve.

When my friend told this story, he finished with the following statement. "I spanked my little boy's seat that day because I wanted to keep him around for a long, long time. I wanted him to grow up to become a responsible adult. And the most wonderful thing about this is...my boy is alive today!"

My friend's children deeply love and respect their Dad because they know he loved them enough when they were little to take the time, exert the effort, pay the expense, and even face the possible wrath and ridicule of others (family and friends) who may have considered him to be overly strict in his correction and discipline. And he did so in order that they might be better prepared along the way as they grew into adulthood.

"Discipline your son (daughter), and he (she) will give you

peace; he (she) will bring delight to your soul!" (Proverbs 29:17 NIV).

Awhile back, I was listening to a so-called child expert on television talking about child discipline and how wrong it is to discipline and correct children. The main focus of her talk centered on her personal hypothesis that all we need to do as parents, while raising our children, is to show them love. Nothing wrong with showing our children love; we should always show them love. The question is: what kind of love?

The kind of love this woman was talking about seemed to be nothing more than a very permissive type of *affectionate* love; what I call a "goo-goo, ga-ga" kind of love. This is the type of so-called love where parents believe that by not saying "no" to their children and by not disciplining or correcting them, they are somehow showing them they are truly loved. These parents seem to believe they can reason with a two year old as to why he shouldn't go into the street or a five year old as to why telling lies is wrong; and that a ten year old child has the mind, character, and ability to make the type of decisions that only maturity, experience, and wisdom can support.

These parents also seem to believe that by telling their children "no," "you can't do that," or "stop this instant" (and mean it) is somehow going to retard or inhibit their children's growth. If we even come close to suggesting corporeal punishment in order to help turn a child around so that he or she might head in a more enlightened or positive direction, forget it! We have just lost the parent's attention and respect (and possible friendship). I say again, what a shame!

Throughout history and especially during the past several decades, we human beings have tried to replace the commandments God set in motion nearly six thousand years ago with our own modern ideas and theories regarding the way to raise children. "There is a way which seems right to man, but in the end it leads to death!" (Proverbs 14:12 NIV). And, "My people are destroyed from lack of knowledge..." (Hosea 4:6 NIV).

Again, we are told, "...but he who loves him (a child) is careful to discipline him (the child)". (Last part of Proverbs 13:24 NIV).

The word *"careful"* is a key word in this proverb regarding correction of children. Webster tells us that the word "careful" means "to be *thoughtful* in a *painstaking way*. Cautious, wary, guarded. Close attention to or *great concern* for whatever is one's work or responsibility. To be meticulous, scrupulous, circumspect, cautious, prudent." Perhaps this might be a good time to ask ourselves if we, as parents, are "careful" when we correct and discipline our children. A lot of parents aren't, and a lot of children are hurt and even dying today because their parents lose self control and aren't thoughtful, meticulous, prudent...careful whenever they punish their kids!

The Bible instructs every parent that child discipline is right and proper when administered God's way. God created us humans with design and protection in mind. He designed the bottom end of a child with protective padding so that when he or she is punished by careful spanking, other than the child's feelings being hurt, there is no physical harm committed. However, God did not intend that a child should ever be beaten or abused! Indeed, child abuse is sin!

Someone reading this might say, "The child's feelings and emotions are indeed affected when a parent uses corporeal punishment as a form of correction, and this is why so many children today are experiencing emotional trauma!" Or, "when we hit a child, we're teaching that child to hit others."

Really? If parents would properly correct their children by first explaining to them why the punishment is necessary and at the same time tell them that they love them more than their very own lives, and secondly; demonstrate this love by example in the way they live their lives with honesty, fairness and compassion toward their children, and finally by the tenderness, encouragement, and respect they give their children on a daily basis, isn't it possible that this will far exceed the momentary hurt feelings a child experiences while being punished? Isn't it possible that this is what really makes a lasting impression on a child's fertile mind? Isn't it true then, corporeal punishment becomes simply a method to help gain a child's attention so that he or she can overcome and turn around whatever their problem may be and then move on to more productive things to

176

learn about and do? Without a doubt. And if you doubt this, take the time and prove it to yourself!

A very important principle we parents need to consider before we correct our children is that we should never discipline or punish them more than the situation requires. We should always - always - carry out the punishment with patience and in love!

One day, I received a phone call from a woman who was terribly upset with her teenage daughter. It seems she had come home later than she was supposed to from a date. The later it got the more the mother worried, to the point where fear and anxiety had taken over. What was the result? How did the mother react? She restricted her daughter to the home for one full year! This girl could not go out with her friends for an entire year!

After helping the mother calm down somewhat by listening to her tell me about the problem with her daughter, she asked me what I thought she should do and if what she had done was correct. It was obvious that this lady had punished her daughter in anger and that the punishment was far greater than the situation required. Not only was the punishment something that could never be kept, it was also very ineffective.

If correction is going to be effective when punishing a child, parents must be willing to fully back up whatever they decide the punishment to be. This is one reason why it is so important we never punish our children in anger. We must always strive to use wisdom and balance when correcting and disciplining a child.

Also, whenever a parent acts too hastily and later has to retract the stated punishment, as in this example, his or her credibility with the child suffers a tremendous loss, especially when the parent must correct and discipline his or her child the next time.

We now understand that our attitude and character as parents, especially when correcting and disciplining our children, must be overflowing with patience, caring, firmness, caution, and unconditional love. But what about the attitude and character of our children? It is important to note that whenever we detect an "I don't care what you do to me," or "So what, it's no big deal!" or "Who do you think you are?!" type of rebellious attitude from one of our kids, wisdom dictates that - after determining that this is actually only a display of arrogance and bad-temper and not some deeper hidden emotional problem - we should never allow this situation to go unpunished. If we do, we will be sorry later. And so will the child!

Arrogance, bad temper, and rebellion are types of diseased cancerous attitude-cells that must be removed early in a child's life, before they become so dominant and powerful that they control a child's emotions, decisions, mannerisms, abilities, character, and thoughts for the rest of his or her life!

Here is another important principle regarding discipline and correction of our children: we must make every effort to correct and discipline our kids at home while always striving to be consistent in our punishment. In other words, we should make every attempt to never punish our children in front of others, nor should we ever deliberately embarrass them in front of strangers, family, or friends. After all, we would never want someone doing this to us no matter what our offense. And, we should never correct our children for doing something wrong the first time, and then when they do it again, simply let it go by. It doesn't work that way. If we are going to be successful parents, we must be consistent in our total approach to child rearing. We must be loving, thoughtful, patient, merciful, and, once again, *consistent!*

Remember, correction and discipline are part of the foundation we are building to support our children as they enter into adulthood - a foundation that will support their every decision, every plan, every hope, and every goal...their very lives!

Whenever I take any of my grandchildren to the store, if they ask for something and I tell them "no", they don't jump up and down or throw themselves on the floor and have a temper tantrum. They simply understand that I mean what I say, and we continue on with the business at hand.

I am not an advocate of making children sit with their hands folded, mouths shut, having to act like little "angels," especially at home. Certainly, I believe children should have good manners, show respect to their elders, and be courteous to those with whom they come in contact. At home, my children were full of youthful mischief (I'm sure they took after their mother). However, whenever we went out to eat, my kids knew how to behave, no matter what their age. In fact, more often than not, our waitress would comment on how well our kids behaved and what a delight it was to serve them. And, today, it is really a pleasure for me to have my grandkids around because I know it's also a pleasure to those people who come in contact with them. And you know why it's such a pleasure? Because my kids have in turn taught and trained their children well!

One time when my children were just tots, the entire family, all eight of us, were traveling some distance from home when we decided we were hungry. Can you imagine eight bellies beginning to rumble and roar all at the same time? Not a pretty sound! So, we decided to stop and eat at a roadside restaurant. We ordered the food and while we were eating the waitress kept noticing our kids' behavior; how polite and quiet they were, especially for such young kids. But after all, they were starved, which probably made a difference! Later, as our waitress was pouring us some fresh coffee, she told my wife and me how much she appreciated waiting on a table surrounded by kids like ours. I admit it made me feel very good.

We finished our meal so I left a tip on the table and told my family I'd meet them out in the car after I went to the washroom.

Well, after traveling about ten minutes down the road, my four-year-old son leaned forward from the rear seat and proudly announced, "Daddy. Here's the money you left on the table."

I couldn't believe it! My little boy was so proud that he had protected me and my money. And all I could think about was how our hard working waitress, who had bragged about my children and had gone out of her way to serve us, was probably thinking not only about how neat my kids were, but how their old man had just ripped her off. I felt proud of my son but at the same time very uncomfortable regarding the situation.

I stopped the car so we could think out our problem. I told my son that I appreciated his help and honesty, and then we discussed how much waiters and waitresses depend on tips for their livelihood. After our discussion, I turned the car around and headed back to the restaurant so my son could return the money to the waitress.

We never knew exactly what our kids were going to do. What parent does? However, whenever they did well and set the right example, I tried to always let them know how much I appreciated them and their efforts. That day on the road, I let my four-year-old boy know that even though we had to backtrack out of our way, nevertheless, I appreciated his thought, protection, and kindness. Whoopee, it was great whenever my kids did things right!

One of my sons called the other day and told me he had taken my grandson fishing and during the course of the day, it seems a fishing pole somehow got knocked into the lake. And guess who did it? My grandson.

"Did you get mad at him?," I asked.

"No way," my son replied. "But I knew you'd get a laugh out of it."

I did get a good laugh out of what my son was telling me. And after I calmed down, I said, "Son, it does my heart good to know that something like this has happened to you, as a father, because of the things like this that happened to me when you were little. I'm especially happy to hear that you kept your cool and didn't scold or punish him. I'm sure he'll learn a lot from this experience."

There was a short pause and then my son, while chuckling to himself, said, "I'm sure he will. I told him he would have to replace the pole by working at odd jobs around the house until he had saved enough money to pay for a new one."

Now here was positive proof that "what goes around, comes around." I was proud of my son and told him I felt he had chosen a very good method for disciplining his boy. Then I added, "Where do you suppose you may have learned the way to properly correct my grandson for his having broken the window pane...ah, I mean, for having lost your fishing pole?!" We both had a good laugh.

Remember, the Bible tells us that there are rewards for doing good, and curses for doing evil; teach your children these principles but put your emphasis on "rewards for doing good." Accentuate the positive in childrearing; accentuate the fact that we all receive a reward of some type - a good relationship, a loving home, health, a feeling of satisfaction, a successful life - whenever we do good.

As I mentioned earlier in this chapter there have been scores of books written about child discipline and correction, discipline vs. non-discipline, punishment vs. non-punishment. And still, the greatest book of all is the one written thousands of years ago for our admonition and edification today, the Holy Bible!

This magnificent book provides parents with knowledge and understanding regarding how to properly teach, train, instruct, correct, and discipline their children. Hosea 4:6 tells us, "My people are destroyed from lack of knowledge..." and yet, more than a few parents would rather read some secular book about raising children written by the latest "child expert" or "New Age Guru" than go to God for His instruction and guidance. What a disgrace!

True knowledge, wisdom, and understanding that parents so desperately need today regarding how to properly raise children, is available. Yet in our present society, we just don't seem to want or desire this knowledge and understanding, and the sad part is our children will eventually pay the penalty. We parents will also pay a penalty of higher taxes, unemployment, more prisons, loss of children, anxiety and despair, higher crime, more violence, and all the while sinking further and further into total decadence and misery. We must strive to keep in mind, "there is a way which seems right to man, but in the end it leads to death!" (Proverbs 14:12 NIV).

DISCIPLINE MUST ALWAYS BEGIN WITH LOVE!

How blessed and wonderful is the parent who disciplines and

corrects his or her child in love, mercy and patience, and by the direction and guidance of our great Creator God.

Parents, raise up your children according to the way God has commanded. Give your kids quality time, love, attention, and proper instruction. Help them now to learn how to overcome small problems, so that when they are older and the problems are much greater, they will have the type of faith, integrity, knowledge, wisdom, empathy, willpower, and determination to overcome these obstacles without falling off track or crashing head on into destruction. Do it now so that you and your children will have long, healthy and prosperous lives. **"Do not withhold discipline from a child..."**
(Proverbs 23:13 NIV)

To help your kids grow in wisdom and understanding teach them to:

"Thank God every morning when you get up that you have something to do which must be done, whether you like it or not. Being forced to work, and forced to do your best, will breed in you temperance, self-control, diligence, strength of will, contentment, and a hundred other virtues which the idle never know." Charles Kingsley

TWELVE RULES FOR RAISING CHILDREN
by
Ann Landers

- **R**emember that a child is a gift from God, the richest of all blessings. Do not attempt to mold him in your image, or that of your father, your brother, or your neighbor. Each child should be permitted to be himself.

- **D**on't crush a child's spirit when he fails. And never compare him with others who have outshone him.

- **R**emember that anger and hostility are natural emotions. Help your child to find socially acceptable outlets for these normal feelings or they may be turned inward and erupt in the form of physical or mental illness.

- **D**iscipline your child with firmness and reason. Don't let YOUR anger throw you off balance. If he knows you are fair you will not lose his respect or his love. And make sure the punishment fits the crime. Even the youngest child has a keen sense of justice.

- **P**resent a unified front. Never join with your youngster against your mate. This can create in your child (as well as in yourself) emotional conflicts. It also produces destructive feelings of guilt, confusion and insecurity.

- **D**o not hand your child everything his little heart desires. Permit him to know the thrill of earning and the joy of deserving. Grant him the greatest of all satisfactions - the pleasure that comes with personal achievement.

- **D**o not set yourself up as a model of perfection. This is a difficult role to play 24 hours a day. You will find it easier to communicate with your child if you let him know that Mom and Dad can make mistakes, too.

- **D**on't make threats in anger when you are upset - or

impossible promises when you are in a generous mood.
Threaten or promise only that which you can live up to.
To a child a parent's word means everything. The child
who has lost faith in his parents has difficulty believing in
anything.

• Do not smother your child with superficial manifestations
  of "love". The purest and healthiest love expresses itself
  in day-in, day-out training which begets self-confidence
  and independence.

• Teach your child there is dignity in hard work, whether it
  is performed with calloused hands that dig ditches or
  skilled fingers that manipulate surgical instruments. Let
  him know a useful life is a blessed one and a life of ease
  and pleasure-seeking is empty and meaningless.

• Do not try to protect your child against every small blow
  and disappointment. Adversity strengthens character and
  makes us compassionate. Trouble is the great equalizer.
  Let him learn it.

• Teach your child to love God and to love his fellow man.
  Don't SEND your child to a place of worship - TAKE him
  there. Children learn from example. Telling him something is not teaching him. If you give your child a deep
  and abiding faith in God it can be his strength and his
  light when all else fails.

"He must manage his own family well
and see that his children
obey him with proper respect"
(1 Timothy 3:12 NIV)

184

CHAPTER FOURTEEN

Teaching Children
about
$$$MONEY$$$

M anaging money is one of the most difficult problems facing mature adults today. In fact, look at the way our government manages (or some would say "mismanages") its tax revenues and how billions of dollars are misspent every day. See the way many adults spend money with little or no regard for savings, retirement funds, or investments for the future. Note how little is taught in school regarding money management or capital investment. Is it any wonder our children grow up not really understanding what money is, what it can produce, why it should be respected, and how it should be properly managed?

How many parents take the time to teach their children about the proper use of money, or how to set up a savings account and then skillfully maintain it throughout their teenage years and on into adulthood? If what we read in Chapter Three regarding how most parents only spend an average of 37 seconds a day with their children is true, then obviously the answer is that not many parents today are teaching their kids how to manage their finances - no matter if we're talking about a few coins in a piggy bank, an insurance policy annuity, or a small savings account.

If we use the present state of our economy as a type of barometer to indicate how well we, as a society, are doing financially and how well we are instructing our children regarding money management, it would seem most adults, parents of teenagers, and government bureaucrats greatly lack an understanding about important financial matters. When we look at this situation as a national issue, there is little doubt it has become a major problem that doesn't appear to be going away any too soon!

For years I have counseled young people about how to manage money, how difficult it is to make it and keep it, and how to properly use it. Believe me, I sympathize with parents because I know first hand this is not an easy subject to instill into the minds of our children.

One of the greatest obstacles I run into as I counsel young people for marriage is a growing ignorance and naivete regarding one of the more important support systems for any marriage and that is the management of and proper respect for money! We live in a money driven society. None of us can live without it. We might be able to live with less money, but, nevertheless, we all need money to provide the basic essentials which enable us to grow, live and survive.

It seems with each new year it takes more and more money to pay our mortgage or rent, buy food, support an automobile, pay for insurance policies, provide personal healthcare (which is beginning to skyrocket out of control), support our children's schooling and extracurricular activities (which more and more schools can no longer afford to provide), supply funds for family recreational needs, attempt to maintain a reasonable savings account, fund our retirement (which many companies are no longer providing their employees), and simply live our lives on a day-to-day basis as best we can! As many of you well know, it ain't easy!

Take a moment and ask yourself, "Do my children really understand the value of money?" "Do they realize why it's so important for them to get a good education so they will be able to support a family; so they will be able to support themselves?" "Do they realize that worrisome financial responsibilities and having too little money to make ends meet are two of the main reasons so many marriages fail?" "Have I properly taught my kids what they need to know about money and how to manage it?" In fact, "Do *I* also need to understand more about how the financial money-management game works; do *I* personally need to become better educated in important life-supporting subject matters such as money management and capital investment?"

Following are some of the more important fundamental principles I have experienced and put into practice over the years which may help you teach your children more about money management and the real value of money:

1- ALWAYS GIVE GOD HIS SHARE BEFORE ANYTHING OR ANYONE ELSE! In almost every book I have read regarding the subject of money management, the author often admonishes the reader to give God His share from the gross of what we earn by our wits and hands.

I learned early in life that we must always pay our tithe to God from our gross revenues. And I taught my kids this very important principle when they were very young. As we begin to understand that we will never out-give God and that He owns everything that has been created (which means every physical, mental and spiritual element, cell or basic component), we then discover that we are on our way to acquiring the wisdom and knowledge we need not only to manage our money but to better manage and direct our very lives.

Putting God first in everything we say, do, or think provides the means for us humans to begin learning how to properly manage our very lives. Teaching our children to give God His tithes and offerings while they are young will help them understand later in life the value of both the spiritual and physical sum and substance that surrounds and supports their lives. This includes their health, marriage, intelligence, talents, the food they eat, clothes they wear, where they live and how they prosper, what they do with their lives, what their goals are, how they will meet and overcome challenges, and yes, even having a proper respect and appreciation for money!

2- TEACH YOUR CHILDREN THE BASICS OF WHAT IT COSTS TO SUPPORT A FAMILY - WHAT IT COSTS TO LIVE!

Most young people going out on their own today don't have a clue as to how much money it will take for them to live and survive in the real world. After all, was it not dad and mom who paid their bills, bought their food and clothes, and financially supported most of their needs?

I find it interesting (and somewhat depressing) that most schools teach our children arithmetic, history, and even what the word "touchdown" means, and yet after graduation so many kids are unable to balance a check book, figure compounding interest rates, or pay their bills on time. Nor, it seems, do they realize, as they begin their working years, that when the money they bring home (*net income*) doesn't cover expenses (*outgo*), the result is that they will soon find themselves in very serious financial trouble (*unable to pay their debts*). And the less they seem to know about money management, the deeper they go into debt. It's just that simple! And it is certainly one more reason our society is in such dire financial straits!

I always try to convey a message to those young people I counsel about marriage that the husband needs to have secure employment (be on the job for a period of time), the two of them should have finished school, and just as important, they should have also saved at least five thousand dollars in the bank before taking on the responsibility of joining in marital union with each. Who can say when the first child will arrive, how long a job will last, if one will remain in good health, or what the outcome will be for those future, unknown variables and potential problems each young person will face in the years ahead. The "unexpected" does happen!

How many young people you know are starting out in their marriage with a good paying job, a completed education, and at least five thousand dollars in the bank? Not many, I'm sure!

3- TEACH YOUR CHILDREN THE VALUE OF PREPARING A FINANCIAL BUDGET AND THEN LIVING BY IT! Sad to say, most children I work with don't even know what a budget is (nor do many of their parents). We just don't seem to be the type of society that lives by the confines and restrictions of a well thought out and thoroughly prepared financial budget. We bring home the paycheck and then see how fast we can spend it!

Here's something I found helpful when working on the subject of money management with my kids: Say you're a parent with a couple of kids in school. Now, no one needs to remind you that almost every day (or so it seems) you find yourself reaching in your pocket to give your kids money for some school function. There are needed supplies, lunch vouchers, and any number of other things. I had the same problem until I devised what I call my "Three Month Child-Funding Budget Plan." It works like this: during the next quarter (three month period) have your children write down in a notebook every nickel, dime, quarter, or dollar they spend, no matter what they spend the money for or why. It won't be easy and if you're a parent who only spends 37 seconds a day with your kids, this will probably not work for you.

Each child should make his or her own list, and the list should include such things as school supplies, snacks (this will give you a clue as to why Susie or Junior has gained so many extra pounds lately), new clothes, movie tickets, gas for the car (if they drive to school or to a part-time job), tune-ups, books, dates, and anything else they spend money on. Also, be sure to remind them to go over their lists every night before going to bed to make sure they haven't forgotten any expensed item for that particular day (it's very difficult to remember something we bought a week ago).

At the end of the third month, you and your kids will have a pretty good idea of how much money they are spending and where they are spending it. You now have a dollar figure that you can average over a period of time so that you can set up a realistic budget for each child to follow. Of course, you will need to make adjustments as certain needs arise and others no longer need to be met.

This type of budgeting works for a child who simply receives a weekly allowance or a teenager who has a part-time job after school and brings home a paycheck. And, guess what? If children get into the habit of keeping expense records on a daily or weekly basis when they are young, as they grow older this will greatly enhance their ability to support themselves and provide for their family - thus helping them to succeed and prosper in life.

I recall a time when one of my daughters wanted a new sweater costing an entire month's budget. After thinking it out, she went ahead and bought the expensive sweater. To pay for the sweater she agreed to do without certain pleasures and nonessential items for the rest of the month. With the exception of paying for any emergencies or necessary toiletries, my daughter got no additional money from either her mother or me. She had to pack her own lunch, forego a movie or two, and stay home while her friends went skating. But to her the sweater was well worth it and we, her parents, felt good because we knew our daughter was beginning to learn about money management and accepting financial responsibility. This experience was priceless!

When my kids were young, one of them might come to me and say something like, "Dad, I want a new bicycle." I would reply, "Great. Now tell me, just how are you planning to pay for it?" I always found this to be a wonderful opportunity for me to sit down with my kid and help him or her begin to understand what money is, why it is important, and how he or she might obtain whatever it is they wanted by learning how to properly save for it.

Instead of simply giving my children something they wanted, (except for those special times when I would surprise them with something I knew they sincerely desired, and at the same time, I also knew their attitude had been positive by the way they helped around the house or acted toward their siblings and mom and dad), I always tried to find ways for them to earn the money so they could buy whatever it was they really wanted...including their choice of a particular style, color, fabric, etc. If we help our children earn the things they want in life, they will no doubt appreciate them all the more. Not only will they appreciate them, they will probably take much better care of them!

I remember the time when my three daughters needed cheerleading uniforms so they could attend a cheerleaders camp. Well, they all came to me hoping I would pay for the camp and the three uniforms. The uniforms alone cost $400 each...times three!

"Sorry, kids. There just isn't enough money in our budget for uniforms and cheerleading camp."

"But, Dad!"

"Sorry."

We had taught our children that if they really wanted something badly enough - and if that "something" was important and had value - with patience, vision, and thought, they would more often than not find a way to get it, even if it meant having to work for it...*especially* if it meant having to work for it! So, later that night, my wife and daughters came to me with a plan they had devised which would allow my girls to purchase their uniforms and also pay for attending the cheerleading camp. Their money-making strategy included their brothers' participation.

The plan called for my girls and their brothers to build one hundred hanging baskets out of some cedar scraps I had been saving in an old shed. After they built the baskets, the girls planned on filling each one with flowers and selling the completed basket for fifteen dollars apiece to friends, neighbors, and family.

I thought for a moment and then asked, "Where are you going to get the flowers? And who is going to sell them?" They immediately realized they had my interest.

"Honest, we'll take care of all of that. We've got it all planned out." My wife nodded in agreement. "So, will you and the boys make our baskets?" Suddenly, I was included in the manufacturing process. Yet, with so much energy and dedication coming from not only my girls but also from their mother, how could I say no?!

The next day, we all decided to make a real family project from the "flower-in-a-basket" money-making scheme my girls had created and developed with the help of their brothers and their mother. We started building baskets...all one hundred of them!

My wife went to the local nursery and explained to the owner what our girls were hoping to accomplish. I don't know if the lady who owned the nursery was a past cheerleader or not, but after listening to my wife's story, she thought for a moment and said, "I've got some plants out back that might be just what you need. C'mon, if you can use them, I'll give them to you for little or nothing." It turned out that what she gave us (for very little money) was nearly a pickup load of some very nice green plants!

To make a very interesting, long story short, my girls sold every basket we had made for fifteen dollars apiece. The money paid for their uniforms, camp expense, and, of course, God's tithe. They even had a little money left over so they could take mom, dad, and their brothers out to dinner!

Think of ways to help your kids earn money; don't just hand it over to them because that's the easy thing to do. We, as a family, would pick blackberries in the fall of the year so our kids could buy new clothes for school, and we helped our boys with money-making projects such as building mailboxes so they could buy some of the things they wanted or needed. There are many ways you can help your children earn money, and if you work together as a family, not only will they learn how to better appreciate what they earn and receive, you, as a parent, will also experience something of great lasting value, *togetherness* - the tremendous joy of working with your kids and getting to know them better!

4- SHOPPING IS A GREAT WAY TO HELP YOUR CHILDREN LEARN ABOUT MONEY. Taking your kids grocery shopping is a great way to share time with them while teaching them more about how to properly manage money (they will also learn the facts of life regarding the ever increasing, basic costs of feeding a family!).

If you decide to teach your kids about how to grocery shop, plan on it taking a little of your time. You just can't quickly walk through a store and expect to accomplish anything. As you shop, take the time to explain why you may purchase one product over another product, or why a certain type of produce may not be as nutritious as some other kind that may even be less expensive. Teach your children how to read the ingredients on the label; tell them what each ingredient means (and if you don't know yourself, look it up at a library or in a dictionary at home; make a family project out of it).

Instruct them as to the proper way to count the grams of fat and cholesterol; help them learn how to buy only quality food and then only the food that will provide them with the nutrients and fiber they need to grow and survive.

Now is the time, while they are still young, to begin teaching your children the principle that the cost of food is a very important part of your family's budget, and that your family's budget is a very important tool that you use daily so that you will have the money to buy the food when it is needed.

Teach your children to be aware of false advertising. Help them to understand there is a big difference between quality and inferior products. When they are out shopping with you and they see a pair of $20 pants on sale for $15, help them realize that (a) the quality of the pants may not be worth $15, let alone $20, and (b) even though the sale sign tells them that they will save $5 if they buy the pants today, what it is really telling them is if they buy the pants today, they will have just spent $15!

I tried to help my kids overcome the temptation to buy whatever it was they thought they wanted at that moment by telling them, "You know, you got by without it yesterday, you can get by without it tomorrow, and you don't have to have it today. Think about what it is before you spend your money!"

Times are changing. Most parents just don't seem to have the amount of money they had in the past when they could go out shopping and foolishly buy whatever it was they or their kids desired. Today, when we are able to buy our kids something, we should make every effort to be sure that whatever it is, it is quality and we can buy it at the best price possible.

5-   DISCOVER WAYS TO TEACH YOUR CHILDREN WHAT IT TAKES TO SUPPORT A FAMILY. Awhile back, I was talking with a father of a very large family (he also had six children), and during our conversation, we discussed just how careless our kids can be at times. For example, when they leave on the lights, play the stereo when no one is in the room, fail to turn off the TV when they are no longer interested in watching it, take too long a hot shower, launder only a few pieces of clothing at a time, use the dishwasher when it's not fully loaded, or thoughtlessly commit many other money-wasting practices.

After getting a good chuckle (each of us thinking to ourselves about a particular time when our kids had done some dumb thing that nearly warped the revolution speed of the electrical meter hanging outside our homes), he told me how he had solved the energy-wasteful problem his children had with electrical appliances.

His plan was very simple: he didn't charge his kids rent while they were attending school and working at a part-time job while living at home. However, he did ask them to pay the electrical bill. His grin widened as he told me how drastic and positive the results were from his little experiment!

After thinking about this man's experiment with the way he taught his kids to better appreciate the cost of home electricity, my wife and I decided to give his theory a try. At the time, we had three children who were working at part-time jobs while living at home. Up until the day of our experiment, I had charged each one of them ten dollars a week for board and room (hardly enough to pay the electricity bill for my daughter's curling iron!).

I got the kids together and told them they no longer had to pay ten dollars a week anymore. Instead, I wanted them to pay the electrical bill. I added that if they were very conservative, they might even save a buck or two.

At first, things went along as usual; the lights were left on, television played to an empty room, long showers were taken, and so on. I didn't turn off the TV, unplug a curling iron, or tell anyone to stop taking long showers. I just waited for the mailman to deliver that month's electric bill.

The day finally came when I handed over the bill (unopened) to my three oldest kids. Man, you should have seen the expression on their faces when they opened the envelope and began reading what they owed the electric company. It was a wonderful sight to behold!

WHAT A WAY TO LEARN A LESSON!

What made this experience even more interesting, the electric bill that month was the most expensive we had ever received - almost double the usual rate!

Almost immediately, lights went out, showers all but stopped, curling irons were unplugged, clothes went unwashed, stereos were turned off...I mean, it was nothing short of a major austerity program. It was fantastic!

And, it was comical. One day before leaving for work, I told

"WOW!"

my kids I would be arriving home after dark and that I would appreciate it if they would leave the outside light on for me. Before I got to my car, my son came out of the house running toward me with a flashlight in his hand. They had figured that this was a much cheaper solution to my request than leaving the outside light on and then having to pay for its use. There were times when the older kids would tell their younger siblings that they had showered long enough or to turn down the heat and put on a sweater. One thing is for sure: this experiment helped all of my children realize that it is not inexpensive to light and heat a home!

6- TEACH YOUR CHILDREN WHAT IT COSTS FOR RECREATION AND PLAY. Everyone likes to play and have fun, especially young people. My family has always believed that "a family that stays together is a family that *prays* and *plays* together". Still, it usually costs a fair amount of money when a family shares recreation and fun times (especially with six kids!). And, my experience tells me that most parents don't take the time to explain to their children just what it costs to pay for family recreation...for the "play and fun" times.

The next time you take the family on a snow-skiing trip, to a movie, to a dinner at the local pizza hut, fishing, boating, or any number of other outside-the-home and pay-for-play recreational activities, keep a tab of what it costs and then show these costs to your kids. I realize this will only make sense if your children are old enough to understand what it is you are trying to teach them. However, if you train them now, while they are still young, when they become old enough to comprehend what it is you have been trying to teach them, the possibility that they will successfully be able to set up and manage their own financial budgets when they become adults and parents greatly increases.

Teach your kids now about the costs of recreation so when they become parents they also will have the wisdom, understanding and financial ability to both *"pray* and *play* together"* as a family.

7- BE SURE YOUR CHILD HAS A SAVINGS ACCOUNT AND IS PROPERLY TAUGHT HOW TO USE IT. It's hard for me to imagine how many children today know nothing of the value of saving money in an interest-bearing savings account. And, sad to say, there are children living in other nations, such as the Japanese, who are taught about the importance of saving part of what they earn for those emergencies and needs that will come their way later in life.

One way to start teaching your kids about saving money is to save spare change in a large bottle. If you haven't already done this, you'll be surprised at just how fast loose coins can add up. This is one way to save up for that particular holiday, night at the movies, or gift for someone special.

With the way our world and society is rapidly changing, it is important that we save as much money as possible and that we teach our kids to save now for their future. Begin teaching your children (no matter what their age) to put aside at least ten percent of whatever they earn (allowance, jobs around the home, or part-time employment) for future investments. Consider this: if you had saved ten percent of what you have earned during the time you have been employed and wisely invested it, would you be financially better off today than you are? You bet you would. So, given what you now know to be true and wish you had done, but didn't, can you see why it's so important to take the time to teach your kids how to save and invest their money wisely?

Here is another important point you need to teach your kids regarding money management before they leave home: when they marry, they should make every effort not to fall into the trap of living on two incomes. This can be a very serious cause for all kinds of woes and family problems. It can (and so often does) become a major cause for marital breakup and divorce.

I certainly realize how difficult it is today to make ends meet on one income. I also understand it's even going to be harder in the future. The simple fact is that companies no longer pay their employees the high wages they once did. And with trade unions beginning to lose their power and influence, taxes ever increasing, healthcare insurance skyrocketing, middle management becoming increasingly more insecure and fearful, more and more single parents working two and three jobs in order to support their kids, and so many qualified people seeking too few jobs, things are not going to become easier for the worker and his or her children in the near future.

However, one way to reduce the dependency of having to live on a multiple income from both a husband's and wife's salary is not to buy into the hype and peer pressure that comes from a society which promotes such great materialism and greed. Far too many people (young and old) have fallen into this deceptive trap, and it seems so many never get free without having to go through some type of major, negative financial upheaval such as bankruptcy or worse.

Just as our children must learn to live within their means, which means living without their every want and desire being met, we parents must also! And yes, it is very difficult. Especially when one hasn't been living this way!

We should teach our children that when they have children, the wife should work only to support a specific purpose...a definite objective such as paying the cost of college tuition for either spouse, or a child; helping to provide additional family income because of a financial impairment due to illness or loss of the husband's job; purchasing something special for the home within a limited time frame; saving for a planned holiday; or some type of other emergency or necessity.

A married mother with a husband who is gainfully employed and whose responsibility it is to care for and nurture her young children, should make every attempt not to work at a full-time job just so that she might help provide her family with an increased level of *life-style.* Ask yourself: "What is more important: a new luxury car or expensive house in the best neighborhood (an increased materialistic life-style), or having children grow up sane and in control of their emotions and minds; children who have been properly taught and trained at home so that when they are on their own they might succeed and prosper with their own families, children who have had the benefit of sharing time with their parents?"

It's hard to understand why so many parents today want to "have their cake and eat it too!" We can no longer go on neglecting our children just so that we can buy more expensive possessions and material playthings. With the type of hedonistic attitude we see throughout the entire western world, is it any wonder why so many of our kids fail in their marriages, end up in jail, commit terrible crimes, or die before they grow old?!

Much of what is happening in such a negative way to our society and to our children is the direct result of a large number of married women, with children, working only to satisfy themselves through materialism and greed, rather than providing absolute necessities for the family and/or its survival. Single parent families are always going to be under some type of financial pressure (unless good ol' uncle Naybob dies and leaves a fortune to his single parent relative), but in a home with both parents where the father is employed, it is important that we begin to live with fewer materialistic things so that mom can spend more time with the kids. Mom is the principal teacher when the kids are young and growing up. Who else is there?

Again, ask yourself, "What is more important to me: seeing my children grow up with great ideals, sound goals and desires, compassion and understanding; or, my being able to buy that new car or take that expensive vacation to some far-off island I feel I so richly deserve?" These may be difficult questions, and they may sound old fashioned and dated; however, just as everything remains the same and nothing of value or principle ever changes, we parents must first put our childrearing priorities together if our kids ever hope to succeed in life. How do I know this is true? Just look around your community, read the newspapers, attend a PTSA meeting, or watch the news!

We must realize that we are living in a society where scarcity is becoming more prevalent, things of luxury less necessary, joblessness the order of the day, and crime and violence something we view nightly on almost every news program. More than a few so-called "child experts" attempt to explain away our problems with our children simply by stating that the reason children are failing to mature while growing more apathetic toward family, friends, and life is simply because that's "the way things are" - society is at fault. What they seem to fail to understand is that WE are society! WE are at fault!

There is no doubt in my mind that our physical and academic world is changing and not necessarily for the better!

A tip for parents: create and develop a modest money-making project for your kids, then fund it with money you have saved just for this purpose. I can't begin to tell you how valuable this has been in our family. As an example: the money for the plants that we had to buy for our daughter's plant-in-a-basket project, and the gas we bought to haul the family to our blackberry picking ventures, was loaned to our kids from our "special money-making project" fund. It helped our children grow and complete their goals (projects), and it also taught them something about money management, because we made them pay back the money they borrowed from the fund; and if the enterprise was successful, they paid back their loan with interest. We must have used this special fund hundreds of times.

Several years ago, I knew a farmer who needed some help hauling his hay. It was hard and heavy work, and before I accepted the job offer for my boys, I asked them if they would be interested in doing the work. They all said they would be more than willing to help haul the farmer's hay (little did they know exactly what they were getting into). So, without any discussion regarding salary and wages, they started work the next day.

I felt it would be good for my sons to help the farmer haul his hay, while at the same time, I figured they would have a lot of fun. They worked the entire week, and I must say they were very tired when they arrived home at the end of each day.

At the end of the week, the farmer paid each boy ten dollars. I didn't expect my sons to be paid at all, but my sons apparently expected to be paid more than what the farmer gave them. They were a little put out with having been paid so little for what they felt to be such hard and difficult work.

On the way home that night, they all expressed their feelings to me about how little they had been paid and how they felt they had been taken advantage of. I listened until my last son finished saying what was on his mind, then I said, "Hold on a minute. Let's see how much you were really paid. Okay?"

"Whatta ya mean, Dad?," they asked.

"First of all, did you boys have any fun?" They all agreed they had had a blast. So far, so good. "Was it worth ten dollars?"

"Yes. But the work we did was worth more than ten dollars."

"Okay. Let me ask you, did you learn anything new, anything you didn't know before taking the job?" They agreed that indeed they had learned several new things such as how to fix the old truck when it kept breaking down and even more important, how to drive it! I pointed out to each of them that what they had experienced with just the truck was more valuable than ten dollars (a young kid getting to drive a truck for the first time is certainly worth more to him than a ten dollar bill. He would have paid the farmer more than that just for the chance to drive it!). "Okay. Let's say your driving education was worth more than ten dollars. Am I correct?"

"Yeah. I would've paid a lot more than ten bucks to get to drive that ol' truck," my younger son replied.

""Did you get to eat anything while you were out there working?"

The wide grins and sheepish looks on all their faces told me they had eaten very well. They replied, "You bet! Both lunch and dinner! The food was great and we ate like kings!"

"What do you think your meals were worth? And before you answer, remember all three of you ate twice a day for a week. Do you think twenty dollars for each of you for the whole week is fair?"

"Yes. That's more than fair," they said.

"Was there anything else you guys did you haven't mentioned?"

There was a short pause and then my oldest son said, "Well, almost every afternoon we got a break and they gave us some cookies and a soda..."

"Yeah..." my second son joined in. "And don't forget last Wednesday when they took us to the county fair and paid for our tickets, all the rides we got to go on, and the food we ate."

"That sounds to me like we should add another twenty bucks for each of you, doesn't it?"

When we added up the total of what my farmer friend had paid or given to my boys while they worked for him, it came to over one hundred and sixty dollars. So I said, "It seems to me that you might have been overpaid somewhat. I don't know if you should even keep the ten dollars he gave you." Boy, did the car get quiet for a minute. I could just hear the rationalization and justification going on in their minds. Surely, they didn't want to return their wages!

The following day, my boys went back to the farm and thanked the farmer again for their week of fun, work enjoyment, and the ten dollars!

Thousands of years ago, a wise king named Solomon wrote, "He who loves money shall never have enough. The foolishness of thinking that wealth brings happiness!" (Ecclesiastes 5:10 Paraphrased Version).

We need to begin teaching our children that they will never be able to buy happiness and that true happiness only comes from obeying the commandments of God!

"The more you have, the more you spend, right up to the limits of your income; so, what is the advantage of wealth except to watch it as it runs through your fingers!" (Verse 5:11).

We must also teach our children how to save and budget their money. Again, King Solomon writes, "The man who works hard sleeps well whether he eats little or much, but the rich must worry and suffer insomnia." And, "There is another serious problem I have seen everywhere - savings are put into risky investments that turn sour, and soon there is nothing left to pass on to one's son or daughter. The man who speculates is soon back to where he began - with nothing. This, as I said, is a very serious problem, for all his hard work has been for nothing; he has been working for the wind. It is all swept away. All the rest of his life he is under a cloud: gloomy, discouraged, frustrated, and angry." (Verses 5:13-17). Some pretty good advice, right?

"Well, one thing, at least, is good: it is for man to eat well, drink a good glass of wine, accept his position in life, and enjoy his work whatever his job may be, for however long the Lord may let him live." (Verse 5:18).

And, "Of course, it is very good if a man has received wealth from the Lord, and good health to enjoy it. To enjoy your work and to accept your lot in life - that is indeed a gift from God. The person who does that will not need to look back with sorrow on his past, for God gives him joy!" (Verses 5:19-20).

It is our obligation as parents to teach our children about money and how to manage it before they leave home and begin living out the awesome responsibility of managing their own lives.

When we begin instructing our kids at an early age about the importance of money (in context with how the *"love"* of money will only produce evil and pain), while helping them maintain a healthy balance between overspending and being stingy and selfish, we provide them with a positive and proper start in life. Believe it or not, what we do now, and how we teach and train our children today, will have an everlasting effect on their lives!

We are living in a time in history when children must be taught how to live their lives in a way that is proper and right. No longer can we parents accept some type of so-called academic theory that declares aloud to the weak and unsuspecting child that there is no right or wrong, no absolutes. No longer can we reject authority and tradition or view morality and truth with skepticism because we have seen the results from such thinking and the results are far from good!

Teaching our children how to manage money is just one of the many things we parents have been given the responsibility to do. If our kids are ever going to succeed in the 21st century, if they are ever going to be able to take advantage of every opportunity that comes their way, they must first of all have the wisdom to see the opportunity and then possess the knowledge and understanding to accept and manage it. The possibility is very great that they will fail if we don't teach them now!

Wealth is a very dangerous inheritance,
unless the inheritor is trained to active benevolence.
C. Simmons

A SAMPLE BUDGET TO TEACH AND LIVE BY:

Over the years, I have used this sample budget during many of my talks with youth groups hoping that it might help them see a more clear picture of what it really costs to live and survive today. Young people need to understand that it takes money to support their life-styles, to support a family. Take a moment and go over this budget with your child; it will be fun and exciting and it might even help strengthen your relationship. As an example: use $10 per hour times 40 hours per week or $400 per week for a total of $1,600 per month as your base income (round numbers are easier for young children to understand and work with), or you might want to use your actual monthly income for a more realistic evaluation.

BUDGET for ONE MONTH:

Income: $_____

Less Expense:

Tithe (10% to God)..$_____

Rent.._____

Electricity..._____

Utilities (water/garbage)..._____

Telephone.._____

Insurance (auto)..._____

(health)......................................._____

Auto (payment).._____

(gas/oil/maintenance)......................................_____

(license).._____

(minor car repair).._____

(.10 per mile for tires, etc.)..........................._____

Newspapers/stamps/magazines, etc.........................._____

Food..._____

Non-edible items..._____

Laundry/cleaners..._____

Recreation.._____

Pet care..._____

Personal care (hair, etc.).._____

Clothes/shoes..._____

Gifts..._____

Retirement (IRA, pension plan, etc.)......................._____

Savings (10%)..._____

Total Expense: $_____

Less Income: $_____

Total Net Income(Before Tax): $_____

Not Much left over is there?!

CHAPTER FIFTEEN

How NOT to Provoke Your Child to Wrath!
And why you should never do so!

How many times have you said to yourself, "If only I had known what was going to happen, I sure wouldn't have done what I did!" All of us have said this sometime in our adult lives, and some of us say it more often than we would like to admit. One area where we, as parents, often seem to have to ask ourselves this question is after having said or done something that may have "provoked our children to wrath!" What parent really wants to cause his children harm? What parent wants to provoke her children to anger?

We are living in a world that is waxing cold, where often times we are overworked, underpaid, unemployed, taken advantage of and not appreciated; and because of this, we sometimes thoughtlessly provoke our children to wrath. We don't mean to, but we do, just the same.

One day, not long ago, a seventeen-year-old girl came to me with tears in her eyes. She told me her sad story about how much she wanted to please her parents, but it just seemed impossible. "I can never do anything to satisfy them," she said. "No matter what I do, it's never right...it's never enough! When my dad comes home, I'd love to go up and throw my arms around him just to show him I love him, but I can't. As soon as he gets home from work, he immediately starts putting me down. He chews me out for everything and anything." She began to break down and cry.

"What do you mean, 'everything and anything'?," I asked.

"If I go some place and don't call right away, or maybe, I even forget, he just yells and hollers at me. I mean, I'm never allowed to make an honest mistake without being screamed at and put down.

I have so many jobs to do after school that I can't get them all done; and, I guess I really just don't care anymore if I get them done or not. I wish I was out of school so I could leave home. I'd do almost anything, just so I could get away!"

"Where would you go?"

"I dunno and I don't care." She stopped for a moment and then looked up at me with pain and frustration outlining her young face. "You know, my dad always expects me to do something wrong, and I'm at a point now where I feel I might just as well. I mean, nobody really cares anyhow!"

This young girl's story can bring tears to the eyes of anyone who has children - especially to those who have experienced this type of pressure and frustration in their own lives. Her story is by no means an isolated case. There are hundreds of young people out there just like her...perhaps, there might even be one in your home!

A young boy at camp once asked me, "I want to love my dad, but he won't let me. I guess he thinks I'm going to end up just like him!"

"What do you mean?," I asked.

"He won't trust me anymore. He doesn't trust me as far as he could throw me. Man, I just can't wait until I can get out of that madhouse!" He began to cry as he continued, "He beats me! I don't mind a spanking when I deserve it, but I don't want to be slapped around just because he doesn't like the look on my face or the length of my hair. I want to love my dad, but lately, I find myself hating him." He hesitated for a moment and then added, "Sometimes, I think I could just kill him!"

Pretty shocking, isn't it? During the past several years, it seems we are reading more and more about an ever growing number of young kids attacking and even killing their parents for some reason or another. This is something that almost no one reading this book probably ever heard of when you were young, but it's happening today.

Another terrible thing that's happening in our society is the

206

large number of kids running away from home. And the number is growing every day! It seems so many young people are running away because they can no longer cope with the pressures and frustrations they encounter at school, at home, on the job, from their peers, or from their parents.

Certainly every kid who runs away from home hasn't been beaten or abused by his parents, but a large number of them have! And this has got to stop before it's too late.

The ironic thing about this situation is that many of these young people who profess to hate their parents, and some who have even killed them, still have a great desire to be loved by them. And, what about Mom and Dad? How do they feel about this situation? I am convinced that most parents truly love their kids, but they just don't know how to show them their love.

Our Creator God tells us that, "Children, obey your parents in the Lord: for this is right" (Ephesians 6:1 NIV). Children should obey their parents. But, let's take a moment to ask ourselves, in direct context with this statement from the Bible, "If we expect our kids to honor and obey us, how difficult do we parents make it for them to honor and obey us?" If we show real love and tenderness toward our kids, it isn't going to be difficult for them to obey what we tell them to do. If we want to really express love in the way we tell our kids to do something, what we say will be said with thoughtfulness and kindness; and the possibility of our kids obeying (and, in turn, honoring us by doing so) greatly increases.

"Fathers, do not exasperate (provoke) your children; instead, bring them up in the training and instruction of the Lord." (Ephesians 6:4 NIV).

The two stories I just shared with you (and there are many other similar stories I could write about concerning this problem) demonstrate that if we don't take the time to give our children a sense of worth and purpose, if we badger and brow beat them at every opportunity, we are not making it easy for them to honor and obey us and, indeed, we are provoking them to wrath.

What is "wrath"? Mr. Webster explains that wrath is 1- intense anger; rage; fury. 2- any action carried out in great anger, especially for punishment or vengeance.

Do we ever cause our children to become so angry, so full of rage and fury, that they commit an action whereby they lose control and harm themselves or some other person or thing? You bet we do!

Ask yourself, "Have you ever demanded something from your kids that you were unwilling to do yourself?" "Are the demands you often make on your children unrealistic - too difficult for their age - too insensitive?" "Do you constantly make your kids do all those dirty rotten menial jobs around the house just so you won't have to do them?" "Do you ever yell at them or put them down in front of their friends?" "Do you set a positive example for your kids by what you say or do, or do you allow the pressures from your own frustrations to determine the manner in which you instruct and guide them?" I realize that simple questions sometimes require difficult answers.

As a father of six, I know that all parents have a certain boiling point where, if not checked, they will eventually lose control of their emotions, patience, and temper. And then, look out! Words are said that hurt and destroy, fists begin to fly that often do physical harm, and the result is the relationship between child and parent (or husband and wife) may become so fractured that it may never heal or, at best, take forever to mend. And why does this happen? Mostly due to lack of self control! Does it have to happen? Certainly not!

There is an old parental law that goes something like this: "In order for our children to be willing to obey us, their parents, we, as their parents, must be willing to set a right example by our actions. We must demonstrate to our children, using our adult maturity and wisdom, how to treat the other person in the proper way; indeed, we should do unto others what we would wish for them to do for us. It is only by our setting a right example and then living that example that we may ever expect our children to succeed in life."

One way we can better teach our children is to often look

back at when we were young and remember what our parents did to turn us on or what they did that turned us off; what caused us to react in a positive way as opposed to our reacting in a negative way. Why we obeyed and why we disobeyed!

As an example: when you were young, what came to your mind whenever you heard your mom and dad fighting (assuming that they ever fought)? Did it hurt? Were you angry? Upset? Frightened? Remember, your children think about things much the same today as you did when you were their age. Granted, television, movies, and certain types of music have caused our kids to become more desensitized than we may have been in our youth. Still, when raw emotion and terror is unleashed within the confines of the home - the one place where our children look to find safety and security - they will no doubt experience similar types of emotions, including fear, anxiety, and insecurity. Just as we did in our youth.

I always wanted my mom and dad to be happy. I wanted everyone around me to be happy! And when my wife and I were married, we made a vow to each other that we would never quarrel or fight in front of our children. And to this day, we haven't. If something bothered either one of us, we would discuss the matter when we were alone. Our children have commented many times how much they appreciated living in a home where there was no fighting; and how stable and secure it made them feel.

Provoking a child to wrath (anger) doesn't always come from a particular assault aimed directly at the child. It can also come from within a home where the parents constantly argue and fight, where dreams and hopes are destroyed by insensitive words and actions, where love is seldom expressed, and where fear often rules the family.

Teach your children by living each day as a loving, thoughtful and caring parent. Believe me, they will love and respect you for it as they begin to learn and grow with a type of attitude that produces strong character. There is nothing more powerful or important to our children's upbringing than the example we parents set for them!

In the book of Genesis, we read about two brothers: Cain and

Abel. Cain is the first person we ever read about who, because of his great fury and anger, gave way to unsound reasoning and committed a violent act of wrath against another person: he killed his brother! What we see here is that unrestrained anger can lead to violence and crime. In this case it led to murder.

Have you ever considered what may have caused Cain to have such anger, such emotional wrath? How did he ever come to have such a troubled mind and violent tempers...such a lack of character? Was he born this way? Or, did he learn about violence and anger from another person? And if so, who? Who might have provoked him to such wrath? Besides his brother Abel, who was righteous (and there may have also been several younger brothers and sisters) there were only two other adults on Earth at the time: his father and mother, Adam and Eve!

Take a moment and try to envision the following scenario: Eve took of the fruit of Good and Evil from the tree that God had forbidden her and Adam to eat and then gave this fruit to her husband, and he also ate. Shortly thereafter, Adam and Eve lost everything they had been given in the Garden of Eden. Their comfortable world drastically changed!

A question comes to mind: could Adam have become so hostile against Eve that his attitude and character changed to a point that he felt only anger, bitterness, and resentment toward his wife from the time he ate the fruit until his death? Genesis 3:12 tells us that the first thing Adam did when God asked him what had happened in the Garden was to blame his wife. And because of Adam's transgression, could his son Cain possibly have felt the tremendous pressure, guilt, and frustration emanating from his father? Could Adam have provoked his son Cain to wrath?

I question if Adam ever let Eve forget that she had let herself become seduced by Satan. And I'm pretty sure they got into more than a few arguments and fights about who actually caused the sin. Men and women still blame each other for their own mistakes, weaknesses, and stupidity; even today at a time when we adults are supposed to be much more enlightened and wiser!

We can assume that Cain had to learn about anger and bitterness from someone. There is little doubt that he was provoked to wrath from having experienced something that greatly influenced him. When Cain was born he knew nothing about wrath, bitterness, anger, or jealously. It had to be something or someone along the way that provoked, inside his mind, a selfish and violent desire that eventually led him to kill his younger brother.

This story from the Bible regarding our first parents, demonstrates how very important the example we set for our children really is. What we do and say and how we say and do it, greatly affects the way our kids think and act throughout their lives. God admonishes His children to, "Honor your father and your mother; which is the first commandment with promise." If our children are to honor us as their parents, then should we not strive daily to become parents worthy of such honor?

I remember once when I got really upset with my dad. I was working for him in his bakery when suddenly he began chewing me out in front of all of his employees for something that wasn't my fault. I was so hurt by what he had done to me that I went into the back room and cried like a little child.

At the end of the day, I approached my dad (still smarting and more than a little embarrassed) and said, "Dad, you really hurt me this morning. You paid no attention to me when I told you I hadn't done what you accused me of doing; you just hollered and yelled at me in front of everybody."

He looked at me and with a slight nod said, "I know you didn't do what I accused you of doing. But you see, son, I wanted to reprimand you in front of my employees so they would get the point. I only used you as my example." I couldn't believe what my dad was saying. He had really hurt me that day just to make a point to his other employees. I couldn't understand why he would do such a thing to me; after all, I was his son!

I always respected my dad, but that day he did "provoke me to anger!", and it took awhile for that wound to heal. Over the years,

I have discovered we sometimes unintentionally hurt our children when we say or do something to them that we would never consider saying or doing to someone else. It is our children whom we should always protect and show our great love and devotion to; it is to our children that we should be very careful in what we say and how we say it!

Most young boys and girls will agree that there are few things in life any harder than working for one's dad! Dads seem to expect their children to work for little or no pay, put in extra long hours and, at the same time, be perfect in all they say and do!

Shortly after my wife and I were married, we needed some additional money so that we might have the funds to purchase a small house, and we needed the money within sixty days.

My wife worked at two jobs and I took on an additional part-time job pitching fish out of boats. Well, it wasn't long before my dad found out that I had taken a second job and, boy, did he ever get hot under the collar!

The main reason he was so angry was that he felt I would be so tired from my second job that I wouldn't be able to fulfill my responsibilities for my main job, which of course, was the bakery. He just knew that I was going to make a lot of costly mistakes.

After considerable plea-bargaining, all to no avail, I had to quit my part-time job. It was harder, but in the end, we managed to save enough money to buy our house. However, my father had once again provoked me to anger. And because of this, I made every attempt as my children were growing up to try and handle things involving them in the same way I wish I had been treated in my youth. It helps to think back to our younger days when we were much more sensitive and easily hurt so that we don't make some of the same mistakes with our kids that our parents made with us!

One way parents can prevent provoking their children to wrath is for them to become "honorable" parents. If we are truly "honorable" (noble, respectable, worthy), we stand a better chance of being honored by our children. And believe me, to be truly "honorable" takes a certain amount of effort and work on everyone's part. For without honor there is no respect; without respect, there is no kindness; without kindness, there is no love; without love, our world waxes cold and its foundation begins to crumble. Much of what we see happening to society today is due to children not honoring their parents and parents unworthy of being honored!

"And you fathers, provoke not your children to wrath: but bring them up in the training and admonition of the Lord." (Ephesians 6:4 NKJV). What a great commandment to us parents! Paraphrased, this verse tells us, "And now a word to you parents. Don't keep scolding and nagging your children, making them angry and resentful. Rather, bring them up with the loving discipline the Lord Himself approves, with suggestions and godly advice."

We are experiencing so much crime and violence being committed by our youth today that before we will ever be able to turn it around, we must first begin to realize that this situation is caused, to a large degree, by parents not properly teaching and instructing their children at home. Also, it is caused by parents who provoke their kids to anger.

There are parents in every neighborhood who confess to believing in God, yet so often deny what He commands in regard to *not* provoking their children to anger. He tells us loud and clear, "Be careful NOT to do it!"

Remember the two young teenagers I wrote about at the beginning of this chapter? They were provoked to anger by their parents, and this caused them to become bitter and resentful. It also cost them considerable loss of their self-confidence and self-esteem.

It is the fury of uncontrolled anger that caused many of the ills of yesterday and more than a few of the problems we see today. It was anger that caused Cain to kill his brother Abel; anger that caused the Jews and Romans to crucify Jesus Christ; anger that murdered Mahatma Gandhi; anger that led to more than fifty million men, women, and children losing their lives in World War I and World War II; and it is anger that causes parents to abuse their children today, anger that causes more and more young people to carry guns to school where they are shooting classmates they once called friends, anger that is ruining the home and society!

Children involved with drugs, guns, gangs, sex, and violence can only experience misery, agony, suffering, and pain. When a kid, in anger and out of control, commits a violent crime, everyone suffers including the school, friends, relatives, law enforcement officers, society, the children themselves, and mom and dad! Still, we parents must continue to question ourselves, wondering all the more, if we, indeed, had anything to do with the behavior of a child gone wrong!

Being a parent and living in a world where our kids have the kind of temptations that we, in our youth, never dreamed of, is more than a little difficult to understand. It is nearly impossible. And being a parent, especially today, is not a job for children, nor is it something immature adults should attempt to do.

When a father worries about losing his job and mother is concerned for the safety of her children; when mom and dad realize that there is very little security in this world and they fear the collapse of banks, pension funds, or social security, it becomes all the more difficult to show patience and love toward another person or even toward a loved one. And until we discover faith in God, until we acknowledge our very own weaknesses and shortcomings, until we mature as adults and parents, we will more than likely fail in our approach to child rearing...and we will no doubt continue to thoughtlessly provoke our children to wrath!

"You were united to your wife by the Lord. In God's wise plan, when you married, the two of you became one person in His sight. And what does He want? Godly children from your union. Therefore guard your passions! Keep faith with the wife of your youth." (Malachi 2:15 The Living Bible). What does God expect from us parents? "Godly children from your union!" Our Father expects us to raise our children in a godly manner and not provoke them to anger.

Take a moment and think about how you act toward your children when they come home from school or when you arrive home from work. Do you have a long list of chores waiting for them to complete before you give them the time of day? Are you so caught up in your own world (and I realize your world can be a very difficult and time consuming) that you deny your children quality time, that you deny them your love? By your behavior, do you give your kids the impression that you are too busy for them, that they don't mean as much to you as they hoped they did? If so, are you provoking your children to wrath?!

Some time ago there was a bumper sticker that really caught my eye. It simply stated, "Have you hugged your kid today?" If you did, you are well on your way to provoking your child to kindness, affection, and love rather than bitterness, anger, and wrath. There is nothing better a parent can do than to show a child how much he or she is loved by a demonstration of hugs and kisses.

When a kid gets a hug and kiss from his or her parents, it sure helps dissolve many of the tests and trials they may have experienced in school or with their peers earlier in the day. Just as we need hugs and kisses from those we love and respect, so do our children. And just as we experience tests and trials throughout the day, so do our children!

Chores and jobs around the home such as taking out the garbage, picking up one's room, dusting, or raking the lawn are a few of the things a child should do to help the family. But the chores can wait until a child is aware of his or her parents love. It's hugs and kisses and then the chores!

My kids hated to pick up rocks out of the garden. I don't like it, and I'm sure anyone with a sound mind reading this book doesn't rate it as something all that wonderful either. However, I knew my kids enjoyed throwing rocks at cans or skipping them across the lake.

So when it came time to clear the garden, I would set up cans on a fence nearby and pay each kid a nickel for every can they hit (I later had to change it to a penny because they got so good!). Taking a particular chore that no one wanted to do (including me) and making it fun produced a garden free of rocks and a family that enjoyed working and playing together. And there were some other benefits that came from this experience. My boys became very good baseball players!

Instead of demanding my kids that they do something they disliked and possibly provoke them to anger, I tried to think about how I would feel if I were a kid and then I applied whatever I came up with. I had some failures, but most of the time, my kids willingly accepted the work I asked them to do and had fun doing it. In doing so, we prevented bitterness, resentment, and anger from raising their ugly heads and causing family strife!

God realizes we parents need all the help we can get. He is also a parent who understands that a child's mind is not mature enough to withstand many of the pressures and temptations they will experience in their youth. So, once again, He inspired His writers to instruct their parents, "Fathers, do not provoke your children to anger lest they become discouraged!" (Colossians 3:21 NKJV).

Children can often become easily discouraged. A young girl told me awhile back, "You know, nothing I do ever pleases my Dad." When a child (or an adult for that matter) feels a sense of discouragement, when life is no fun and days pass by without laughter, enjoyment, or pleasure, when home life is more than difficult and parents just don't seem to care anymore, then it's only a matter of time before a child will go elsewhere to find pleasure and enjoyment. Wouldn't you?

And where might a child go to find enjoyment and pleasure? To movies, clubs, gangs; or, through music, sex, and drugs. And you know something? Most of these avenues can help provoke your child to wrath...especially if you aren't doing your part at home!

How do we *NOT* provoke our children to wrath? We take time - quality time - to listen to what they have to say - we must listen to our kids! Believe me, you'll be surprised at what you will hear.

Kids love to talk. Mine still do. My phone bill to my kids proves it! Show them how much you love them by listening to what they have to say and chances are your kids will never be provoked to anger...not by you anyway!

Another way to avoid provoking our children to wrath is by our showing them how much we love them. And it must be honest and truthful love (kids know the difference between "phony" love and "*real* " love). "*Real* love is not easily provoked!" (I Corinthians 13:5 NKJV). *Real* love toward our children is when we are careful what we say and how we say it; when we put their welfare before our own; when we spend quality time with them at home, on a walk or at play; when we give them our undivided attention, respect, and appreciation.

Real love also means there will be times when we parents need to correct and discipline our children. However, we should never forget that when we correct and discipline our kids, we must do so only with caution and only in love (see Chapter 13).

Due to something we say or do in a moment of weakness, we all provoke our children to anger at one time or another. And when we do, we should have the courage to apologize so that they will not become bitter or angry..so they will not hold a grudge or allow hurt feelings to fester.

Finally, we should know our children inside out. The better we know and understand our kids, the better the chance we will avoid provoking them to anger. God tells us that anger causes mistakes and sins. It matters not if we are fifteen or fifty years of age, if we become angry and make mistakes and subsequently sin, unless repented of and overcome, we open a door for major problems and difficulties to enter into our very lives. And if, as parents, we ever hope to encourage our kids in a way that will help them overcome the evils of this world, we must do everything in our power, including prayer and supplication to our Lord Jesus Christ, to prevent provoking our children to the point where they commit "any action carried out in great anger" - that **we never provoke our children to wrath!**

YOU'RE NEVER TOO YOUNG
TO MAKE A DIFFERENCE
by
Mark Graham

Once there was a lad who told his mom
he had to go and hear what Jesus had to say;
She gave him his wishes, packed him loaves and fishes
and sent him on his merry way.
When someone in the bunch said, "Hey, what's for lunch?"
he marched right up there unafraid,
One boy tried to make a difference,
and what a difference he made!

You're never too young to make a difference,
Never too small to help a friend.
There will always be opportunity just around the bend.
People all need love and understanding.
It can start with me.
If we all tried to make a difference,
What a difference there would be!

There was a girl whose mother put her baby brother
in a basket in the river Nile;
Pharaoh's daughter found him,
sister hung around for a little while.
And when the lady said, "Hey, how's this baby fed?"
she marched right up there unafraid,
One tried to make a difference,
and what a difference she made!

You're never too young to make a difference,
Never too small to help a friend.
There will always be opportunity just around the bend.
People all need love and understanding.
It can start with me.
If we all tried to make a difference,
What a difference there would be!

THE DIFFERENCE BETWEEN LITTLE BOYS
AND
LITTLE GIRLS!

BY

CARN CATHERWOOD

It's interesting; people who study the developmental stages of the fetus tell us that the male and female brain are virtually identical in the first several months. During the first three or four months of gestation, they can't find any real differences. But, around the end of the fourth month, they begin to notice some differences. It puzzles them; they analyze it. The tiny brain of the male fetus does seem to be modified, and there are different explanations, different things being elucidated by most of those researching this phenomenon.

I am reminded of something a fellow minister mentioned in one of his sermons about five years ago. He told us the human brain is divided into two halves. By the way, he didn't come up with that idea, it's a truism. The left hemisphere and the right hemisphere, the left half and the right half; the brain is sort of shaped like a walnut. It seems, so the researchers tell us, in each half of the brain there are certain tendencies or potentials; there are differences in what goes on in the left side as well as in the right side. Presently, there are a lot of analyses being done, and different people say different things; some of it I understand, some of it I don't. But, I'd like to pick out a few areas that have a general consensus to help us discover more about the differences between little boys and little girls.

During the sixteenth week (approximately), the left hemisphere of the brain of the male fetus does seem to be modified. Some researches feel there's an injection of certain hormones; some of them talk about a hormonal bath. However, it doesn't seem to happen to the female fetus to the same degree. Even though there's disagreement among scientists regarding this subject (but, I'm certainly not going to get hung up on the disagreements in those areas), there is a consensus that the part of the left brain which contains the speech center and the verbal skills slows it's growth in the brain of the male fetus and doesn't develop quite as much as in the female at that stage. Some say it catches up when the little boy is eight or nine years old. There is a growing consensus along that line of reasoning to the point that some of the major schools and school districts are reorienting their educational systems to take into consideration these changes.

What we do know is there is a very clear decreased ability to verbalize which characterizes the young male child. His ability to verbalize develops a little more slowly than it does in the young female child.

At about four months of age, it's been demonstrated that little baby girls respond much more enthusiastically to the sound of their mother's voice than do little baby boys. Some specialists have even measured the length of time baby girls remain excited when their mother enters the room. Babies will kick their little legs and arms, breathe fast and get excited. When they hear their mother's voice, little girls do this, on average, three to four times longer than little boys. Why do little girls respond to the sound of the voice of a parent with more excitement than do little boys? It's a question we need to think about.

In like fashion, it is demonstrable that baby girls will tend to imitate sounds a little sooner than baby boys. Now again, there is overlap. Some little boys imitate sooner, some little girls take longer, but in general it's quite demonstrable that little girls will begin forming words and making sounds that are understandable a few weeks or even a few months sooner than most little boys. Little boys have a harder time articulating sounds clearly; stuttering is almost exclusively a problem of male children - very few little girls stutter. Those that deal with speech problems recognize this particular phenomenon. (As a side note, in part, this also explains why many women have a different approach to talking. It's true women tend to talk more than men do. It may be a little easier for women to talk and may be a little more habitual for them).

Another major change occurs to the male fetus during the fourth or fifth month that doesn't happen to the same degree to the female fetus. It would seem that during the fourth or fifth month some of the fibers that join the left, or analytical side of the brain, to the right, the emotional side of the brain, apparently undergo a chemical process that removes or shrinks some of the fibers that link the two sides together. This is an area where there is more than a little controversy. In the European press and European bookstores and schools, there is a consensus that this does occur. And, in Canada there is also a consensus that this does occur. However, in the United States there is more hesitancy because the feminist lobbies view it as a political issue, and because of this, it's a little more sensitive.

Nevertheless, something seems to happen; shrinkage or removal, I don't know exactly. But whatever it is, it appears to slow the male's ability to move from the analytical left to the emotional right and vice versa. The male can still move from one side to the other, but it's simply a little harder. And, the indication seems to be that this does not happen to the same degree or, according to some, at all, to the female fetus. So the little girl can move from the analytical hemisphere to emotional hemisphere more easily. The result (or, so we are told) is, men tend to specialize more on one hemisphere than the other because it's simply easier. Where women can use both sides quite effectively, men tend to stay on one particular side and become specialists in their interests.

This is why eccentricity often tends to be more of a male characteristic. How many eccentric women have you met in your lifetime? You tend to meet more eccentric men. Little boys will tend to be more stubborn and harder to take into areas not of interest to them. They are a little less flexible. Did you know that "nerd" is basically applied to males and little to females. How many female "nerds" have you seen? Men tend to get a little specialized in their appearance and also in that which interests them, and this single focus can be viewed, by some, as eccentricity.

We can see all kinds of applications here. Is it possible that this may be the reason why men can tune out or unplug so easily while women have a harder time doing this? Men just sort of stay in tune with whichever hemisphere they are most comfortable with, while women keep moving back and forth.

You know the scenario. The man, the husband is reading the newspaper (the sports section, the business section, looking at the mutual funds or whatever seems to interest him); he's totally engrossed in what he's reading. Meanwhile, all around him, pandemonium breaks loose. Children begin to scream, he doesn't hear; the dog begins to bark, he doesn't hear; phones begin to ring, he doesn't hear; soup begins to burn, he doesn't smell. And by now, the wife is in tears because she's heard the phone, she's heard the kids, she's heard the dog; she's heard it all, and she can't regulate everything. Who can?! Dad's engrossed in his paper, totally tuned out, and now his wife is upset because she feels he doesn't love her, or the kids, or the dog, or respect what's going on in the house. He doesn't do his part and she's had it; he's just too selfish to put up with!

Is it possible that he's not all that selfish? Is it possible that there may simply be fewer connectors between the two sides of his brain. I don't know; I mean, I'm not into the connector theory all that much. However, I do look at the results and think about the possibilities. I'm quite sure God designed and constructed the brain of little boys in such a way that they do tend to concentrate in certain areas of interest to them. Just as He designed little girls to be a little more aware of things and have a broader base of interests. It might be said that men tend to be specialists and women tend to be generalists. Obviously, men can be generic and women can specialize. But, no doubt, there are those who will find this type of reasoning offensive. However, as a generic concept, it's definitely something to consider.

Let's look at a couple more differences. It's demonstrable that the part of the brain that contains spacial perception ability will

222

tend to develop a little more in male fetuses. And, there is considerable evidence of this. Spacial perception is the ability to identify distance between yourself and an object...the distance, such as between the football you're kicking and the goal post. The ability to do that is a spacial talent.

What happens as a result of that? Some very interesting things. A baby boy at four to six months of age will tend to focus on any object that is three dimensional, a mobile hanging above his crib or maybe a knob on the crib or something like that. He can become very excited as his little feet and arms begin moving in a jerking motion, while his bright eyes stare at the mobile moving back and forth. They've timed how long little boys will find this exciting, as opposed to how long little girls will. And again, it's three to four times longer for a little boy than for a little girl. What does it mean? In part, it means that the female child is not seeing exactly what the male child sees in quite the same way, nor does she respond in quite the same way, nor does she learn in quite the same way. And the results?

It would seem that little girls have the edge in learning reading and writing in the early years. They are usually ready to do this by the time they are four, five, six years of age. They enjoy these things. However, many little boys are not ready as early as their female counterparts. It's a truism that little boys tend to be victims of dyslexia in percentages much higher than do little girls. I talked with a teacher in New York City who reconfirmed that 90% to 95% of remedial reading classes in elementary, middle and high schools consist of boys. Some of this is attributed to the result of a female dominated educational system that often focuses on the better developed verbal skills of little girls in the first two or three grades, and ignores the better developed spacial abilities of little boys in the same grades. That's why little boys will sometimes get unnerved and agitated in those early grades, while little girls sit in class very happy and content. The girls enjoy what's going on in class, and the boys are ready for action. The problem is the boys aren't allowed to run and play while in class which can then cause part of their agitation.

Little boys do need to develop their spacial abilities. If they are taught in the early grades of school to build a model plane, take apart a clock, or something of the kind, they'll love school. They'll enjoy it because in this way the school is dealing with their male specificity, not just dealing with the specificity of little girls. However, the school is dealing with the specificity of both the sexes...boys and girls. Therefore, it's up to the school to educate in such a manner where little girls are inspired to grow while little boys have the opportunity to use their spacial abilities. If they don't, they can easily turn off a male child's education early in the learning process.

Another phenomenon to notice in children as they get older: little male and female children will express almost the same level of emotion in a visceral way. That is, they will both cry. Little boys and girls will both cry very loudly. The question becomes, "why don't adult men and adult women cry the same amount and just as loudly"? Little boys do and little girls do! There is no difference between how much or how loud a little boy will cry compared to his female counterpart.

Researchers tell us that the seat of the emotion is on the right side of the brain in both the male and female. Babies of both sexes seem to be able to express emotion, physically and viscerally, to about the same degree when they are very, very little. But, around age four or five there is a slight emotional change in the boys. Some of this may be because of something God has created (the result of the way the brain is put together) or it may be something society does (a result of reinforcement and conditioning by society). I think it's true that society teaches little boys that it's unmanly to cry or show emotion while it doesn't teach little girls this.

There are some other things that inhibit emotional development in little boys because of the fact that little boys will gravitate towards physical activities such as sports. They do this because sports meet their spacial needs. A ball and a field with a goal post has distance in it, and there is something in the mind of the little boy that says this is exciting. For some reason not every little girl finds playing football or soccer exciting. Some do. There is always an overlap. But, still, girls who like playing football with the boys would tend to be a minority.

Again, I'm generalizing when I say that because boys need to use their spacial abilities, they get involved in activities that don't have a great deal of emotional basis. Little girls, of course, tend to want dolls. And, by the way, have you ever noticed that the most popular dolls are the dolls that cry. Crying is important and little girls want to hear their baby dolls cry, and they want to hear them talk. So, little girls reinforce that side of their brain by spending a lot of time with little miniature people called dolls that cry. Nothing wrong with crying, but the emotional side is going to be reinforced as a result.

This doesn't happen to little boys to the same degree as they get older. Little boys, when they are two or three years of age, might play with dolls, but by the time they are six or seven, they are too embarrassed to play with them any longer and this desire begins to fade out of their lives.

Another thing to think about is this: because boys' verbal abilities are less developed than girls', as they mature it becomes harder for them to verbalize their feelings...that is, to express them openly. Certainly, they feel them, but it's simply harder for them to verbalize. So, they begin building a wall around themselves for protection. And, as they get older, their wall gets higher and higher. This is not to say there aren't any feelings beyond the wall, there are plenty of feelings...God has put them there. Still, they build walls around themselves because it only gets harder to verbalize what they feel, and it's a lot easier to take the path of least resistance.

On the other hand, little girls have fewer such obstacles to overcome and slowly they continue to learn how to express their emotions. They don't construct any high walls because they don't have to. This, too, sharpens the differences between little boys and little girls. It appears that nature and nurture sort of intertwine...they just seem to work together with each other. What do I mean? Maybe a personal example will help crystallize some of these differences.

Several years ago I gave a sermon on child rearing. In it, I stressed the fact that corporeal punishment should be restricted to times when a child has been truly rebellious...a last resort for very serious infractions and should never be used as a cure-all for parents to punish their children. I now refer to myself as having been the wrong type of example in how *not* to discipline children.

When I was a young father, I took my three little daughters to see the movie "Bambi." My oldest daughter was almost five and the twins were going on three. We were living in Paris, France at the time. I discovered a theatre on the Champs Elysees in the middle of Paris where Bambi was playing. So, I took my girls to see the movie. My wife went shopping at an inexpensive women's shop (she likes those places because they have bargains) and I took our three little daughters to see Bambi.

They loved the movie until it got to the part where the hunters shot Bambi's mother. I'm sure you remember the scene. You hear the shot ringing out while the hunters began to yell, "we bagged the doe, we got one!" And then there was the sad plaintive voice of little Bambi crying, "Mother, Mother, where are you?" Mother, of course, was dead, shot by the hunters, and Bambi was now alone. Suddenly, at that moment, my three, tiny daughters burst into tears all at the same time. They were overwhelmed by the emotion of the death of Bambi's mother. They hadn't expected it; it was a nice movie until then. And the problem was, I couldn't get them to stop crying. The people in the theatre began to look around...soon discovering where all the commotion was coming from. There were a few other little kids who were sniffling and wiping their eyes, but I had three of them, all crying at the same time! When you have twins, they reinforce each other. When one cries, the other cries! So, by now, they were all crying very loudly, and the more I told them to stop, the worse I made it because they couldn't stop. And by trying to stop, they cried even harder. It was quite a commotion and people were looking rather angrily. So, finally in desperation I told them "if you don't stop I'll have to spank you". Well, they didn't stop so I picked them up and walked out of the main part of the theater to the bathroom where I spanked them for disobeying me when I told them to stop crying.

I now recognize it was inappropriate and wrong for me to do that. My daughters were simply in mourning, they were grieving for the death of Bambi's mother. It's natural to cry when you grieve and that's all that they were doing. They were grieving; death (real or on the screen) is a shock to a little child. I was too young and immature to recognize that. I have brought out this example because none of us should ever do things like this to our children. Whenever I tell this story in public, people look shocked and often give me the "cold eye", and I deserve it. Any parent who paddles their children for anything other than a major offense deserves to be admonished (at best!).

There is a sequel to this story; I call it Bambi, Part Two. My eldest daughter who was five years old when she saw Bambi, now has her own little five-year-old boy named Jeffrey. About a year and a half ago, Mommy and Daddy were given a video copy of the movie "Bambi." Of course, they have a VCR and they could play it for little Jeffrey at home. But, there was a concern; my daughter remembered her and her younger sister's reaction when they first saw the movie...especially the part where Bambi's mother gets shot. So, she and her sisters were concerned that little Jeffrey might become just as emotionally shocked as they had been before. After some discussion, they decided to play the tape and if he had an emotional reaction they would stop the VCR and talk about death and explain that animals also die. They had some anxiety, but they felt it might be an appropriate learning experience, so they decided to go ahead and run the movie. Little Jeffrey loved the story, just as his mommy and aunts had twenty-two years previously. When the plot approached the crisis point where the shots rang out and the hunters began to shout they had bagged a doe and Bambi began to cry, "Mother, Mother, where are you?," all eyes were on little Jeffrey. How would he react? Would he lose control? Well, Jeffrey didn't disappoint anyone. He never does. On cue, he stood up, eyes wide open and proudly said, "Daddy, Daddy, can you buy me a gun so I can go hunting, so I can go hunting and shoot animals too?" You say there's no difference between little boys and little girls...that it's all just culturally derived? Sure!

You see, while his mommy and his aunts focused on the relationship between Bambi and his mother, Jeffrey focused on the action of the hunt. Later, it struck him that Bambi and his mother were going to be separated and he was sad about that. But his ability to focus on the action enabled him to bypass the emotional content of the story for awhile. And, you know, as he gets older, Jeffrey's ability to bypass his feelings and to focus, not on the emotion of the circumstance, but on the action of it, will get even stronger because of some natural things that are there from birth. In part, as well, because of the pressure and conditioning a male society will place upon him. As children move into their teens, the differences really kick in. Teenage girls are much more emotional than teenage boys, at least on the surface. Under the surface, who really knows. But, on the surface, most definitely!

Teenage girls form friendships with other girls. They have confidants, they share secrets, and there is a lot of talk about feelings. At that point, however, teenage boys have moved to the other side of the pendulum. They have friendships with other males their own age, to be sure, but it mainly involves sharing activities, they don't tend to share secrets. See the difference; the boys don't tend to share secrets, they tend to share activities. They hunt together or play basketball together, but rarely do they discuss personal things. Girls share everything, including their emotions.

This is the period of life when adolescent males begin building their protective walls even higher; adding brick upon brick, constructing a moat, putting up "No Trespassing" signs - these are my emotions, so don't trespass - or "Keep Out; I'm in control!" Sometimes they lose that control, but they try hard to keep it. And, girls? They don't put up any walls and they very seldom hang up signs telling the another person Not to Trespass. They don't try quite as hard in general to protect their emotions, nor are they all that concerned with their spacial perception!

At about the same time all of this is happening, boys get interested in girls and girls get interested in boys. Some boys even get interested younger than others just as some girls wait until they are older before they give a boy the eye. For the most part, it seems teenage boys are from Mars while teenage girls' are from Venus. But the nice thing about this is they don't know it! Also, the boys don't know that the girls favorite activity is tearing down their signs and scaling their walls, while talking about feelings and emotions which is the last thing most boys want to hear - let alone talk about! But, for the sake of his overpowering desire to be close to a girl who has captured his heart, a boy will listen quietly and at length, while, at the same time, he will no doubt be thinking about his latest victory on the ball field, his car engine, or how he's going to try and get out of having to read his essay in front of the class.

So, now we ask the question, **"Are there differences between little boys and little girls?" You bet there are!**

Every child born into the world is a new thought of God, an ever-fresh and radiant possibility.
-Kate Douglas Wiggin

It is refreshing to find a clergyman willing to defend the youth of today. Unfortunately the defense of the youth today is too frequently made by lawyers.

-Crane

CHAPTER SIXTEEN

DATING!
That **Phase** in a Child's Life that
Parents Fear
More Than Almost Anything Else!

D ating is a subject that worries most parents. And why shouldn't it? Something is certainly wrong when so many young girls - some even in their preteens - are becoming pregnant with unwanted babies more and more every year. The result? A tragic number of abortions being performed on young girls each and every day, a tremendous loss of life for the unborn children, and a horrible ruination of life for the mothers!

As a parent of a teenage girl or boy, I'm sure, when you think about it, you realize your child is probably not prepared for the pitfalls and possible failures that are closely associated with teenage dating. Have you ever asked yourself, "Is my kid mature enough to go out on a date with another person of the opposite sex?" "Does my child know enough about himself or herself to handle the type of pressures that often arise during the course of an evening when two young people strongly believe they are in love?" "How's my kid going to handle the situation if the subject of doing drugs, committing some illegal act, or having sex comes up?" "As a parent, how am I going to handle my kid beginning to date?!"

Dating is as much a part of a young person's life as is eating and sleeping. But before we allow our children to begin to date (and, sooner or later, they are going to date with or without our consent), it is our responsibility, as their parents, to help prepare them for this prodigious event as best we can. And believe me, this will not be an easy task!

The very first thing I always advise a parent to do, before allowing their children to date, is to go before God, on hands and knees, to ask for His guidance, direction and help, including His divine protection, for both the young people who want to go out on a date and their parents. I also strongly suggest that parents ask their Maker to guide and direct their efforts in the proper way of raising their children, including what they tell their kids about dating and how they say it.

There is no doubt that our kids need to have both male and female friends. The need to understand how the other sex thinks and acts is very important. Kids need to be prepared while they are young so that when they marry, they will have a better understanding about the opposite sex. This will provide a better opportunity for them to experience the rewards resulting from having a successful marriage.

The problem is this: too few parents stop to realize that one day their offspring will leave home, marry and begin raising their own family. Unless Junior and Susie are instructed and prepared while they are young - to have respect for the opposite sex, including how to listen, how to be patient, how to properly provide for a family, how to be gracious and well mannered - their survival rate for a successful and happy marriage is not going to be all that good. And the sad part is the probability that their children will grow up ill-trained, unprepared for life and parenthood, and poorly educated. Like father, like son!

So how do we prepare our kids for marriage and parenthood? We begin by preparing them for the time when they will begin dating. Did you just say, "MY SON OR DAUGHTER WILL SOON BE DATING?! I'M NOT READY FOR THIS! I WANT MY LITTLE GIRL TO REMAIN HOME, CLOSE TO THE FAMILY AND MY SON TO ONLY THINK ABOUT COLLEGE AND HIS CAREER. HOW CAN I KEEP THEM YOUNG AND INNOCENT? HELP!"

Remember, mom and dad, just like when you were young, the time comes when things that were important to you suddenly no longer seemed to mean as much; so, the hugs and kisses you give to your children today will no longer mean as much to them as they did when they were younger. It's the hugs and kisses from the boy at school or the girl down the street that are going to become increasingly more important to your kids as they grow older. And although it hurts to admit, some other person's demonstration of love is going to have a more profound affect on your teenage child than the love you demonstrate to them at home. Believe me, you'll no doubt feel disappointed, hurt, and possibly a little angry at your son or daughter. After all, weren't you the one who changed all those diapers, bandaged all those cuts and bruises, denied yourself so that Junior or Susie might have a new pair of shoes or badly needed school books; aren't you the one who put up with so many fits of temper or broken hearts and stayed awake many nights during the times when he or she fought a cold or the flu?

"I think I'm in love."
"Me, too!"

"You know, Mom, after the dance last night, I felt kinda funny inside when Billy Joe kissed me good night. I mean, it was outta sight! It was sure different than when you or dad kiss me good night. You know what I mean?"

This is the time most parents dread, when their children become so involved with their friends and out-of-the-home activities that they lose interest in their family and become absorbed with their peers and even the families of their peers. And no matter how we try, there's little or nothing we can do about it. The concerns and curiosity of our children greatly changes as they grow older because of the influences, pressures, and importance they feel toward their friends and schoolmates. And when they fall in love with that one certain individual, the situation becomes all the more explosive!

In fact, it seems the more we try to prevent our kids from spending so much time with their friends - *away from home* - the more we force them toward their peers and away from us. This is why it's so important that we understand the minds and character of our children and also how best to prepare our little ones for the time when someone of the opposite sex begins to show a special interest and concern toward them - the time when we might possibly lose them if we haven't done our part to provide proper training and instruction!

As a parent, I spent a lot of time trying to decide when the right time should be for my kids to start dating. I had three girls and three boys and even though I tried to show each one of them the same kind of affection and love, I admit when it came to my daughters, I treated them somewhat differently. I wanted to protect each daughter from that certain young fellow who would simply enter and then leave her life; who, during a very brief moment of contact, would convince her that he loved her - telling her all those beautiful and wonderful things that girls want to hear and only boys on the prowl can conjure up - and then finally break her heart when he leaves.

This experience of protecting my daughters helped me to better understand the difference between the way a father feels about his daughter dating, as opposed to the way he feels about his son dating. In the dating game, boys seem to be more the aggressor, whereas girls most often find themselves in a more defensive position. It shouldn't be this way, but it is. If boys had a greater respect for girls and girls had a greater respect for themselves, there would be considerably fewer problems of date rape and sexual abuse. I realize girls are becoming much more aggressive toward how they approach dating; however, it still remains a fact that most dates are initiated by the male, and most males are more aggressive on a date than their female counterpart.

What I taught my boys about dating had some similarities to what I taught my girls, but, believe me, there were also some major differences! I never wanted my boys to take advantage of a girl, and I required that each of my sons honor and respect their girl friends as they would their mother (more about this later).

My wife and I spent considerable time discussing what we felt should be the proper time for our children to begin dating. We considered how we should go about teaching them the proper way to date; what dating really means; the responsibilities and consequences (good or bad) that anyone dating another person will experience; the importance of honor and respect toward the other person; and how we might best prepare our kids for dating right from the start.

One of the main questions we asked ourselves was, "How old should our kids be before we allow them to date?" Over the years in counseling parents, this is probably the question I am asked most often. "How old should my child be before he or she begins to date?"

Although age is relevant and very important, it isn't nearly as important as how mature the child is before going out on a date...especially if the date includes only a boy and a girl and no other friends or family members!

My friend Daniel Webster tells us that to "date" (in the context we are discussing) means, "a social engagement with a person of the opposite sex." We all know this. However, the words here that capture my attention are, "social engagement" and "opposite sex." Hopefully "social" should mean out in the public with friends and not in the back seat of the boy's car, and "opposite sex" should pertain to the gender to whom a boy or girl dates.

Let me explain my "tried and true" concept of dating. First of all, I am not in favor of single dating until a child is fully capable of handling himself or herself in any type of difficult or potentially harmful situation that may (and often does) arise. This is what I mean about age being secondary to maturity. An analogy might be something like a child taking a college-level examination before he or she ever enters high school. Most children just aren't prepared to take the test, let alone pass it!

An analogy for dating might be where children attending school gradually begin to learn by slowly developing patterns of behavior by and through their relationships with their male and female peers. It takes time to develop an understanding and appreciation of those of your own sex, so developing an understanding and appreciation of the opposite sex can (and often times does) take a lot longer.

Let's use the above analogy to bring this point home a little further: just as most seventh grade students will not even come close to passing a college midterm exam, neither will they succeed at single dating if they try it before they are ready! And failing at single dating can have consequences that are a lot worse than simply failing a school examination.

On the other hand, if parents work with their kids by helping to prepare them for the time when they will be going out on that first date alone, chances are they will pass the dating test with flying colors. It's no different with every other aspect of childrearing: if properly instructed and trained, a kid will more likely than not overcome peer pressure to take drugs, join a gang, rob a store, commit suicide, or engage in illicit sex on a date.

Take a moment and think about this: when you were young, did schools pass out condoms to the boys or the "pill" to the girls? Did you have the type of peer pressure from your schoolmates that our kids experience today? You did? Really? You mean when you were young there were kids carrying guns to school and, at times, fatally shooting each other; selling powerful illegal drugs such as heroin and cocaine on the school grounds; running around with violent street gang members, destroying school property, while at the same time pulverizing their fellow students just for the fun of it. Did your girl friends have abortion after abortion and did they "put out" almost every night so that they might have a most favored status position with the jocks and school studs; and did your school have a number of violent students who beat up their teachers whenever they were admonished? Unless you graduated from high school in the past few years, your answer must be "no"!

How many unwanted pregnancies or abortions do you remember any of your girlfriends having when you were in high school, or when you were in junior high (middle) school? Who prepared you for dating? Who instructed you about the dangers of "necking" and "going all the way"? Who explained to you about what happens to you and your girlfriend after she becomes pregnant? Who provided you with a mature understanding about why you should never drink and drive...especially when you are driving a car loaded with other kids? Who was it that prepared you for life's tests and trials? Your parents? Your teachers? Your school chums? Some person on the street? Playboy Magazine? No one?

Like so many of us, you probably did what comes naturally when you were young. But today, as we enter the 21st century, where morality, proper values, and high principles seem to be on the wane; where love is waxing cold and people think more about themselves than they do their fellow man or even their own kids and family; where children are beginning to question if indeed they even have a future; and where hope and faith seem to be harder and harder to come by, do you really want your children to experience life from "what comes naturally?" If you don't, you had better take the time now to teach and instruct your kids about such things as sex, honor, respect, and dating before it becomes too late!

When my kids were young and beginning to think about dating, I devised the following three-stage dating plan to help guide my wife and me, and our children, through this monumental (and often times frightening) experience. This plan has worked well for my family and for those whom I have counseled over the years.

The three stages include:

(A) <u>GROUP</u> <u>DATING</u>
(B) <u>SMALL</u> <u>GROUP</u> <u>DATING</u>
(C) <u>SINGLE</u> <u>DATING</u>

Earlier, I wrote about Mr. Webster's definition of "dating". My definition of "dating" is simply stated: "any time a boy and a girl get together for a social activity, it's a 'date'." I can almost guarantee you that this will not be your child's definition of a "date," but nevertheless, when a boy and a girl get together as a social function (this doesn't mean they have to smooch or hug each another), it's a "date."

Let's take each particular stage of this three-stage dating plan and examine it more closely.

(A) GROUP DATING: My wife and I often allowed our children to invite their friends - both boys and girls - to our home for group activities. This gave our kids and their friends the opportunity to begin to understand how to properly act around someone of the opposite sex. It also gave us the opportunity to know that our children were being chaperoned and supervised and not simply left alone to their own devices. We would direct the evening's fun and games and then, after everyone went home, my wife and I would talk with our kids regarding the fun they had had with their friends and some of the things they felt they had experienced during the course of the evening. What came out of this conversation with our kids was pretty amazing sometimes. They told us how they felt about their friends; what so-and-so was up to; why someone wasn't going to be invited ever again; and how they each felt about the activity as a whole. And we listened. It was family sharing time!

In an earlier chapter regarding the "Assembly Line Concept" (see Chapter 2), we concluded that we only have so much time to help assemble (prepare) our children for adult life after their life at home. Well, the same principle of the assembly line concept holds true for our kids as they prepare to go out on that single date (with a person who is, no doubt, the love of his or her life!). It takes time to properly teach a child about dating. It takes time to help a child know the difference between the way he or she may think as opposed to the way their date (the opposite sex) may think or rationalize about the same subject. We found that one of the best ways to teach our kids these important principles was by group dating.

Here is an example of how we helped guide our kids during group dating events: One evening we had a few of our kid's friends over to the house for dancing lessons. My wife and I decided we were going to teach our kids and their friends how to dance.

It came time for a snack break, so all the kids went upstairs to find their favorite place to sit; all the kids, that is, except my fourteen year old daughter. By the time she got upstairs, and all the seats were taken, so she decided to sit on a boy's lap while everyone ate and drank their refreshments.

I admit, Ol' Dad didn't really appreciate this very much. However, at the time, I didn't want to make a scene or embarrass my daughter in front of her friends. But when the opportunity came (and it came sooner than one might expect!), I found a chair for my daughter. Was it all that important that I didn't allow my daughter to sit on a young man's lap? If I were going to help her, it sure was!

A young man can get "turned on" and become easily aroused just by a pretty, young girl touching him with her body ever so lightly. It's a simple fact that this is the way the male gender was created to react to the female gender. It's been this way since Adam and Eve.

I'm sure God planned it that way and I'm thankful He did! But, I'm also sure that God didn't plan for two immature children to arouse one another with powerful sexual desideratum - the type that is difficult to control and often leads to sexual misconduct - just so that they might satisfy their own lusts and childish desires.

After the party was over and all the kids had left for home, I took my daughter aside and we discussed the importance of why girls and boys need to be aware of the way they conduct themselves toward one another, whatever the circumstance, but especially during social events or when dating as a group or individually. We also discussed how one should behave and react in those situations when things might get out of hand and how frequently boys will think about having sex with his girlfriend, especially when she snuggles up to him and he feels her body next to his (something that a lot of girls cannot readily identify with). I told her there are times when young men have difficulty controlling their developing sexual urges, and the result, if not suppressed and controlled, can be very damaging and possibly lead to pregnancy, abortion, or even rape.

I then explained to my daughter how to overcome such situations by simply staying away from body contact; by telling the other person how you feel about whatever it is you like or don't like;

by gently changing the subject of conversation; or, as in the case with my daughter, by simply finding another chair to sit on.

This experience gave my daughter and me the opportunity to talk about dating, sex, flirtation, and her relationship with boys in a more serious and profound way than either one of us had expected. I went on to explain what body language is and how it can tell the other person something she might not want to say aloud. We talked about flirting and teasing and how wrong it is when a girl who has no interest in dating a fellow (my kids call it "not having eyes for the guy or gal") strings him along. Often this happens simply because she doesn't have a date, wants to go out but doesn't have the money to do so, wants to show off in front of her friends, or any number of other selfish reasons. Whatever the reason, it's wrong!

I tried to spell out the fact that when she accepts a date from a young fellow, she is basically telling him, "I really like you". I mean, if she didn't, she wouldn't really want to go out with him would she? And then, what about the guy? What does he think? No doubt, he believes that when the girl accepts his offer to go out with him, she does so because she really cares about him; she really likes him.

I also explained that when a girl goes out on a date with a guy and after they get into his car she slides over near him, he automatically begins to reason to himself that she must feel something special for him.

"Wow! She really likes me!," he tells himself. And before long, his mind shifts into high gear as he wonders, "What will happen if I put my arm around her? Will she tell me no? Or, will she let me do it? All she can say is no!" And so he does it.

Right then and there, if the girl doesn't show that she isn't interested in his advancement and moves over, while removing his hand away, and instead she allows him to keep his arm around her, then his mind immediately shifts into overdrive! "This is gonna be my lucky night! I think she's gonna wanna go all the way!"

By now, the situation is getting more and more out of control. But who's the person that's out of control? The girl? No! She's just sitting there feeling comfortable, thinking that she's going to have a pleasant evening with a boy who is taking her to dinner and then a movie. And the boy? By now, he most likely has an entirely different idea about what he hopes will be the night's entertainment!

Girls have to become more aware of the way most boys think and react, especially the way they react toward girls when they hit their teens. And boys have to learn how to control their emotions (i.e., libido!) and become more sensitive to the fact that the girl sitting next to him most likely isn't even thinking about sex, "getting it on," or "making out." Granted, some girls may be thinking about these things, but most girls aren't!

Young girls like to be held and so do our daughters. I love to hold and hug my daughters, even to this day, now that they are married adults with children of their own. But as everyone reading this book knows and understands, there is a very big difference between a father's hug and a boyfriend's hug. Ask your daughter, she'll explain the difference.

"Did it hurt when you sat on his lap?" I asked my daughter as we cleaned up the kitchen.

"No, Daddy. Are you kidding?!," she replied.

"Do you understand, when you are sitting on his lap, you could be telling him, 'Don't stop. It's okay!'"

"Well...uh..."

I could tell from her stuttering that she hadn't thought it out. So, I continued. "Do you understand that if you were out on a date with your friend...just the two of you on a single date...how one thing can easily lead to another and before you know it, things suddenly get out of control? Do you realize that your actions, as honest and trusting as they may be, can easily lead a boy to misunderstand what you are saying verbally, because he is only "listening" to your body language? And, that he might want to hold more of your body - other parts of your body - than you want him to hold?"

Suddenly, my daughter's eyes widened as she blurted out, "Hold on, Daddy. I sure didn't intend to tell him THAT!" She was now beginning to get the drift of my message. "I mean, are you kidding?!"

"Honey," I said, not wanting to scare her or cause her to become anxious, "I know you didn't. But can you now see how easy it is to communicate to another person by what we do with our eyes and our body rather than only by what we say?"

"I'm beginning to see what you mean, Daddy."

My daughter and I were sharing such a wonderful moment as we talked to one another that I decided to take our conversation a little further. "Remember, Honey. I realize you and your sisters like to be held and I know it feels good. I mean, I even like to be held." She smiled, as I continued, "It's not wrong for a fellow to put his arm around you to escort you or help you over some physical object. But keep in mind, when you allow a boy to hold you close, your body can be telling him it's all right to hold more of your body than you want held. And the reason you allow this to happen is because your body is telling you it likes to be held."

(B) SMALL GROUP DATING: The next step we must take as we teach our children the proper way to learn how to date another person - and more important, how to control every facet of the dating activity - is what I call "small group dating." We always tried to prepare our kids for this second level of dating by entertaining them and their friends in a smaller group dating atmosphere. The result was our children had so much fun dating in a smaller group that, until the time arrived when they eventually became serious about one certain individual, they seldom wanted to go out on a single date. Even after high school, they preferred being with a group of friends.

As parents, we should make every effort to teach our children the value of family and friends and a profound appreciation for being part of such a group. This second phase begins to help a child increase his or her level of understanding the responsibility regarding how he or she must act when dating that special someone, that special someone our child may believe (at the moment) he or she truly loves! This level provides the parents with certain controls over who the person is their kid dates, where their son or daughter goes on a date, and what time the date ends. It also provides their offspring with flexibility and a degree of autonomy.

There is no doubt that, as our children grow and mature, they are going to experience a magnetic, physical attraction for someone of the opposite sex. It's almost impossible for parents to realize, just because their kid is a certain age or the nerd of the senior class, very involved in his computer work or her political science class, that he or she isn't going to "fall in love" sooner or later. When two kids "fall in love" there is usually no set time frame, no particular place for it to happen, and very little parents can do about it. It just happens! However, the one thing parents can do is to help prepare their kids for the time when this does happen.

When our kids were going through the "small group dating" phase, my wife and I would encourage them to invite the person they were particularly interested in over for dinner. We allowed our teenage children to couple up, as a foursome with two of their other close friends, and my wife and I would serve them a formal meal. Later, we would all play family-type games and usually have a very enjoyable evening.

Because of this experience, we were able to teach our kids the value of communication, respect, and family togetherness. At the same time we helped them to overcome the temptation where they might suddenly find themselves alone with the other person in a situation where passions can become overheated and uncontrolled emotions take over, and nine months later a baby is born to two very unprepared, uneducated teenagers.

Someone reading this might very well be thinking to himself or herself that what I am suggesting regarding "small group dating" is old-fashioned, behind the times, or yesterday's news. I can only respond to this type of suggestion as follows: at a time in history when parents have little control over their children; when schools no longer are able to teach and train our kids for the future; when movies, pop music, and television programs more often than not promote premarital sex, violence, and disrespect for parents and adults; when young girls no longer have to tell their parents about their pregnancy or, in some states, aren't even required to get their parents permission before having an abortion; and where many public and private high schools around the country now hand out condoms to young students, not so much to prevent unwanted pregnancies but to help prevent AIDS, do you really believe that my counseling parents to spend time with their children and their children's friends is illogical and that I'm old-fashioned and naive?

If we parents don't take back the control over our children, if we don't prepare them now for the real world tomorrow - which includes teaching them why the type of dating that leads to necking, caressing, fondling, and having sex (which often results in having an unwanted child to care for) is dangerous and something to avoid - then who will? What will happen to our children's lives if they blow it during their youth? What will happen to our society in a few years if we continue to neglect our child rearing responsibilities today? Just because we are heading toward the 21st century doesn't mean the values and principles we were raised with - the high morals and strong character our parents taught us just as their parents taught them - are no longer important, no longer relevant, no longer something to be honored and respected!

I realize what I am writing may be thought by some to be old-fashioned and out of date. However, my years of experience with counseling numerous parents and children tells me that when parents take charge of their responsibility for raising their kids, the chance that their kids will experience success in their youth and later in life greatly increases!

Unless you, as a parent, begin teaching your son the proper respect toward girls including why it's important for him to ask her folks for their permission to date their daughter, how not to take advantage of his girlfriend's weaknesses and emotions, and why he must control his passions while on a date; unless you, as a parent, begin to teach your young daughter the value of self-respect and the importance of remaining in total control of her mind and body when she's on a date - including how not to let her emotions (heart) fall prey to the amorous pressures she will no doubt experience from a boy with an overly aroused libido - then who will? What will be the consequences for your children, your society and for you personally if you fail to properly carry out this great parental responsibility?

(C) SINGLE DATING: Now comes the big one! Hopefully, when our children come to a point in their young lives where they begin to want to share their ideas, dreams, hopes, and aspirations with someone with whom they feel a very special fondness or even perhaps real love, we will have prepared them to handle this situation in a very mature and distinguished manner.

We must teach our children when they begin to date that they must date a person with their minds and not only with their hearts, that they must rely on their intellect and not just their emotions. Jeremiah 17:9 reminds us that, "The heart is deceitful above all things and desperately wicked; who can know it?!" Do we parents really understand how fallacious we are when we allow our kids to begin dating before they are mature enough to exercise their minds and intellect?

The main purpose behind most movie themes, musical scores, stage plays, and television programs is a desire by the writer, actor, singer, director, and producer to control the "heart strings" of the audience. Many films are written and produced about young love prevailing over the objections of "old fashioned" and very "naive" parents; about how something that seems right to do at the time must be okay; about how looking out for "number one" is more important than caring for another person; and about the notion that pre-martial sex, adultery, and fornication is normal, relevant, and something to be valued by our modern and enlightened society.

More and more, screenwriters, film directors, and producers seem to be telling our youth (the largest of any group going to movies) that they should live only for the moment; that marriage is something no longer valid or relevant, no longer something special to be respected and honored; and that pre-martial, bisexual or homosexual intercourse is normal, healthy, and part of today's enlightened way

245

of life! Did you ever stop and consider that many films are written by men and women who often write about their own fantasies and desires which may have evolved from some past negative and/or abusive experience? Or that screenwriters and filmmakers usually have their own agendas which they hope to sell and project to a mass young audience? Do you realize that a trashy story in the form of a book, novel, song, or film makes the creator and writer millions of dollars (Francs, Marks, Yen, Pounds, Lira, etc.)?

Also, have you ever stopped a moment to consider that children believe what they see on television or at the movies, that most often they believe the story a screenwriter has written is true? Can you see the possibility that children might become so engrossed in the film's story that it could cause them to do something they might not have done had they not see the film?

I know a man who, when he was a teenager, went to see a movie at a time in his life when everything seemed to be going wrong. His parents left him to fend for himself when he was in his junior year of high school. He didn't have the maturity to understand the situation or what he should do next. Then one night, after seeing a very emotional movie (with a heartrendering musical score), my friend suddenly decided to pack up his belongings and move to a state far away from his friends, his hopes, and dreams. His life drastically changed and not for the better. Today, this man tells me that the film he saw that night had everything to do with his decision to move, to run away, to leave his friends, and dreams. He realizes now that his decision caused him a lot of problems in his later years, and it had much to do with the bitterness and resentment he felt toward his parents during most of his adult life.

This man simply altered his life by moving to another state. But what about the kids today who see so many graphically illustrated, violent movies who later try to emulate the same evil vulgarities and violent acts they watched some actor perform in the film? There is a definite reason as to why we, as a nation, are experiencing so many more murders, rapes, robberies, and other violent crimes today. Is the heart wicked and most deceitful above all things? You bet it is!

And this is why it's so important to teach our children to let their minds - their intellect, not their emotions - guide their decisions, especially regarding the subject of dating.

Single dating often leads to going "steady." And one of the main problems that comes to the surface when two young people go steady is the enormous possibility that sexual intercourse will become part of this ritual and then one or both of them will end up having to suffer a painful broken heart, a shameful experience, guilt from having an abortion, and/or the devastating effects resulting from unprepared and immature parenthood; or, worse yet, the likelihood that they may get AIDS or contract some serious type of venereal disease that often leads to premature death. Single dating and going steady just isn't as safe as it used to be!

When my kids were younger, I asked them not to go steady with any one person until such time as they, and the particular person they had fallen in love with, were willing to make a total commitment to one another in marriage. I realized this type of total commitment could only survive if a young person had reached a certain level of maturity. I knew my children well enough to know who had reached maturity and who still had much to learn.

Facts bear out that when two young people who haven't reached a competent level of maturity go steady, more often than not they will end up in some kind of trouble, and the entire family will suffer.

What does the word "maturity" really mean? D. Webster tells us: "the state or quality of being full grown, ripe, or fully developed. Being perfect, complete, or ready. A state of full development - a person of mature age."

Using the above definition as our guide, we can now begin to see that without maturity, the possibility of a young person achieving victory and success while going steady or single dating without experiencing some type of emotional and/or physical dilemma, is very remote, if not downright impossible.

247

Illicit sex covets privacy and dim lights. When two young people are going steady, it's only natural that they would want to be alone together, especially at night! And given the "wrong" time, the "wrong" place and the "wrong" situation, many children (teen and preteen) will fall under the temptation to commit fornication. A young body and adolescent heart wants affection and attention from a person of the opposite sex almost more than anything else. And when passion between two young people (or adults for that matter) is heated up to the boiling point, only maturity and the common sense that comes from mental growth and experience will help both individuals overcome the temptation and overwhelming desire to do what is wrong; to sin! This is when maturity really comes into play; when being prepared and completely in tune with one's mind (intellect) is *the* thing that counts most!

Whenever I teach a young, dating class, I try to explain to them that they have real physical and emotional needs regarding the way they desire - the way they yearn - to belong, to be respected, to be honored, and to be loved. I explain that these physical needs can sometimes be so overwhelming to the point where they will suddenly find themselves questioning whether or not their minds can handle and overcome the situation. I also try to stress the importance of always remaining in control, holding on to what one knows to be real, genuine, honest, and true principles.

I tell my young students that I realize it's so much easier to say these things than it is to actually do them. And because it's so difficult to remain in control and hold on to what is honest, genuine, and true, we cannot expect our children to behave accordingly if we fail to teach them what these words mean; and if we fail to also live by them.

If we parents have difficulty or embarrassment when it comes time to instruct our kids about such things as dating; what sex is all about; what fornication means; why it is important to understand where VD and AIDS comes from (and that the best method of prevention is abstinence); how little babies are created and then what usually happens to both the child-parent and the baby after the baby's birth; then it is necessary, indeed vital, that we seek qualified guidance and help from someone with the experience and credentials to teach us.

Our kids need our instruction and guidance if they are going to be able to overcome the pressures they will no doubt face when dating or going steady. So, parents, do whatever needs to be done to help them. Even if this means having to study a few college courses so that you might gain valuable knowledge and understanding regarding the best way for you to teach and instruct your children!

Note: A Good book regarding what happens when a young girl's physical and emotional needs spins out of control is, "The Stork Is Dead!" by Charlie Shedd.

Here are a few examples of what our kids experience today and what they need from their friends and family if they are to successfully grow into adulthood:

(1) GIRLS OF ALL AGES NEED ATTENTION: It's simply the way they were created, and it's wonderful! Let's take a moment and see how needing attention might affect your daughter's attitude when on a date.

Mom, think back a few years ago to when you were younger. When you were in school, did you enjoy getting attention from your peers? From the boys? Did this desire for attention ever cause you to make a mistake or error in judgment? Well, your daughter is no different today than you were then. Just because she's young and living in a faster world which is considerably more evil and therefore a more dangerous environment in which to live, nevertheless, she still needs - requires - attention from her family, her friends, and especially from that special someone of the opposite sex.

What happens when your daughter doesn't receive any attention at home? The answer is, she will probably find it from some other source - a friend (whom you may not know), a boy (who may take advantage of her simply because she is so vulnerable), a teacher (whom you may not agree with regarding religion, politics, or redeeming social values), or someone on the street she just happens to meet by chance (whom you realize is the worst of all possible alternative sources for providing your daughter with attention).

This problem can easily become critical when a girl needs attention so much she is willing to do almost anything to get it. Sooner or later, she may be out on a single date when her boy friend, the one with the aroused libido, suddenly begins to put on the heavies by showing her the wrong kind of attention; by camouflaging his desire for sex and self-gratification over her need for attention and love. And the result can be a lack of self-esteem, depression, pregnancy, AIDS, or worse.

This is why we must take the time to teach our daughters about what physical needs are and how they intertwine with very powerful emotions and sexual urges that are experienced by both male and female. This is just one example of how we can help our children overcome the type of ignorance that often causes every one of us to make mistakes...sometimes very costly and devastating mistakes!

(2) JUST AS GIRLS NEED AFFECTION, LOVE, AND ATTENTION, SO DO BOYS! Affection, love, and attention are vital elements in a young boy's emotional, physical, and mental development.

Over the years, I've counseled men and women with severe marriage problems. The one problem area in the marriage that constantly keeps raising its ugly head is how often husbands fail to show their wives love and affection.

It may be that husbands fail to show their wives love and affection because they were never shown or taught these fundamental principles at home. Now, this doesn't mean when they were young boys they didn't also want and need affection; but it does mean they were probably never given proper attention and affection from those whom they trusted and loved - their parents!

If a man is ever to show his wife (or anyone else) proper

respect, or if he is ever going to be able to demonstrate his love for his wife by giving her the type of honest affection and attention she both desires and needs, he is, first of all, going to need to learn what love and affection really is. He is going to have to learn how it comes about and how to give it without condition. And the best people to learn from, especially anything of principle and value, is mom and dad!

(3) GIRLS LIKE TO BE HELD! Boys also like to be held. That is until they suddenly reach an age where roughhousing with the old man wins over being held and caressed my mom. Then a few years later, this turns around when teenage boys discover how great it feels to be held and caressed by teenage girls. Once this happens, the relationship between a boy and his mom and dad is forever changed. He may hold or even kiss his parents, but it will never be the same as when he was a small boy.

On the other hand, girls never seem to come to the point in their lives where they stop wanting to be held by the person they feel closest to at the moment - mom and dad in their youth, a husband throughout their marriage, and children in their December years. Remember the bumper sticker that read, "Have you hugged your kid today?" Well, every kid needs to be held and hugged daily. And, the need we parents have for hugging our kids, as well as the need our kids have for being hugged, never grows old.

Earlier in this chapter, I wrote about the time when I counseled my oldest daughter regarding what can happen when a young girl's emotional and physical needs cry aloud, "I want to sit close to this boy! I need to be held!" She then allows her heart to rule her head and finally succumbs to her own passionate pleas. And all too often, the result can be tragic!

Mom, when you were a teenage girl, didn't you enjoy sitting close to your boyfriend? When you were on a date, didn't you enjoy hugging and kissing him before you said good night? Sure you did. The problem is, today things are much different than when you were young. Your boyfriend probably didn't have a condom tucked away

251

in his wallet; movies and music didn't fill his and your mind with notions that it was all right to have premarital sex (or if they did, it wasn't as obvious or out in the open as it is today); many of your friends didn't smoke dope or snort cocaine or shoot heroin; girls weren't becoming pregnant while still in high school (or even junior high school); and, abortion wasn't as easy to come by, nor was it handled in such a cavalier manner, as it is today. Things such as attitude and character of young people were much different when you were young!

If you teach your children while they are young to appreciate the difference between the male and female gender, and if you instruct them as to the proper way to behave while on a date (while at the same time enjoying the company of that certain someone of the opposite sex), then my counsel to you is: you can rest assured that when the time comes for your child to be tested (and we all face tests and trials throughout our lives) - to face and overcome the temptation to commit fornication, smoke dope, take illegal drugs, or perpetrate a crime - he or she will fall back and rely on the firm foundation you have provided by your instruction, guidance, and example. And, if you have set the right example, given proper guidance and instruction, taken enough time for training and play, the probability that your kid will achieve success in overcoming, doing what is right, and becoming a solid citizen, will be very high!

(4) GIRLS AND BOYS LIKE TO BE NOTICED! Why does it take as long as it does for our daughters (and wives) to get ready whenever they are going some place? Why do they spend so much money on clothes and accessories while trying to maintain a certain style and chic appearance? Why do they purchase so many beauty and fashion magazines every month? Why do you suppose our daughters (and wives) support the cosmetic industry the way they do by buying enormous amounts of expensive products that high paid models endorse? Why do young women wear the type of scanty bathing suits that they wear whenever they go to the beach (especially when, more often than not, the suit never touches or even goes near

water!)?

Isn't it interesting how many girls hate to take showers where other girls might see their naked bodies; however, they don't hesitate for a moment when the time comes to head for the beach wearing a frock some call a bikini that barely covers certain parts of their bodies. Do you suppose the reason for this show of immodest behavior might just have something to do with the fact that they hope to attract the attention of some young available hulk who may also be at the beach...who may be there for more than just a day of playing in the surf and sand? If you're honest with yourself, you know it is!

I tried to inspire my daughters to consider the way they dressed by pointing out to them that "most young men believe that those young women who show it all are willing to give it all". You see, the vast majority of the young women whom I have counseled have no idea how easy it is for a young man (or older man for that matter) to become sexually aroused.

Why do you suppose girls want so much to be noticed? From the conversations I've had with a great many young girls regarding this subject, I have come to believe that most girls don't really know why they want to be noticed. Nor do they realize that by their actions - including what they are or aren't wearing at the time - they can cause another person, male or female, to look at them with less than pure or positive thoughts. Kids today are being molested and severely injured simply because they are at the wrong place at the wrong time and often wearing an inappropriate style of clothes! My advice to parents is that we teach our daughters how to be well groomed; how to dress appropriately within the limits of a clothing budget and to be modest in appearance...not showing off her body, not tempting a young man, teasing him by the way she is dressed. There is nothing wrong with modesty (I Timothy 2:9). Our sons should also be taught the art of being well groomed and how to be modest in their appearance.

Lately, kids wearing expensive sports jackets and tennis shoes are being mugged by those who want what they are wearing. It doesn't only have to be skimpy or revealing clothes that can get a child in trouble today; it can be any style of clothes or shoes that some other less fortunate or deranged kid carrying a gun or knife decides that he or she wants.

Also, our kids need to understand that a person with a perverted mind, hoping to attract and then attack a young girl for his sexual pleasure; or that young man or woman who plans to steal the clothes off Junior's back, doesn't always look like some Gothic character living in Transylvania who flies out of his or her cave when the sun goes down. Most men committing sexual crimes against young girls or mugging a child on his or her way home from school are neatly dressed and fairly well groomed. Teach your children to be aware of where they are at all times, whether on a date, at school, taking a shortcut home, or shopping at the mall.

At my summer youth camp, the girls on my staff wear one-piece bathing suits. I kidded them, on the square, when I told them I didn't want any of the young boys attending camp falling off the end of the boat dock because they were distracted by some pretty, young girl in a bikini. It's happened in the past. Boys of all ages are definitely distracted when it comes to a pretty young girl walking by wearing a bikini bathing suit (what I call two Band-Aids and a piece of gauze).

Every girl wants to be noticed, no doubt about it. But shouldn't the main reason for wanting to be noticed be that she has a bright mind, a positive attitude, and Godly character? Simply dressing in a fashion or modern style so others will notice her form and figure can be very superficial. Just as a style of dress changes, so does a woman's figure. But a positive attitude, a bright mind, and Godly character, if cultivated with the degree of energy and time a woman spends with her cosmetics and fashion paraphernalia, only blossoms and grows...it only gets better!

In much the same way boys are attracted to girls who are neatly groomed and dressed, and who present themselves with style, elegance, grace, and a decor of modesty; girls also appreciate and are attracted to boys who have good manners, dress well, and possess positive and strong character.

So, parents, it is our responsibility to teach our kids, boys as well as girls, how to act, how to dress, and how to live, so that they don't go through life wearing some kind of superficial mask just so they can be noticed. Teach them the value of good manners, a well-groomed appearance, a bright mind, a positive attitude, and Godly character!

(5) GIRLS (AND BOYS) WANT TO BE LOVED! We parents must take very special care regarding this subject of how our children want to be loved. We must be aware of our daughter's emotional feelings and her vulnerability to the negative side of wanting so much to be loved. A child (especially a girl) seeking someone to love (or someone to love her) has some very strong and tenuous pulls to overcome...the type of pulls that can lead to a lot of pain and suffering if not controlled at the very beginning.

Children need to be loved. The point is, "by whom?" Whom do you want your children to be loved by, and where do you expect them to find this love? Hopefully, it will come from you, their parents, before it surfaces on the scene from someone else. It is up to us parents to teach our kids the difference between what "real" love is and what sexual gratification is and how to handle love in the proper way.

There comes a time in every young person's life when love from someone other than mom or dad is much more important and exciting. It's at this point in their lives we hope and pray that those things regarding love, sex, and life, which we taught them in their youth, will hold up...including how to react properly to whatever situation they will face in life by using their heads and not simply doing what their heart tells them.

Remember, God's prophet Jeremiah warned us that the heart can be very deceitful above all things! Ask yourself, as a parent and guardian of your children, do you really want only their hearts (emotions) dictating what they do with their lives? Or that they allow their emotions to determine many of the major decisions they will have to make as adults? Or that they might also allow their hearts (emotions) to direct the way they act or react toward others...especially on a date? If not, the only one sure way your kids will ever be able to properly direct their lives by using their minds, and not just their hearts, is if they have been taught how to do so at home...by you, their parents!

Proverbs 3:13-18 explains, "Blessed is the man (or woman or child) that finds wisdom (knowing right from wrong), the man who gains understanding, for she (wisdom) is more profitable than silver and yields better returns than gold. She is more precious than rubies; nothing you desire can compare with her. Long life is in her right hand; in her left hand are riches and honor. Her ways are pleasant ways, and all her paths are peace. She is a tree of life to those who embrace her; those who lay hold of her will be blessed!"

Wouldn't you feel successful as a parent if your children applied this type of truth and understanding in their lives? Wouldn't it be great, especially where dating, marriage, and raising children is concerned?

Well, in the world where we live today, the only way your children are ever going to learn this type of knowledge and wisdom is if you take the time to teach them...they certainly won't get it from school, classmates, friends, or on the street!

An important point parents should take the time to teach their children is the reality that "Love is Love" (a deep and tender feeling of affection for, or attachment or devotion to, another person or persons, - a strong interest or liking for another person), and "Sex is Sex" (not to be confused with the word meaning "love"). Love should always be the foundation for physical sex; however, sex as in "having sexual intercourse" has nothing to do with the word or meaning of love.

The phrase, "I want to make love to you" has no real meaning. It is simply a colloquialism. One does not *make* love, one *has* sex. Therefore, the more correct way for someone telling another person, "I want to make love to you" is, "I want to have sex with you!" How many girls do you suppose would become turned on to some guy if he simply said, "Hey Babe, I wanna have sex with you"? I think most girls would reply, "Sure, right! Take a hike!"

Love and sex are two separate, yet not completely unrelated, elements of life. You can have one without the other, but you shouldn't! Love and marriage, including proper sexual conduct, is a blessing from God. He created the union between a man and his wife. Sex outside the marriage vow is fornication. Fornication between a man and woman who are not married to one another, but married to some one else, is adultery and sin. And the penalty for this sin results in divorce, destruction of the family, mental and physical illness, and even death. (For a better understanding about this subject including how we should teach and prepare our children for life, read the entire chapter of Proverbs 5 in your Bible.)

I try to encourage parents and their children to be aware of the many pitfalls, snares, and dangerous traps going steady and single dating presents. Just like the undetected traps hunters use to snare their prey, the traps used to snare our children usually can't be seen by them until it's too late. We parents have been given the responsibility to provide proper road maps so that our kids will not fall prey to destructive snares, nor will they be harmed by well-camouflaged pitfalls or traps!

One way we can help our kids is to teach them the dangers of going steady and why they should not date the same person more than once, before they are prepared to deal with the emotional and physical trials that so often come into play whenever two young people begin to seriously think they're in love.

As parents, we need to teach our sons and daughters about the dangers of going steady with only one person. We need to teach them while they're still in their youth, so as they grow and mature, they will begin to understand exactly what we expect of them. Not only will this type of training and instruction provide them with an understanding concerning the advice we give them regarding a particular situation, such as single dating or going steady, but it will also provide them with a solid foundation of needed knowledge for other situations they will encounter throughout their youth and on into adulthood.

Don't wait until they're older, more independent, and going steady with someone before you begin teaching your kids about dating. By this time, they probably won't listen to you because they will no doubt feel they know better, or they will think you are telling them not to date simply because you don't like their friend...you just simply want to break up their relationship for whatever reason (and the reason doesn't matter!).

Believe me, when teenagers go steady, it's a very dangerous situation. I have counseled so many young people who have experienced tremendous problems because they decided to devote all their time and attention to one individual. These problems can easily begin to manifest themselves into dangerous and profound situations because so often the individual our child is smitten with misleads or corrupts him or her to the point where sex becomes part of the relationship. In fact, more than sex can be the snare; drugs, alcohol, theft, rape, murder, and other violent crimes often result from two immature young people spending all of their free moments with one another.

Now, to those who would jump in here and accuse me of being too conservative or too rigid with my assessment regarding how we should teach our children about the dangers of going steady, I can only point out the fact that so many kids today are in deep trouble in school, at home, and with the law because they haven't been taught, disciplined, and properly supervised at home. They haven't been instructed about what going steady means or what a responsibility it is to be alone with another young person without any supervision or guidance. Read the papers and watch the nightly news; our kids are in trouble as never before! And there's a reason why!

Perhaps it's the way we have allowed our kids to get away with things, such as lying and cheating or being lazy and idle; perhaps we've allowed them to watch too much television or listen to too many CD's containing violent and harmful lyrics; maybe we have failed to properly teach them how to honor their elders, their parents;

perhaps we didn't care if they stayed out late at night, or we didn't care where they went or with whom; and perhaps we listened to too many so-called child experts tell us that to punish and discipline our kids is abusive and wrong. Could it also be we have failed to provide an important instructional road map to help them avoid the various traps and snares, the dangerous pitfalls they will encounter along life's path? Or perhaps the reason our kids are in such trouble today is we parents just don't give a damn! Perhaps we are too concerned about our own welfare, our jobs, our money...our own lives!

Parents, seize the moment now to begin teaching and preparing your kids for tomorrow. Help them to avoid being emotionally or physically harmed because of someone whom they think they love decides to date another person, demands to have sex, promotes the use of drugs and alcohol, or even attempts to destroy their very lives. It happens every day!

Realize that the values and principles you've taught your kids, by not allowing them to begin dating while they are still too young to understand the consequences of their mistakes, are priceless and certainly something to be honored and desired. Also realize that just as you were immature when you were young, your children are also immature. However, let them grow up slowly, don't force them to be adults; let them be kids!

We parents should never allow television, music, films, or our children's peers the opportunity to influence them in an adverse manner. What recent TV show, movie, or music tape have you seen or heard that you would feel comfortable in allowing to instruct your children regarding marriage, sex, religion, money management, respect for others, dating, or discerning right from wrong? I doubt if you can name very many. What about your children's friends and peers? How many are left alone to decide for themselves the difference between right and wrong? Should a young child left alone, often frightened and sorely in need of companionship, be the one who instructs your child about such important things as love, truth, sex...life?

In Chapter 4, we discussed the importance of how to work with and instruct the mind of a child. One of the main topics of that chapter concerns the importance of why we should take every precaution to make sure we allow only the highest quality seeds, i.e., values, principles, wisdom, and knowledge, to be planted into the minds of our children. The seeds we plant include how we teach our kids about dating, sex, and marriage, and how we teach our kids about God.

WHY TEACH OUR KIDS ABOUT GOD?

Whenever we parents bring up the subject of God and how He sees things, does things or wants things done, we stand the risk of turning off our kids. So many young people today don't believe there is a God. And when we, as a people, do away with God - His principles, His laws, His love - what then is left to form the basic foundation that supports our great society? If not for our trust and belief in a great Creator God, then what are we to rely on? Our own selfish desires and greed? Our own man-made theories and ideas that more often than not begin to crumble when put to the test? Our own finite intelligence? Without God, what becomes of us? How do we govern society? How do we maintain and obey the laws that protect the small and weak as well as the strong and the mighty? How do we prevent anarchy if we fail to obey the laws of the land? Where do we find strength and understanding? And without faith in God, how can we parents discern what is right from what is wrong? How do we teach our kids the right way to live?

Unless those reading this book realize there is a wise and all-powerful and all-knowing God, then most of what I have written will have little or no meaning. For what I have written is based on the principles of the Word of God! And it's these principles that will provide parents reading this book the type of knowledge, wisdom, courage, understanding, and unconditional love to successfully rear their children while at the same time help to prepare them for their future lives as undefeated and victorious adults!

Chastity enables the soul to breathe a pure air in the foulest places. Continence makes her strong, no matter in what condition the body may be. Her sway over the senses makes her queenly: her light and peace render her beautiful. -Joubert

IN DEFENSE
of a
LITTLE VIRGINITY!

a message from Focus on the Family

Incredibly, the "safe sex" gurus and condom promoters who got us into the present-day problems we have with so many of our young people now experiencing sexually transmitted diseases, including HIV/AIDS, abortions, which are increasing annually, and so many other diseases hard to understand and pronounce, are still determining our policy regarding adolescent sexuality. Their ideas have failed, and it is time to rethink their bankrupt policies!

How long has it been since you have heard anyone tell teenagers why it is to *their* advantage to remain virgins until married? The facts are being withheld from them, with tragic consequences. Unless we come to terms with the sickness that stalks a generation of Americans, teen promiscuity will continue, and millions of kids...thinking they are protected...will suffer for the rest of their lives. And many will die of AIDS!

There is only one safe way to remain healthy in the midst of a sexual revolution. It is to abstain from intercourse until marriage, and then wed and be faithful to an uninfected partner. It is a concept that was widely endorsed in society until the 1960's. Since then, a "better idea" has come along...one that now threatens the entire human family.

Inevitable questions are raised whenever abstinence is proposed. It's time we gave some clear answers:

Why, apart from moral considerations, do you think teenagers should be taught to abstain from sex until marriage?

No other approach to the epidemic of sexually transmitted

diseases will work! The so-called "safe-sex" solution is a disaster in the making. Condoms can fail at least 15.7 percent of the time annually in preventing pregnancy[1]. They fail 36.3 percent of the time annually in preventing pregnancy among young, unmarried minority women[2]. In a study of homosexual men, the *British Medical Journal* reported the failure rate due to slippage and breakage to be 26 percent[3]. Given these findings, it is obvious why we have a word for people who rely on condoms as a means of birth control. We call them..."parents."

Remembering that a woman can conceive only one or two days per month, we can only guess how high the failure rate for condoms must be in preventing disease, which can be transmitted 365 days per year! If the devices are not used properly, or if they slip just once, viruses and bacteria are exchanged and the disease process begins. One mistake after 500 "protected" episodes is all it takes to contract a sexually transmitted disease. *The damage is done in a single moment when rational thought is overridden by a moment of passion!*

Those who would depend on so insecure a method must use it properly on *every* occasion, and even then a high failure rate is brought about by factors beyond their control. The young victim who is told by his elders that this little latex device is "safe" may not know he is risking lifelong pain and even death for so brief a window of pleasure. What a burden to place on an immature mind and body!

Then we must recognize that there are other differences between pregnancy prevention and disease prevention. HIV is 1/25th the width of sperm[4], and can pass easily through even the smallest gaps in condoms. Researchers studying surgical gloves made out of latex, the same material as used in condoms, found "channels of 5 microns that penetrated the entire thickness of the glove[5]." HIV measures .1 microns[6]. Given these findings, what rational, informed person would trust his or her very life to such flimsy armor?

This surely explains why not one of 800 sexologists at a conference a few years ago raised a hand when asked if they would trust a thin rubber sheath to protect them during intercourse with a known HIV-infected person[7]. Who could blame them? They're not crazy, after all. And yet, they're perfectly willing to tell our kids that "safe sex" is within reach and that they can sleep around with impunity.

There is only one way to protect ourselves from the deadly diseases that lie in wait. It is abstinence before marriage, then marriage and mutual fidelity for life to an uninfected partner. Anything less is potentially suicidal!

That position is simply NOT realistic today. It's an unworkable solution: Kids will NOT implement it.

Some will. Some won't. It's still the only answer! But let's talk about an "unworkable solution" of the first order. Since 1970, the federal government has spent nearly $3 billion to promote contraception and "safe sex." In 1993, $450 million tax dollars will go down that drain[8]! (Compared with less than $8 million for abstinence programs, which some in Congress have sought repeatedly to eliminate altogether.) Isn't it time we ask what we have gotten for our money? After 22 years and nearly $3 billion, some 58 percent of teenage girls under 18 still did not use contraception during their first intercourse[9]. Furthermore, teenagers tend to keep having unprotected intercourse for a full year, on average, before starting any kind of contraception[10]. That is the success ratio of the experts who call abstinence "unrealistic" and "unworkable."

Even if we spent another $50 billion to promote condom usage, most teenagers would still not use them consistently and properly. The nature of human beings and the passion of the act simply do not lend themselves to a disciplined response in young romantics.

But if you knew a teenager was going to have intercourse, wouldn't you teach him or her about proper condom usage?

No, because that approach has an unintended consequence. The process of recommending condom usage to teenagers inevitably conveys five dangerous ideas: (1) that "safe sex" is achievable; (2) that everybody is doing it; (3) that responsible adults expect them to do it; (4) that it's a good thing; and (5) that their peers know they

265

know these things, breeding promiscuity. Those are very destructive messages to give to our kids.

Furthermore, Planned Parenthood's own data show that the number one reason teenagers engage in intercourse is peer pressure[111] Therefore, anything we do to imply that "everybody is doing it" results in more...not fewer...young people who give the game a try. Condom distribution programs do not reduce the number of kids exposed to disease...they radically increase it!

Want proof of that fact? Since the federal government began its major contraception program in 1970, unwed pregnancies have increased 87 percent among 15-19 year olds[12.] Likewise, abortions among teens rose 67 percent[13]; unwed births went up 61 percent[14]. And venereal disease has infected a generation of young people. Nice job, sex counselors! Good thinking, senators and congressmen! Nice nap, America!

Having made a blunder that now threatens the human family, one would think the designers would be backtracking and apologizing for their miscalculations. Instead, they continue to lobby Congress and corporate America for more money. Given the misinformation extant on this subject, they'll probably get it.

But if you were a parent and knew that your son or daughter was having sex, wouldn't you rather he or she used a condom?

How much risk is acceptable when you're talking about your teenager's life? One study of married couples in which one partner was infected with HIV found that 17% of the partners using condoms for protection still caught the virus within a year and a half[15]. Telling our teens to "reduce their risk" to one in six (17%) is not much better than advocating Russian roulette. Both are fatal, eventually. The difference is that with a gun, death is quicker. Suppose your son or daughter were joining an 18 month skydiving club of six members. If you knew that one of their parachutes would definitely fail, would you recommend that they simply buckle the chutes tighter? Certainly not! You would say, "Please don't jump. Your life is at stake!" How could any loving parent do less?

Kids won't listen to the abstinence message. You're just wasting your breath to try to sell them a notion like that.

It is a popular myth that teenagers are incapable of understanding that it is in their best interest to save themselves until marriage. Almost 65 percent of all high school females under 18 are virgins[16].

A few years ago in Lexington, Ky., a youth event was held that featured no sports contest, no rock groups-just an ex-convict named Harold Morris talking about abstinence, among other subjects. The coliseum seated 18,000 people, but 26,000 teenagers showed up! Eventually, more than 2,000 stood outside the packed auditorium and listened over a hastily prepared public address system. Who says kids won't listen to this time-honored message?

Even teens who have been sexually active can choose to stop. This is often called "secondary virginity," a good concept that conveys the idea that kids can start over. One young girl recently wrote Ann Landers to say she wished she had kept her virginity, signing the letter, "Sorry I didn't and wish I could take it back." As responsible adults, we need to tell her that even though she can't go back, she can go forward. She can regain her self-respect and protect her health, because it's never too late to start saying "no" to premarital sex.

Even though the safe-sex advocates predominate in educational circles, are there no positive examples of abstinence-based programs for kids?

Thankfully, some excellent programs have been developed. Spokane-based *Teen-Aid* and Chicago's *Southwest Parents Committee* are good examples. So are *Next Generation* in Maryland, *Choices* in California and *Respect, Inc.* in Illinois. Other curricula such as *Facing Reality; Sex Respect; Me, My World, My Future; Reasonable Reasons to Wait; Sex, Love & Choices; F.A.C.T.S.* etc., are all abstinence-themed programs to help kids make good sexual decisions.

A good curriculum for inner-city youth is Elayne Bennett's

267

Best Friends Program. This successful "mentoring" project helps adolescents in Washington, D.C. graduate from high school and remain abstinent. In five years, not one female has become pregnant while in the *Best Friends Program*!

Establishing and nurturing abstinence ideas with kids, however, can be like spitting into the wind. Not because they won't listen, because most will. But pro-abstinence messages are drowned out in a sea of toxic teen-sex-is-inevitable-use-a-condom propaganda from "safe-sex" professionals.

You place major responsibility on those who have told adolescents that sexual expression is their right as long as they do it "properly." Who else has contributed to the epidemic?

The entertainment industry must certainly share the blame, including television producers. It is interesting in this context that all four networks and the cable television entities are wringing their hands about the terrible epidemic of AIDS. They profess to be very concerned about those who are infected with sexually transmitted diseases, and perhaps they are sincere. However, TV executives and movie moguls have contributed mightily to the existence of this plague. For decades, they have depicted teens and young adults climbing in and out of each other's beds like so many sexual robots. Only the nerds were shown to be chaste, and they were too stupid or ugly to find partners.

Of course, the beautiful young actors in those steamy dramas never faced any consequences for their sexual indulgence. No one ever came down with herpes, or syphilis, or chlamydia, or pelvic inflammatory disease, or infertility, or AIDS, or genital warts, or cervical cancer. No patients were ever told by a physician that there was no cure for their disease or that they would have to deal with the pain for the rest of their lives. No one ever heard that genital cancers associated with the human papilloma virus (HPV) kill more women than AIDS[17], or that strains of gonorrhea are now resistant to penicillin[18].

No, there was no downside. It all looked like so much fun.

But what a price we are paying now for the lies we have been told.

The government has also contributed to this crisis and continues to exacerbate the problem. For example, a current brochure from the federal Centers for Disease Control and the City of New York is entitled, "Teens Have the Right," and is apparently intended to free adolescents from adult authority. Inside are six declarations that make up a "Teenager's Bill of Rights," as follows:

- I have the right to think for myself.
- I have the right to decide whether to have sex and whom to have it with.
- I have the right to use protection when I have sex.
- I have the right to buy and use condoms.
- I have the right to express myself.
- I have the right to ask for help if I need it. (under this final item is a list of organizations and phone numbers that readers are encouraged to call. The philosophy that governs several of the organizations reflects the homosexual agenda, which includes recruitment of the young and vigorous promotion of teen's right to sexual expression. Certainly, our tax dollars are at work!

When we stop to ponder the enormity of this present crisis, it is not difficult to recognize the growing danger now threatening an entire generation of our best and brightest. It seems quite evident that if we parents are to ever experience the "Joy of Raising Our Kids in the 21st Century," we must return to teaching our children some of the tried-and-true principles that have endured for generations...one being an old-fashioned value called "virginity." Now more than ever, *virtue is a necessity!*

Data Sources: 1) Elise F. Jones and Jacqueline Darroch Forrest, "Contraceptive Failure in the United States: Revised Estimates from the 1982 National Survey of Family Growth" Family Planning Perspectives 21 (May/June 1989); 2) Ibid., p.105; 3) Lode Wigersma and Ron Oud, "Safety and Acceptability of Condoms for Use by Homosexual Men as a Prophylactic Against Transmission of HIV During Anogenital Sexual Intercourse," British Medical Journal 295 (July 11, 1987); 4) Marcia F. Goldsmith, "Sex in the Age of AIDS Calls for Common Sense and Condom Sense," Journal of the American Medical Association 257 (May 1, 1987); 5) Susan G. Arnold et al., "Latex Gloves Not Enough to Exclude Viruses," Nature 335 (Sept. 1, 1988); 6) Nancy E. Dirubbo, "The Condom Barrier," American Journal of Nursing (Oct. 1987); 7) Theresa Crenshaw, from remarks made at the National Conference on HIV, Washington, D.C., (Nov. 15-18, 1991); 8) "Condom Roulette," Washington Watch 3 (Jan. 1992); 9) William D. Mosher and James W. McNally, "Contraceptive Use at First Premarital Intercourse: United States 1965-1988." Family Planning Perspectives 23 (May-June 1991); 10) Cheryl D. Hayes, ed., "Risking the Future: Adolescent Sexuality, Pregnancy and Childbearing," (Washington: National Academy Press, 1987); 11) Planned Parenthood poll, "America Teens Speak: Sex, Myths, TV and Birth Control," (New York: Louis Harris & Associates, Inc. 1986); 12) "Condom Roulette," In Focus 25 (Washington: Family Research Council, Feb. 1992); 13) Gilbert L. Crouse, Office of Planning ad Evaluation, U.S. Dept. of Health & Human Services (March, 1992); 14) U>S> Congress, House Committee on Energy and Commerce, Subcommittee on Health and Environment, 102nd Congress, 2nd session, March 19, 1991; 15) Margaret A. Fischl et al., "Heterosexual Transmission of Human Immunodeficiency Virus (HIV): Relationship of Sexual Practices Seroconversion," III International Conference on AIDS, June 1-5, 1987; 16) U.S. Dept. of Health & Human Services, National Centers for Health Statistics, Centers for Disease Control, "Percent of Women 15-19 Years of Age Who Ate Sexually Experienced by Race, Age and Marital Status: United States, 1988; 17) Joseph S. McIhaney, Jr., M.D., "Sexuality and Sexually Transmitted Diseases. (Grand Rapids, Baker Publ., 1990); 18) A.M.B. Goldstein and Susan M. Garabedian-Ruffalo, "A Treatment Update to Resistant Gonorrhea," Medical Aspects of Human Sexuality, (Aug. 1991).

CHAPTER SEVENTEEN

ANTICIPATION!

For Our Children's
Welfare
and
Success!

Anticipation is sometimes a difficult concept for parents to understand because we cannot always anticipate or foresee the many problems and various situations that will happen to our children as they grow older. Still, using our past experience and the knowledge we gained from it, we try to protect them from those mistakes we have made in our youth, as well as the ones we make as adults. However, try as we may, we will never completely be able to protect our kids from every bad thing or every evil that they will come their way. We can only hope that we will teach them well enough so that when they do face their trials and difficulties, they will be able to overcome them and go on with their lives.

Anticipation and anxiety often go hand-in-hand. And this is especially true for parents who have children of all ages. We worry when our kids are ill; when they are late coming home from school or a date; when they take their school exams; when they go to their first party (or their second, third, fourth...); when they go to camp; when they begin to date; when they graduate from high school; when they head off for college; when they meet that special someone they want to marry; when they marry; when they have kids; when they lose their job; when they begin getting old. It's true that most parents worry about their kids until the day they die!

How do we parents learn to anticipate what our children are going to think or do? This is a difficult question, but let's see if we

271

can find an answer. Let's begin our search by using an analogy of a child lying to his or her parents as an example. As a parent, are you always able to anticipate or foresee when your children are going to lie to you about something they've done wrong but don't want you to know about it? Oh! Your kids never lie, you say? Believe it or not, every kid lies to his or her parents (big lies, little lies; white lies, or dark lies) at some time or other.

What child wants to readily admit to something he or she has done wrong; something terrible such as breaking your favorite antique vase or perhaps losing the money you gave him or her to buy groceries? Which one of your children will stand right up and admit that he or she ate both bags of the cookies you were saving for your Bridge club? Or, will your son or daughter admit to breaking the living room window without your having to prod or threaten them before you get your answer? And by the way, did you ever tell a lie to your parents when you were a kid?

In Chapter two, we discussed the assembly line concept and how children are "molded" by what they see their parents doing - how their parents act and behave in various situations. Here, we begin to understand that if we parents lie or cheat, our kids will probably lie and cheat as well. In this regard, the old adage, "like father, like son; like mother, like daughter" certainly holds true!

A major problem in child rearing, I have witnessed over the years, is the way parents seem to force their children to lie to them simply because they approach a problem or speak to their kids in a very negative and often abusive manner. As an example: a flower pot has been knocked over and there is a pile of dirt lying beneath it on the floor. However, the pot has been put back into its place on the table. It is obvious that someone knocked over the pot and then replaced it. But who?

"Honey. Did you knock over my flower pot in the living room?" You ask your husband.

"What pot?" He replies. "I don't know what you're talking about."

You immediately eliminate your spouse from your list of

possible culprits because you know he probably didn't do it (he was busy watching the football game in the family room!). So, now, who's left? You call up to your children (who are quietly playing in their rooms). "Hey, kids. C'mon down here for a minute." Suddenly, you begin to anticipate that you may be on to something as you hear them whisper to each other as they slowly come down the stairs. You realize any other time you would have to be yelling at them to be a little more quiet.

You are now confronted with two ways to approach this problem. Without taking the time to think out this situation with patient understanding, you can anticipate (foresee) that your kids are probably going to lie to you and so without giving them the chance to speak, you say, "Okay. I know one of you knocked over my flower pot and whoever did it is going to be punished, but good!" (Some parents have even been known to say something like, "I'm gonna beat the stuffing out of whoever did it!") Wow! This is certainly one way for you to help your kids muster up the courage to stand right up and announce, "I realize you are going to beat me within an inch of my life, but just like my teacher read to us about our founding father, George Washington, I can't tell a lie. I confess, I did it!" If you believe your kids are ever going to admit to something they did wrong, while at the same time realizing they're going to be punished or abused, I know some people who have a bridge in New York they would like to sell you as soon as possible. The fact is: it just isn't going to happen.

The other way to handle this situation, even if you have cause to anticipate that your children are going to lie to you, is to simply say, "Someone knocked over my flower pot and didn't pick up the mess. How about you taking the time right now and go into the living room and clean up the dirt off the floor."

"But, Mom!" Your daughter moans. "I didn't do it, Junior did!"

"I didn't do it!" Junior retorts. Susie did!"

"It doesn't matter who did it, you both go in and clean up the mess." You wait for a moment and then add, "And the next time one of you makes a mess or does something wrong, don't wait for me to discover what you did. Come to me right away and tell me what happened. That way, we can work it out together and you don't have to worry about being punished. Okay?"

Even though neither child confessed to having committed the infraction, both of them knew exactly who it was that knocked over the pot. They will no doubt deal with this situation between themselves. And because you, the parent, handled the problem in a calm, patient, and understanding manner, the possibility that your kids will handle a similar situation much better, the next time they do something wrong, has greatly increased.

The example you set during this type of exercise would provide your children with an awareness as to why they should trust you in the future to be understanding and patient with them. And why they should not be apprehensive or fearful that you might over react and harm them by verbal abusive or physical punishment.

Take a moment and visualize yourself as a small child. You just did something wrong and your mother and father are standing over you yelling and screaming at the top of their lungs about whatever it is you did; and, at the same time, threatening that they're going to "beat you within an inch of your life." Now how would you feel? Would you jump up and confess to the crime, such as our example of knocking over a flower pot? Or would you play dumb, asking "What pot? Did a pot get knocked over somewhere?" When children believe they are about to get the stuffing beaten out of them, their imagination can suddenly leap into warp-speed resulting in a most frightening and fearful experience. Is it any wonder then that they would lie to possibly save their hides?

Lying is part of growing up. It is not something children are born with; it is something they acquire along the way to puberty. Lying is part of a child's character that needs to be worked with and changed while he or she is very young. When confronted by something they may have done wrong or when they find themselves in a tight situation where fear and anxiety may overwhelm them, most young kids are going to try and lie their way out of it. So, we parents must work at becoming very sensitive to our children and their problems, learn to anticipate their needs, fears, and weaknesses before things get out of control. By taking the time to truly understand them, which results in our being able to anticipate their needs and fears, our ability to help our kids manage their emotional and physical problems will be greatly enhanced. This will help us to help them overcome those weaknesses that can prevent growth in a young person's life!

I remember an incident when I was young that might help to better explain what I mean about anticipation in context with our example of children lying.

I had stolen some money from my dad when he was not looking. Later, as I was nonchalantly playing with the silver coins in my pocket, my mother heard the sound of the coins and asked, "Son, what do you have in your pocket?"

I hesitated for a moment, hoping to change the subject. "Nothing. When's dinner gonna be ready?"

"What do you have in your pocket?" She wasn't buying my trying to change the subject. "I know you have something in your pocket. What is it!"

"It's just some money." I figured I didn't want to give her anymore information than I had to.

"Where did you get it?" She asked.

Man! All of a sudden, I knew I was in trouble! If I told the truth about stealing it from my dad's pocket, I knew I was going to be punished. So, I figured the best way to get out of this predicament was simply to tell my mother a lie. After all, who really wants to get caught stealing...especially from one's own father!

I thought for a moment and then told my mother I had earned it from a neighbor lady for some work I had done. By now, I was beginning to feel uneasy and hoped she would believe me and go on to some other subject.

Mom was quiet for a few moments as she looked down at me, studying my body language. I must have been convincing though because she simply said "Okay" then went on with her cooking.

The next afternoon when I got home from school, my mother

was waiting for me at the front door. Without skipping a beat she said, "The money you had in your pocket last night, where did you say you got it?"

Suddenly, I felt the hair standing up on the back of my neck; I immediately began sensing trouble on the horizon. I wasn't too concerned because I thought I could carry on with my deception, remembering the story I had told my mother the night before. So, I repeated my lie, "I earned it from our neighbor."

My mom looked at me slowly shaking her head, softly saying. "I spoke to our neighbor this morning and she told me she didn't give you any money."

I knew I was trapped. "You did?!"

"You got the money out of your dad's pocket, didn't you?"

At that moment, fear and all, I thought how smart my mother was. I mean, how did she know I had taken my dad's money. Did she see me do it? She couldn't have. I had been very careful. I made sure no one was around when I committed my dastardly deed. It also hit me, "Does my dad know I stole his money?!"

Now that I had been found out, my crime discovered, my back up against the wall, I told my mom the truth. And was it ever embarrassing! I knew then and there that I never, ever wanted to go through that kind of experience again!

As we look back on so many of our experiences during our youth, when we were often foolish and we did things that were mischievous or perhaps downright hurtful, we can see how easy it is for our children to do the same kind of things today. Our kids are no different than we were, except, in today's world, some of the more mischievous things they do can result in much greater consequences and penalties. Our kids have grown up with Sesame Street, new math, and computers, but they still have a fear of punishment; they still want to have their own way; they are still selfish, often arrogant, and a little bit greedy; and, like us, when we were young, they tend to lie when they feel the occasion warrants it.

Until we stop and realize that our kids are most likely experiencing some of the same types of things we experienced as children, we will never be able to gain complete access to sound reasoning with them nor will we be able to anticipate their very next move - what they will say or do before they say or do it. The best way we can help our children overcome their fear of telling the truth is by giving them our unconditional love, honest consideration, and a firm foundation to support their faith and trust, no matter what their age, thus avoiding abusive punishment, embarrassment, and guilt.

Let's take a look at what Daniel Webster tells us about the words "anticipate" and "anticipation." To "anticipate" means to (1) look forward to; expect, (2) to make happen earlier; precipitate, (3) to prevent by action in advance; forestall, (4) to foresee and perform in advance, (5) to use and enjoy in advance, (6) to be ahead of in doing or achieving, (7) to pay before due. "Anticipation" means (1) foreknowledge; presentiment, (2) something expected or anticipated.

Here we begin to see that if we are to help our children grow and mature, we must first of all anticipate (expect and foresee) what they are thinking, feeling or wanting to do and then show them the right and proper way to handle the situation.

As an example: I often left money laying on top of my dresser or desk. So, when my kids were just little tots, I would tell them, "This is your dad's money and I want to feel free to leave it here without anyone taking it. Okay?!" What I was saying to them is, "this is someone else's money, so your responsibility is to leave it alone!" I didn't leave the money on my desk deliberately just so I could test my kids; however, this exercise did help me to teach them how to respect other people's property, and it also helped them to learn more about honesty, values, and a number of other important principles.

I never punished my children for telling the truth; however, I did punish them for lying. In Chapter 13, I wrote about child discipline and punishment. And, I say again, I realize we live in a society that believes corporal punishment is wrong (some even think all punishment is wrong). Still, something is really missing in the way we train and educate our kids when so many of them are running away from home. And there are kids still at home who are in serious trouble with their parents, their school and the law.

Why is it parents just don't seem to realize that discipline and proper punishment is really about caring and showing love. The type of caring and love that causes us to take the time to educate, correct, and discipline them. Ask yourself, doesn't God the Father correct and discipline those whom He dearly loves? Absolutely! Take a moment and read Deuteronomy 8:5; Psalms 94:12; Proverbs 3:11; Proverbs 3:12; John 15:2; Revelation 3:19 NIV to see just how often He does chastise us, His children, whenever we need correction.

Since I became a grandparent, I have discovered that, as a group, grandparents seem to know what to "expect" and "anticipate" from their grandchildren much more so than when they were raising their own kids. We just seem to know what our grandkids are up to before they do it. I suppose it has everything to do with the experience we gained from our having raised the parents of our grandkids. Practice makes perfect, so they say. The problem is, so often it takes a very long time to reach perfection, and then when we think we've got it all together, we discover we still have a ways to go. It's kind of funny how we never seem to quite get it right!

It's a shame that the way we work and play with our grandkids isn't the same as the way we were with our own children. However, for those of you reading this book who are young parents, or about to be parents, you don't have to wake up some morning, after your kids are gone, and think to yourself about how you wish you had handled things differently while they were still at home. You can begin teaching and training your children now so that after they leave home, you will feel good and secure about how you raised them; and you will probably also have a very warm and close relationship with them.

The question is, "How do I go about accomplishing this?" It's a relative simple answer but not necessarily easy to put into practice. You must first begin by studying everything you can about child rearing. Then toss out all those editorials, articles, and books that promote inconsistent theories contrary to your religious beliefs,

278

or well-camouflaged illogical philosophies that simply feed your mind with watered-down pabulum while, at the same time, neglecting the more sagacious and satisfying meat you will need in order to nurture and produce the knowledge and intelligence required to be a parent. In large part, you will accomplish your goal by listening to the common sense of your elders - your parents, grandparents, older friends, pastors - those whom you acknowledge as having successfully raised their children.

The more young parents study about how to become a successful parent, the closer they will come to the point of being able to anticipate (foresee) the daily problems and situations their children will experience. For example: if we read and study about the symptoms a child shows just before he or she comes down with a cold or the flu and suddenly we notice our kid has some of these same symptoms, chances are, our little one will soon be in bed with a cold or the flu and our diagnosis will be correct.

When we learn how to read our children - how they act, what they do and how they do it, what makes them moody, what makes them laugh or cry, what turns them on or off, what makes them tick - we soon discover that we can begin to expect or anticipate certain things to evolve in their lives. It doesn't matter if our kid catches a cold, loses a ball game, or anything else, we can help him or her simply because we have anticipated the next step, that next part of the natural order of things. And when we accomplish this, we have just experienced the meaning of anticipation!

Parents, you need to realize that if your children are ever going to have good manners and be well behaved, if they are going to respect one another as well as their elders, if they are going to honor mom and dad, if they are going to reject and overcome the temptations from those who would harm them, you must help them by first learning how to anticipate these situations before they happen. And to do this, you need to be sensitive, patient, and empathetic with your kids so that you can see more clearly just what it is that you need to anticipate - those obstacles that are waiting just ahead for your kids to stumble over.

Finally, there comes a time in every parent's life when anticipation becomes reality. We anticipate the day our little boy knows how to feed himself, and it becomes a reality; we look forward to the time when our baby girl is potty trained, and we know the time is coming when Junior will be able to tie his own shoe strings - and, sure enough, it becomes a reality. Perhaps we don't necessarily look forward to the day when Susie begins wearing her training bra, but, sooner or later, it becomes a reality. We dread the night when Junior stays out late or his sister comes home from a date in tears and this, too, will most likely become a reality. We hope our kids always make straight A's, but we know that it's probably only wishful thinking on our part and more often than not, this, too, becomes a reality. We expect our children to work hard and graduate from school, and we know the day is coming when they will marry and have children of their own, and, hopefully, with our prayers and proper guidance, this, also, will become a reality.

How we handle the way we work and play with our children today, how we anticipate the things that will happen in their lives, how we apply what we know to be sound and true by the way we teach and train them has everything to do with how well they will succeed in life.

The manner in which we employ and put to use our anticipation and foresight, good or bad, for our children will largely determine how well we measure up as parents. Likewise it will also greatly determine how well our children will measure up as parents when the time comes.

Here are a few book titles you might want to pick up at your local library regarding childrearing:

"The Stork is Dead" by Charlie Shedd
"Intended for Pleasure" by Dr. Wheat
"Shaping Your Child's Sexual Identity" by G. A. Rekers
"How to Really Love Your Teenager!" by Ross Campbell
"How to Really Love Your Child!" by Ross Campbell

These books should help you gain a deeper understanding about how to become a better parent in today's world. It's simple logic that the more we know and understand about our kids and the world they are living in, the better job we will do as parents.

So far, I have tried to help you, the reader, gain a greater understanding regarding some of the things your kids are experiencing today. It doesn't matter how old you are or how well educated or wealthy you may be, the fact remains that your society today is a lot different than it was when you were young.

It's a violent world our children face each day. Some might say that we live in a world gone mad. But it doesn't have to be this way. If we parents begin to deny ourselves some of our lesser important pleasures for a moment and begin spending quality time with our kids; if we learn to say "no" and also how to properly correct and discipline our children; if we become sensitive enough toward our kids so that we begin to anticipate their needs and the problems they will soon be facing, before the problems take hold and can't be corrected or managed, we will not only help our children and our family to survive and prosper, we will also help our neighbors, our fellowman, and our nation. However, if we fail to carry out this tremendous responsibility, the end result for our children, our families, and our society will be nothing less than disastrous!

The next chapter is addressed to our kids. In this chapter, we will discuss *how they can help rear us*...their parents!

We speak of educating our children.
Do we know that our children
also educate us?
-Linda H. Sigourney

CHAPTER EIGHTEEN

ESPECIALLY FOR THE CHILDREN:
HOW To Raise YOUR Parents!

How many articles and books have you read, how many TV talk shows have you seen, or how many sermons have you heard regarding childrearing? Probably hundreds, right! Let me ask you this question: How many articles, books, talk shows, or sermons have your children read, seen, or heard regarding how to rear you, *their* parents?!

Let me suggest you read this chapter with your kids. And after you read something that captures their attention, let them ask whatever questions come to their minds and then you answer them the best you can. If you do this, you will soon discover that you probably know more about whatever it is your kids ask than you thought you knew. You will also learn more about what makes your son or daughter tick and how and why they think the way they do. You will grow closer with your children simply because you have taken the time to academically and intellectually communicate with them. There is nothing like having mom or dad (or uncles, aunts and grandparents) take a moment of their valuable time and spend it with Junior and/or Susie talking about those special things which greatly interest their young, fertile minds.

Okay. Are you ready? So, let's begin reading together as a family.

My first question to you young people is, "Do you realize that your parents have only been parents since the day you were born?" They really didn't know much about what it means to be a parent until the day you came into existence. So, take a moment and calculate how old you are now and then equate your years on earth with the years your mom and dad have been rearing you - the length of time you have been their children and they have been your parents. It's not very long, is it?

A way to look at this subject of children rearing their parents is to begin by understanding that once you, as a child, have reached an age of reasoning, you are offered the opportunity to help rear your parents in a way that you and mom and dad will discover some very wonderful things about each other. Wonderful things such as feelings, emotions, dreams, desires, fears, and so much more that make up our very lives.

It's true, your parents will always have the edge. After all, they are your parents. They have already gone through their terrible two's, puberty, adolescence, and seven difficult teen years when, finally, they reached adulthood. And along with each one of these growing phases, your parents experienced ups and downs, highs and lows, fear and rejection, love and hate, including a vast assortment of problems, heartaches, and joys which, when knit together, provided the kind of knowledge and wisdom they needed to survive and succeed in life. Without this most valuable experience, they would probably have failed to be where they are today.

And again, remember, your parents have only been your parents for the same amount of time that you have been a child. When you work, study, or play, each new day brings some unique discovery that captures your attention, and it's no different with mom and dad except they've been doing it longer. And just like you, they also learn new things every day. But because they have been at it a little longer than you have, they will always have the edge. There's no way to get around it!

Mom and dad are not perfect (or, perhaps I should say, I have never met a mom or dad who is perfect) and so they also make mistakes. Do you ever say anything you wish you could take back? You do? Well, guess what? You're not the Lone Ranger! Mom and dad sometimes say things they wish they hadn't said. There are many times they wish they could take back something they have said or done. And, you know what? Every parent, until the day they are no longer walking on earth, will continue to say dumb things once in a while. The trick is to narrow down these mistakes to the point where we parents blow it less often, or not at all! Do you ever do some stupid thing that you later feel embarrassed about and then wish you could take it back and start all over again? Welcome to the club; so do your parents.

"OK! Which one of you broke the lamp?!"

So now that you understand that mom and dad are human and they really need your help to become better parents, what can you do to help them? There are a lot of things you can do to help your parents grow and mature in the right way. So, let's explore some of them.

Following are several points that will help you to better understand what your job and responsibilities are as a child and how you can help mom and dad become very loving compassionate, understanding, patient, forgiving, and devoted parents. It makes no difference if your parents are together or if one of them is raising you as a single parent. What does matter is that you learn how to properly rear your parents so that your home life will be a better place to live.

To really understand how to rear your parents, you must first go to the instruction manual God gave His children a long time ago. This book is about life and how each of us should manage it. And because God knew children would desire a better understanding regarding how to act toward those who brought them into this world - their parents - He instructed those who wrote the Bible to write: "Honor your father and your mother, so that you may live long in the land the Lord your God is giving you." (Exodus 20:12 NIV).

All parents want their children to live long and have fruitful lives. But how can children live long and have fruitful lives? By heeding the following: "Children, obey your parents in the Lord, for this is right." God then repeats, through His apostle Paul, "Honor your father and mother - which is the first commandment with a promise - that it may go well with you and that *you may enjoy long life* on the earth." (Ephesians 6:1-3 NIV). You can see from what we have just read that when you honor and obey your parents, God promises that you will have a long and fruitful life...a life you will enjoy!

But wait a minute parents! There is a catch! In order for our children to really want to, indeed, be able to, honor and obey us, we must first of all be "honorable" as parents! We cannot expect our children to honor us if we lie, steal, or cheat; or if we abuse them or put them down at every opportunity.

We are very special in the eyes of our children. It's important that we conduct ourselves - by what we say and do - in a way that helps our kids appreciate us so they will honor us - so they will do what we tell them to - that they might escape the terrible dangers facing them every day.

Kids, raising your parents will not be an easy thing to do. For the most part, they're pretty set in their ways, you see. What do I mean, you ask? Well, they can sometimes be very stubborn. Over the years, they've made a habit of wanting to do things their way, and you might as well realize that it'll be a little difficult for them to change. So, I'm letting you know now this is not going to be an easy undertaking. God, with all His love, mercy, and patience, has been working with your parents for years, and even He has had problems with them at times. So, it just isn't going to be easy!

However, to help jump start you on the road to rearing mom and dad, I'm going to give you ten points of instruction that should help you to raise happy, caring, loving, and honorable parents. Read what each point says, think about it when you're alone, talk it over with mom and dad, and then put it into practice on a daily basis.

Point Number One: *Encourage Your Parents Often!* You can encourage mom and dad by showing them how much you are growing up in the way you behave; the way you study and what you do at school; how truthful and polite you are; the care you give when you do your house work; how you handle money and other people's property; the way you appreciate what you have been given; the way you take care of your toys and clothes; and the way you carry out and manage your responsibilities. It all comes down to character and attitude. Do you have strong character? If not, why not? Do you have an attitude problem? If so, why? How do you change a poor attitude into a positive way of thinking, or lack of character into becoming an honest and reliable person? By learning what is right and then doing it! Sounds simple doesn't it, but it isn't.

Whenever you demonstrate by your actions that you're overcoming a difficulty or major problem, you encourage your parents. Whenever you try as hard as you can to do something - even if you don't succeed at the moment - you encourage your parents. When you say, "please" and "thank you", you encourage them. When they hear a good report from your teachers, you encourage them. When you do what you're told without stomping off and pouting, you encourage them. When you say, "I love you" and mean it, you encourage them!

Your parents desperately need encouragement. They work and live in an adult world that is waxing colder and colder and they don't get a whole lot of appreciation from those around them. And yet they still have the responsibility to not only work away from home (often at boring and unpleasant jobs) to pay the rent and put groceries on the table, but also to help get you (their pride and joy) through school and into adulthood. So, remember, just a little encouragement from you can do wonders in raising joyful, caring, loving, and honorable parents!

Point Number Two: *Don't Be Too Strict with Mom and Dad!* And don't demand that everything be done your way! Let your poor ol' parents listen to what they want to hear on the radio or watch on television once in awhile. Let them have some peace and quiet without your nagging or complaining about something you don't have (but know you'll just die if you don't get it), or without your losing control of your emotions and yelling and screaming around the house like you do sometimes.

We all have those difficult moments when we lose it. Believe me, there is a proper time and place to let it all hang out. But it doesn't always have to be at the precise moment when mom or dad are paying the bills, reading a report from the doctor, signing your school report card, or when they're busy cleaning the house. Pick and choose the right time to talk with your folks about those things that are annoying you, causing you to suffer, or simply something you want to get off your mind. You'll find that it works a whole lot better, and that you'll get more accomplished if you have a good attitude, without causing a family quarrel, if you carefully choose the time and place to discuss your problems. Also, it's always better to handle any problem situation with elegance, style, and grace.

If you do what I've suggested, you will be more than a little surprised at how your parents will help you in return. Remember, "What goes around, comes around!"

Point Number Three: *Tell Your Mom and Dad "Thanks" at Least Once a Day!* "Thanks for what?!", you ask? I'll bet if you really think about it, you'll find a lot you can be thankful for, especially where your parents are concerned. Let's see what we can come up with. How about simply, "Thanks for being my mom and dad?" Or, "Thanks for providing my clothes, food, shelter, school supplies, entertainment, spending money, support, protection,...your very love!"

When you tell your parents "thanks," and really mean it, you'll find your life will suddenly become a whole lot easier...especially the next time you ask for something you might not have gotten had you not been thoughtful enough to thank mom and dad for some of the other things they've done for you.

Don't take your parents for granted. In today's world, mom or dad's health can deteriorate very quickly; dad can lose his job overnight, mom can end up having to take on another job just to make ends meet, and this could cause you to be affected in a way you probably wouldn't appreciate all that much.

No matter what your present circumstance might be (the family financial situation, your ethnic and racial background, the color of your skin, or the level of your education), never think for a moment that your parents owe you a living simply because they brought you into this world. Yes, they do owe you their abiding love, guidance, direction, instruction, time, and protection, but they don't owe you a living. You owe yourself a living! You are the one responsible, as a young person, to learn how to make do with what you have; to appreciate what you have been given and make the most of it. How you handle this responsibility will greatly determine how you succeed as an adult. Don't blame mom or dad because you don't have the same things your friend down the street has. Your parents are probably doing the best they can with what they have to work with. The idea is to take what you have been given and run with it; make it work for you no matter how hard the task or how many times you have to try something before you succeed!

Believe it or not, we are living in a much smaller world today than when your parents were your age. The television set, airplane, fax machine, satellite, and telephone have brought the world much closer together. When the wall in Berlin fell, we watched it on television at the moment it happened. When communism ended in Europe and Russia, satellite dishes instantly carried the news into our homes via radio and television. And a few years ago when thousands of students revolted and chaos exploded in Tiananmen Square, again, we watched it all happen.

What else do we see on TV besides music videos and late night pornographic movies? We see nearly one quarter of all children living on earth today not having enough food to eat or clothes to wear to survive. We see children, the same age as you, without a mom or dad to protect them, going to bed at night under a bridge or in some darkened alley, hungry, cold, and afraid. We see more and more children caught up in drugs, gangs, sex, and violence who are also being abused by their peers, family, friends, and society. We see a terrible evil affecting a growing number of children throughout the world!

But you know something? The fact that your parents care enough about you to take time from a busy schedule to read a book like the one you are now reading - hoping to become better educated as loving, devoted, honorable, and involved parents - this should give you cause to appreciate them all the more; and, certainly, you should never simply take them for granted.

God tells every one of us to be thankful for what we have been given. "...and be thankful!" (Colossians 3:15 [last part] NIV). If you really want to help raise happy, understanding, and loving parents, don't forget to say *"Thanks"* once in a while. I promise you, if you do, they'll really appreciate it and love you all the more!

Point Number Four: *Do Something Very Special for Your Parents Today!* The key to point number four is to do something very special for your parents before they have to ask. And not just today, but every day (or at least once a week!). If you always have to be asked to do something, what have you freely offered and what is so special about your doing it? The answer is, not a whole lot!

I can just hear you saying to yourself, "What can I do for my parents that will be special?" Well think about it for a minute. Keep in mind when we started this chapter, regarding how to raise your mom and dad, I explained that it wasn't going to be easy! It requires thinking and then doing (work!) on your part. However, for the sake of time, I'll give you a few hints of what you can do that will be very special to your parents...things you can do without being asked.

CLEAN YOUR ROOM. (Neatly put away your clothes, pick up your toys and/or school books, make your bed, dust and vacuum your room.)

HELP CLEAN THE HOUSE. (Dust and vacuum the house, especially if mom has to work away from the home. Boy, will she be delighted to come home to a clean house. And, you'll experience a wonderful feeling of having done something very special!)

WASH and DRY THE DISHES. (Tell your mom, before she asks, "You sit and relax and I'll do the dishes tonight." Man, will she be thrilled! Remember, do this more often than once a year. The more often, the better.)

CLEAN THE GARAGE. (Now here is a way to win your dad's heart! Not only this, but you will probably find some old baseball mitt, fishing pole, or doll you forgot about long ago. It'll be like getting some new toy or plaything just because you decided to help your dad by cleaning up the garage.)

FIX DINNER. (The meal you prepare doesn't have to be an expensive dinner of bottled wine or Cordon Bleu. Just a nice fresh cooked meal of hamburger, beans, soup, or spaghetti will do very nicely. Hey, you can even put a TV dinner in the oven. I mean, it's still fixing dinner! Right?)

Let your parents know that you really love them by not only telling them that you do, but by doing something very special for them. When you do this, you will soon discover that you are on the way to raising some really neat parents!

Point Number Five: *Apologize When You've Done Something Wrong!* Don't be afraid to tell mom and dad that you're sorry when you have done something wrong. If you are sincere when you apologize, your parents will surely forgive you. I mean, if a friend of yours does something that you don't like and then later comes to you and apologizes, don't you accept his or her apology? Don't you also feel a lot closer to your friend after the air is cleared and whatever it is he or she did is forgotten? Sure you do. And it's the *same* with mom and dad. When you blow it and do something wrong, you just don't feel good until you tell them that you're sorry. And after you do this, not only do they feel better, but a dark heavy burden suddenly lifts off your shoulders and you can, once again, go about your work and play feeling good about yourself.

It takes courage to be able to apologize to anyone, even your parents. And what makes it even harder is, there is always going to be a Mister Macho or Gloria Valleygirl type who get their kicks making fun of others, calling anyone who apologizes to another person, especially to their parents - "wimps" or "buttheads." And you know why most people act this way? Simply because they don't have the courage or manners to say they're sorry when they do stupid things. You see, the problem is, they don't think they ever do stupid things. But they do! A lot! The real "wimp" or "butthead" is the person who's afraid to tell another person that he or she has done something wrong and then apologize. And, you know what? The more we apologize when we are wrong, the easier it becomes and the better liked we'll be by our friends and family. It's as simple as that.

It's not wrong to make a mistake, but it is wrong to make a mistake and then not apologize to the person or persons (classmates, teachers, best friends, or parents), we have wronged!

When you learn how to apologize to mom and dad, it will definitely help you along the way to reaching your goal of raising a couple of very understanding and loving parents. And, if you're being raised by a single parent, it will not only help him or her to better understand you, it will also make his or her day very worthwhile and a lot easier!

Point Number Six: A Very Important Point to Ponder: *Never do anything to betray the love or trust of your parents or cause them to question your honesty!* Let me repeat this: Never do anything to betray the love or trust of your parents or cause them to question your honesty! This is just about the most important thing you, as a young person, can do if you really want to help raise your parents in the best way possible!

Your most valuable and precious possession is your name and what it stands for. And a name to be valued and desired is a name that stands for honesty and trust! If you ever lose the value of your name, you will have lost something that will be very hard to replace...some say, it's almost impossible to replace a tarnished name or reputation.

Honesty and trust are without peer. There are very few other things in life that are as important as telling the truth no matter what the consequences, no matter what happens to us. There are times when we know if we tell what really happened or what it was that we did wrong, we will no doubt get into serious trouble with our parents, teachers, or even the law. Still, even when we realize what we've done is going to cause us to be disciplined and punished, we must always tell the truth! Easy to say, but difficult to do!

I realize that some, maybe even many, of your friends don't tell the truth. They lie to their teachers, friends, classmates, and parents so they might escape punishment, make themselves out to be something they're not, or simply get their own way. And they often cheat on exams or slander (lie about) those they once called their friends. But you know something? In the end, they will be the loser; they will be the ones who have difficulty holding on to a job, making a marriage work, being promoted on the job, or so many other parts of our lives that become more important as we grow older.

In school, if you expect to get a high grade on a test, you've got to give the correct answer to the teacher. Right? Well, it's no different if you expect to ever gain the respect and trust from your friends and parents. You've got to tell the truth, no matter what anyone else thinks or says. No matter what the consequence, you've got to give the correct (honest) answer!

God tells us, "You shall not give false testimony (you shall not lie) against your neighbor." (Exodus 20:16 NIV). A neighbor can be a friend, a teacher, a classmate, a boss, and/or a parent.

God also tells us we must always "do things in such a way that everyone can see that you're honest clear through" (Romans 12:17 Paraphrased). As an example: if you are going to be late coming home from school, call your mom or dad and let them know why you'll be late; where you are when you call; who you're with; what time you'll be home; and any other pertinent information that might ease their minds. Remember, your parents are concerned about you.

If you handle this properly, it probably *won't* be a "big deal". But if you blow it and your folks find out you were lying about why you were going to be late, it probably *will* be a "big deal!" But it shouldn't be. Not if you are honest and tell the truth.

Here's an example of a difficult situation you may experience some day (if you haven't already): you get a letter from some special person and your mom or dad asks if you'd mind if they read what your friend has to say. Instead of immediately demanding your rights to privacy, let them read it. If the letter contains something you're either embarrassed by or ashamed of, you probably have a problem in the making and it might help solve your problem if you share it with your parents then and not later.

Honesty and trust between children and their parents is a two-way street. If you trust your parents and you're honest with them, they'll trust and be honest with you also. If you're not honest with them, they'll still be honest with you; however, you will have seriously injured their trust in you. Parents are given responsibility over children because they're supposed to be mature and intelligent enough to help their kids handle all those difficult problems that come up from time to time. Honesty and trust play a very important part in how well parents are able to help their kids overcome their problems. Sometimes it depends on how open and trusting a child is as to whether or not a parent can help solve a problem.

Honesty and trust are two great treasures. Guard them with your life. If you do, you'll discover you're raising the kind of parents that will allow you to do the good things that are most important to you. Did you catch the word "good" right before the word "things"? Parents aren't going to allow their children to do some dumb thing that might harm them, nor should they.

When you learn to trust your parents, you'll be surprised how enjoyable your life, indeed, the lives of everyone in the family, will be. Doing all the things you do at home or away from the family in a way that mom and dad will always be able to put their complete confidence and trust in you will help you raise the kind of parents you will be very proud of!

Point Number Seven: *Don't Think of Yourself as Being Perfect!* As we begin this point, keep in mind, your parents aren't perfect either! Try never to become so upset at mom and dad's shortcomings that you fail to realize that you, too, have things you must overcome. Remember the Bible story about how we shouldn't worry about the "speck of wood" in the other person's eye, but rather, we should be very concerned about the "large plank or beam of timber" in our own eye? It's really no different with you and your folks, or anyone else. We all have some amount of "timber" caught in our eyes; we all have things we still need to overcome before we're able to judge the other person.

Whenever you see some of your parent's faults (shortcomings), remember, sometimes it's pretty difficult being a parent; in fact, sometimes it's pretty difficult just being an adult! As a young person living at home, you probably don't yet have the responsibility for raising a child. It's not up to you to provide the necessary clothes, food, shelter, and many other essentials children need in order to survive (let alone succeed!). Think about it: are you ready to take on the responsibility of raising and caring for a child the same age as you? Really?

Sometimes parents become extremely angry when they shouldn't. And when they become that angry, they often do or say things in the heat of the moment that may hurt the child they dearly love. This is definitely inappropriate and wrong! Parents should never harm their children no matter what the cause for their anger. Parents need to grow and mature, as both guardians and defenders of their children, just as children need to grow and mature into adulthood. It's one step at a time. And, it seems the staircase every parent has to climb is never ending. When we miss a step or two, we discover, sooner or later, that this may be the reason we have failed at whatever it was we were attempting to do. If we ever want to get it right, we have to go back and realize the importance and purpose of those steps we failed to take. This is what is called an absolute.

Maturity is very relevant and sometimes difficult to understand. One kid can be ready to take on the world when he or she is still in their teens, while another young adult in his or her twenties can barely get through the day without blowing it completely.

The point is, it's wrong when parents and their children are unwilling to listen to one another; unwilling to change. It is wrong for the child and it's wrong for the parent. We all have to do our part in overcoming and changing our ways if we are ever going to succeed as a family and as friends! So kids, don't be too hard on your parents when you think they've blown it. Stop what you're doing for a moment and try to understand why they might be so upset with their work, their studies, themselves, or even you. If they show signs of anger toward you for something you're not guilty of, something you haven't done (we're not talking about verbal or physical child abuse here), wait until they've settled down and then explain, in a calm and patient manner, how you feel about whatever it is that has been said or done to you. Sometimes you're the one, not necessarily your parents, who will have the patience during an emotional display of anger in the family. So use it wisely.

Finally, after you realize mom and dad have all kinds of emotional warts and character blemishes (faults and shortcomings that neither you nor they are very proud of), forgive whatever it is they may have done or said and move on with your life. It takes a forgiving child to rear happy, loving, and forgiving parents!

Point Number Eight: *Don't Be Afraid to Ask Mom and Dad for Advice!* The next time you have the opportunity, ask your parents for advice regarding anything that is especially important to you. By doing this, you will not only gain their trust and a deeper concern about you and whatever it is that may be troubling you, you will discover that your parents have something more than a glob of gray matter suspended inside a skull sitting on their shoulders. You may also discover that their experience, and the wisdom that comes from such experience, might just help you solve your problems. And by going to mom and dad for advice, the chance of you sharing a deeper and more sensitive and considerate relationship with your parents is very good.

When I was in my teens, a man whom I greatly respected gave me some wonderful advice one day. He told me, "Ride your success on the shoulders of giants!" In other words, let those who have succeeded in whatever it is you want to do in life, help you to achieve your goals and desires, your own, personal success.

Think for a moment. Do you realize that there are "giants"

who have already succeeded in their quest for success, right in the midst of your family? Mom and dad are the greatest "giants" you will ever know. Learn how to use their experience, their wisdom and knowledge, their maturity and talents as a basis for gaining a deeper understanding about what it is you wish to do in life; what it is you hope to accomplish.

Remember, your parents were also kids at one time in their lives. They played in the mud and had to have their noses wiped. And, as they grew and matured into adulthood, they experienced much of what you're experiencing today. So, do yourself a favor and listen to them when they give you advice. You'll be amazed at what you'll learn. Going to your parents for advice may, in the long term, save you a lot of heartache and misery, both now and into the future.

There is no one who loves or cares for you any more than your parents. No one! So why not give them a shot at trying to help you solve some of your problems before your problems grow any bigger and suddenly spin out of control? Your folks realize that solving these problems is very important to you; they also understand that those situations that often come our way that we refer to as "difficulties" are just that - difficult - and that they're real and need attention. And they need to be dealt with before they become major problems that can harm our lives.

Best of all, by asking mom's and dad's advice, you will be helping to rear happy and loving parents who, in turn, will be pleased and very proud of their kids!

Point Number Nine: *Take Mom and Dad into Your Confidence!* As hard as you think it might be to do, nevertheless, it's very important that you take your parents into your confidence. When you have problems, don't be afraid to tell your parents about them; let them know how you feel about whatever it is that's bothering you. You will find that by doing this, you will most likely resolve your problems with less difficulty and pain.

Talk to your parents like you would a friend. After all, you don't have any greater friend in all the world than your parents. Make it a point every day to treat your family, especially mom and dad, as you would your closest friend. And this means confiding in them about those things that are important to you; those things that frighten you, upset you, bother you, or even please you.

To really confide in your parents, you must first of all trust them. If your parents have passed the "honorable" test that we discussed a few pages back, then why not trust them to understand and help you with whatever it is that is bothering you? It doesn't matter if you tell them you're scared to go to school, you've stolen something from the cookie jar, or you hit Bobby Joe and got into trouble with the principal. Or, your problem may be you've done something really stupid like smoking a marijuana joint, snorting cocaine, or becoming pregnant (or getting a girl pregnant). Whatever your problem is, talk to your parents about it. And the sooner, the better!

Let's use a really big problem as our example: pregnancy! You're two months late and you think you might be pregnant. Who better to talk it over with than your folks? You think you'd rather talk about this with your girlfriends? Your (ugh) boyfriend? Your teachers? The old woman down the street? Not hardly. However, if these are the only people you can talk to, then it's better to get some advice than no advice at all. It's very important that the advice you get is quality advice. The question is whether or not the *quality* of the advice you're getting from those with whom you are discussing this problem is sound and morally correct? If not, talk to your parents!

Okay, okay, I can hear some of you beginning to yell, "Are you kiddin'?! You want me to tell my folks that I've done something as stupid as letting myself get pregnant?! You've got to be crazy!"

Well, I'm not crazy (or, for the most part, I don't think I am. Of course, the crazy person is always the last to know. Right?) Neither are your parents crazy. Sure, if you tell them something such as how you think you might be pregnant, you better believe it's going to upset them. Why wouldn't it? After all, you're their little girl (and you'll always be their little girl!). But just because they become upset, and maybe even say some things they don't want to say, doesn't mean that they won't help you handle your problem. It doesn't mean that the don't love you. Becoming pregnant, as an unmarried teen, is definitely wrong. But don't you realize your parents love you so much that after they settle down, they'll realize the magnitude of the situation and help you in any way they can?

"But what if they don't?", you ask. Once again, let me point to the fact that your mom or dad (or both) are reading this book (and hopefully other books regarding childrearing) so they can become better parents. By this demonstration of their love for you, you should realize that even though they may have certain fears and anxieties resulting from the overwhelming pressures and responsibilities that are part of what being a parent is all about; nevertheless, they want to help you grow and prosper any way they can.

If your parents are ever going to overcome these fears and anxieties, not only do they have to study about how to be a better parent, they have to apply this knowledge and deeper understanding in their daily lives. And you, as the main focus of their attention and the one person they would gladly give their very lives for, have the responsibility to help them achieve their desire to become a better parent by the way you act and behave. And one way to help them is for you to *not be fearful* of confiding in them. Give your parents a chance! Talk to them!

No matter what you do with your life, your parents will always love you. Sometimes we have a peculiar way of showing just how much we really love our kids, but, nevertheless, we do, and we always will!

If you really want to help raise mom and dad in a way that everyone in the family benefits, you must first of all, do your part. This means, no matter what your situation, no matter what your problem or difficulty, you must confide in mom and dad!

Point Number Ten: *Don't Be Afraid of Your Parents!* Don't be afraid to talk with them, work with them, joke with them, and play with them.

Whenever you talk with your folks and suddenly things

become a little tense, don't give up. In a gracious and polite manner, finish whatever it is you have to say. Whenever you work with mom or dad, finish what you have started...don't leave your work half done. When you joke and laugh with them, don't be afraid to be the object of the joke. Be able to take kidding from others in the same way you give it out. And, when you play with your parents, have a ball. Let yourself go and really enjoy the moment because one day you'll realize that precious moments like these aren't lasting, they end all too soon.

It takes a lot of work and effort to properly raise your parents, just as it takes a lot of work and effort for them to raise you. But the rewards when everything is said and done - after you grow into adulthood and realize how wonderful your parents are and that you had something to do with the fact that they are so wonderful - are tremendous!

"What are the rewards?" you ask. It would take an entire book to answer this question completely. So let me just say that they include how well you succeed in life - because of the way you were taught as a child; how well you do as a parent - because, when you were young, you learned how to properly help raise your parents; and how well you will do on the job - because you had the opportunity, as a kid, to help your parents around the house. Finally, the greatest reward you will receive, resulting from the way in which you helped raise your parents, will be the positive impact you will have on society as an adult. "Even a child is known by his actions, by whether his/her conduct is pure and right" (Proverbs 20:11 NIV).

Stop for a moment and consider the points we have just examined.
1- Encourage your parents often.
2- Don't be too strict with mom and dad.
3- Tell your parents "Thanks" at Least Once a Day.
4- Do something very Special for your parents.
5- Apologize when you've done something wrong!

6- *Never Do Anything* to *Betray* the *Love* and *Trust* of *Your Parents* or *Cause Them* to *Question Your Honesty!*

7- Don't think of yourself as being perfect.

8- Don't be afraid to ask mom and dad for advice.

9- Take mom and dad into your confidence.

10- Don't be afraid of your parents!

So ask yourself, how well have you applied these points in your daily life? What does each point of instruction really mean to you? And, after considering what you have just studied, do you think you might need to work on adjusting your attitude or gaining a little more character to do a better job in helping rear mom and dad?

All human beings have been created with a desire to have a great family relationship - the special love, trust and honor that happen between children and their parents. "Children's children are a crown to the aged, and parents are the pride of their children (Proverbs 17:6 NIV)." However, in order to achieve this magnificent family experience, we must <u>all</u> do our part to make it happen. It takes a lot of hard work and effort, but in the end it's worth it. Our children reap a reward; we parents reap a reward; and society, as a whole, reaps a reward. So, hang in there kids, and *never give up in your quest at helping to raise your parents!*

The
smallest
children
are
nearest
to
God,
as
the
smallest
planets
are
nearest
the
sun.
-Richter

CHAPTER NINETEEN

FOR THE PARENT
Some Final Thoughts

As we've continued our study regarding childrearing, we have addressed many of the problems facing our kids today. We have come to realize that parents who truly care for and love their children are concerned about their future and whether or not their children will succeed in life. And in more and more cities and towns across the United States, Asia and Europe, parents are not only concerned that their children will succeed, they are witnessing more and more children losing their lives because of drugs, suicide, gang killings, and disease, and this is causing them even greater concern.

Today, parents in their late twenties, thirties, and older cannot really identify with what their children are experiencing at school, the mall, on the street, or in homes where violence rules the night. It's difficult to relate to children having to cope with gang violence and murder; illegal drugs that obliterate the mind; herpes, VD, and a killer called AIDS that is destroying more and more young lives; fellow classmates carrying weapons and often using them, killing or maiming both teachers and students alike. It's difficult, especially when one hasn't grown up living in this type of environment.

How many parents do you suppose would be a little more than embarrassed or confused if they were to take the time to understand the music their children are listening to or what they are watching on programs such as MTV? When I was growing up, a friend staying overnight might sneak a copy of some "girlie" magazine into my bedroom. After making sure no one was around, we would look at the bare-breasted models and fantasize about what it would be like to be on a date with her. Today, children still fantasize, but instead of looking at bare-breasted models, they now look at models exposing every part of their bodies while often being photographed in lurid, suggestive sexual positions. The so-called "girlie" magazines today tempt young male minds to want to do more than just date the model.

Also, where my generation only had magazines exposing (exploiting) the female body, today we have male nudity magazines that are photographed just like the "girlie" magazines, only the idea is to "turn-on" the female reader. The question is, "turn-on to what?!" And it doesn't stop there. We have child pornography magazines, girl-to-girl, boy-to-boy magazines, magazines depicting every kind of sodomy, rape, and murder. And this obscenity and pornography is being published and sold as valid written material (some even call it educational) and protected under the First Amendment! Never mind, so the advocates of filth tell us, "It matters not the tremendous devastating effect this has on the minds of our children!" Never mind the fact that: "what goes into our minds, stays there." Really?! Remember, although it may be dormant, what goes into the minds of our children will be there for the rest of their lives! Is it any wonder crime is rising at such an alarming rate?!

A FEW MORE STATISTICS REGARDING OUR CHILDREN TODAY!

MORE AND MORE CHILDREN TODAY EXPERIENCE DRUG AND ALCOHOL RELATED ACCIDENTS, SUICIDE, HOMICIDE, AND DEATH!

MORE THAN ONE MILLION KIDS RUN AWAY FROM HOME EVERY YEAR! THIS AMOUNTS TO 1 OUT OF EVERY 240 PEOPLE LIVING IN THE UNITED STATES!

MORE THAN ONE MILLION UNWED TEENAGE GIRLS GET PREGNANT EVERY YEAR! YOUNGER GIRLS (SOME AS YOUNG AS

ELEVEN AND TWELVE) WHO BECOME PREGNANT IS ON THE
RISE! MORE AND MORE TEENAGE GIRLS ARE HAVING
ABORTIONS EVERY YEAR!

600,000 TEENS ATTEMPT SUICIDE EVERY YEAR. 5,000 TO 6,000
SUCCEED!

BOYS AND GIRLS WHO ARE NOT YET TEENAGERS FEEL PEER
PRESSURE TO DRINK ALCOHOL AND USE DRUGS SUCH AS
HEROIN AND CRACK!

VIOLENT GANG CRIMES ARE RISING, AS IS GANG MEMBERSHIP!

MORE AND MORE CHILDREN ARE SUFFERING FROM AIDS, VD,
HUNGER, AND HOMELESSNESS!

TEENAGE MURDER OF PARENTS, TEACHERS, CLASSMATES, AND
CO-WORKERS IS RISING EVERY YEAR!

So, what are we parents to do if we are to ever experience
"The Joy of Raising Our Kids in the 21st Century?"

During the past several years, we have witnessed an increase,
indeed, a tremendous acceleration, in crimes of every type committed
by our youth. We see a more militant group of kids attempting to tear
down the fabric of our society while another group of positive, morally
well-adjusted kids work to build it up. Why? Why do some kids want
to destroy their lives and the lives of others, while other kids (some
from broken homes and poor families) want to make the system work
and succeed for themselves and their society? It all has to do with the
way children are reared. Why will one little boy say it was wrong for
his neighbors to set a building on fire while another little boy thinks
it's no "big deal". Or why does a teenage girl tell a reporter it was
wrong for her friends to physically beat up her classmate to the point
where she may lose an eye or possibly even die while others couldn't
care less? It has everything to do with the way in which children are
brought up by their parents.

305

It has been said that if one wants to truly destroy a nation, all he has to do is destroy the family unit. But, how does one go about destroying the family unit? By first destroying the minds of parents which, in turn, will destroy the minds of their children. An example might be how, during the past couple of decades, our society has ridiculed and put down the sanctity of marriage and motherhood; i.e., a woman as mother, guardian, and wife in the home. It seems that during the 1960's, while we were busy doing away with certain values and principles we had been raised with - I mean, after all, we had wisdom and perception that our parents lacked...we had gone to college! - we sought greater truth and a deeper enlightenment and many of the values and principles our forefathers and parents had given us no longer seemed relevant or of value. In our quest for greater "wisdom and truth," we exchanged what our parents had taught us for modern man-made theories and Eastern philosophies and we forgot that "the hand (mother) that rocks (guides and directs) the cradle (both child and family) rules the world!" This saying is as true today as it was when the first person uttered those words centuries ago!

When children are born, their minds are like a blank sheet of paper. There are certain genetic characteristics comprising some of the elements which form the basis for the brain. But, the mind is relatively uninhabited and void of intellect, vision, reason, and education. As each child grows older, all kinds of things will be written on that sheet of paper (mind). Some will be good, some not-so-good. The problem is, there is no eraser! What goes on that sheet of paper, stays on, like it or not.

Children are learning all of the time. Whether or not we, as parents, are making a concerted effort to teach our kids is not the point. They are acquiring knowledge from every available source; they are being taught by someone, somewhere, all the time. So, if we care about the quality and character of what goes into the minds of our kids, it's up to us to guide and direct their education, environment, and experience.

Two of the most important things in the lives of our children is the music they *hear* and what they *see* on TV or at the movies. Their "pop" culture, their "own thing," is what they seem to value most. On an average, kids watch television more than seven hours a day and listen to music more than ten hours a day! Some say today's generation of young people are music addicts! (I would also include films and electronic games).

The problem is, when a young person drives up next to you at a stop sign and his or her radio or tape deck is so loud that their car convulses in time to the rhythm of the music, is it possible that they can really be thinking about anything constructive? It might not be so bad if they only listened to music in their cars (although it couldn't be worse for their hearing, especially in later years!) but, kids listen to music most of the time. They listen at home, on head sets at school, and at social events with friends. And usually their music is very loud!

Music captures a person's mind to the point where, while listening, they don't want to think about anything else. If they do, they think only about what they are hearing in the lyrics of the song. And here comes the rub. Parents, take a moment and listen to some of the lyrics your children are listening to in their music! Do you realize there are some performers who sing about, or rap to music that explain how good it feels to "kill a cop," rape a woman (in graphic detail), rob a bank, mug someone, shoot heroin, or "stomp" a parent. Did you know that lyrics to songs your kids listen to state in gutter, street language such notions as "the Jews are wicked and we can prove this," "F— the Police," "he's someone who is as happy as a faggot in jail," "Niggers get outta my way, don't wanna buy none of your gold chains today," and so many other lyrics to songs that promote bigotry, sexual perversion, street crime, rebellion, and violence. Do you think this doesn't have an effect on a young, fertile mind? Of course it does! Think about how many songs you know the lyrics to that you never made a conscious effort to learn. When you hear the music, you can sing the lyrics. What goes into the mind, stays there!

What about the horror films, violent movies, and provocative television sitcoms we see advertised today? If we ask ourselves the question, "do these movies and TV shows support strong family values, positive attitudes, and high moral character?" Most of the time our answer would be a resounding, "no!" Because much of what we see on the screen, at a theater or in the home, attempts to destroy what we deem to be important - to be of value - simply for the sake of our entertainment and someone else making a buck.

How many films have you watched lately that depict fornication and adultery as being something which is okay to do? How many movies have you gone to that picture a homosexual relationship as being something of value and an acceptable alternative life-style? How many prime time television shows use illicit sex as the main theme of the story? How many movies resort to graphic violent acts and gore (more realistic today than ever before) simply to bring a young audience into the theater? If you look at the movie listings in your Sunday paper, you'll be amazed at the number of 'R' rated movies as compared to "G" and "PG".

For every CD we listen to and every television show or movie we see, someone has scored the music, performed or acted the part, and written the dialogue or lyrics. And when asked why they have written, performed, or produced such baneful, mindless, offensive, and vulgar *divertissement*, more often than not, they will say that they are only providing the audience what it wants to see or hear. Really? If this is true, then we, as a nation and people, are in serious trouble! That is unless we begin to do something about it today!

Someone is teaching your kid whatever it is they (the person teaching) personally believes to be of value, (either intellectual, educational, and/or financial). It can be a teacher in school, a musician/song writer, an actor on stage or in the movies, a screenwriter, a novelist, a family member, a politician, a social worker, a friend, a foe, or even his or her own parents. And what we see our children's minds being exposed to is not necessarily intellectually or academically proper, nor is it always morally right. Much of what our kids see on TV and at the movies or listen to on tapes, CD's, and radio can only be best described as garbage for the mind. Is it any wonder then that our children are misbehaving the way they are? As a parent, ask yourself, "where is *my* responsibility in all of this? What can I do to help guide, direct, and protect my kid from such amoral and immoral influences?"

Awhile back an author wrote that "the connection of youthful ignorance and pop music bigotry may not be readily apparent, but both flow naturally from a culture which is suffering from a severe shortage of grown ups (parents)." What we are seeing today is a society made up of extremely selfish people, including parents, and this is reflected all too often in the actions and character of our children.

Practically every talk show on television, childcaring book written during the past several years, sermons given on Sunday mornings, lectures and seminars by well known childrearing experts, and/or literature handed out by social organizations and well-intended "do-gooders" send out the message to parents that if we are ever to raise children to become normal, well adjusted adults, we must "loosen up," "chill out," "don't be square." No matter what our children do, including using foul language, experimenting with drugs, engaging in premarital sex, or having an abortion, we must above all else "be tolerant."

We are told over and over it's unwise for us to be like those stiff, uptight parents of the fifties and long ago...*our* parents! Rather, we are to be loose, non-caring, and cool. By no means are we ever to discipline, admonish, or punish our children. After all, to do so is very uncivilized. So, we listen and do what the experts tell us to do. And the result?

The result from our being so "civilized" is we have replaced proper discipline and punishment with physical, verbal, and mental child abuse; our children are so uneducated that many cannot find major countries on a map nor can they read, write, spell, or complete difficult math problems. Many young people seem only to find enjoyment by going to movies, playing an electronic video game, listening to a new CD recording by the latest singer to come along; walking the mall scoping out the action; or wearing some hyped-up style of clothing as an act of rebellion. And all of this is only going to be pleasure for a moment. Soon it will evaporate like a mist at midday.

If you still believe that what a child sees or hears doesn't affect his or her mind, perhaps you should talk with the parents of a six-year boy who, after watching wrestling on TV, decided to throw his baby sister to the floor with a body-slam. It killed her. Talk to the parents of a young man in Montana, who, after reading a particular passage in a recent horror book written by a very successful and well-known author, decided, like the character in the novel, to go to school and kill his teacher. He did, she died, and now he is in prison for the rest of his life! Or, talk to the parents of a five year old boy who burned down their house after watching a couple of cartoon characters on TV do the same thing. And, what about the parents? Not a day goes by that their minds and emotions aren't adversely affected because of what their children have done. What a tragedy!

So, let's stop for a moment and ask ourselves, "As parents, what's our part in how our children behave or misbehave? What can we do about it?"

When we see or read about the large number of parents who marry and then divorce five or six times while trying to raise children from each marriage, is it any wonder why so many kids are mixed up, out of control, and doing terrible things against themselves and society? It's sad to realize that some parents regard their children as unnecessary baggage...having little or no value. Why even have children if we aren't going to take care of them, nurture them, and love them?!

A story comes to mind which a close friend of mine witnessed the other day that might help illustrate just how poorly some of us are handling it as parents.

It seems a little boy had fallen and hurt himself just before the family was going to have lunch. The mother had arranged to meet her husband (with all four of their children) during his lunch break. However, before they could sit down and eat, the little boy had fallen and hurt himself.

They went to the nearest emergency room and while the mother was trying to fill out the forms and take care of the payment for the doctor's services, she asked her husband to help their youngest daughter put on her coat.

After sarcastically asking his wife why she didn't do it, he then scolded his older daughter (maybe three or four years of age) for not being able to help put the coat on her younger sister. When he finally decided to help his little girl with her coat, he did it in such a way that he hurt her, making her cry. Apparently, he was so angry because he had missed his meal, he lost all patience and understanding and the entire family suffered because of it.

Instead of thinking about how his wife must have felt under such trying circumstances or how his two little girls must have been confused and upset by all the commotion, the father regarded his own self-interest as being far more important than those of anyone else...including his family. Apparently, the father wasn't overly concerned that his little boy might have had a brain concussion or that having stitches sown into his head wasn't any fun and very painful. And that this caused his son to cry which made both of his little girls cry. Nope, ol' dad was totally self-absorbed! The sad thing is, we see this type of self-absorption, lack of patience, and waxing cold happening more and more every day by parents toward their children.

Have you ever considered how much of a real miracle your child (or child to be) really is? Believe it or not, we all began as a dot too small for the naked eye to see. In that little dot was a blueprint for everything about us - every feature regarding the genetic makeup of our very lives. This little dot (sperm to the fertilized egg) determined whether or not we would have male pattern baldness, how big our ears would be, how long our nose would extend in front of our face, the color of our hair, the color of our eyes, if we would have freckles and fair skin or dark skin and curly hair, how tall we would be...how we would look! All this was mapped out in a tiny dot smaller than the head of a pin!

By the time we reach adulthood, there is somewhere in the neighborhood of thirty trillion cells constituting the complicated chemical network composing the structure for our physical human bodies. We go from a small fertilized egg inside a womb to a full grown adult with over thirty trillion cells going every direction, while at the same time maintaining order both mentally and physically. Some miracle! And yet, even with the miracle of our physical growth, we still must acquire everything we learn...everything that goes into our minds that results in our ability to reason, think, create, inspire, and teach!

We are not born with the basic instincts that animals possess. Little babies don't immediately stand up and shout, "Where's the milk? I'm hungry!" If they're not directed to their mother's breast soon after birth or given a bottle at certain intervals, they would starve and eventually die. And look how long it takes for a toddler to begin learning how to walk...it takes a while, and this experience includes a lot of bumps and bruises along the way. We must learn how to speak the language of those who teach us. We must learn how to think, to reason, and to create. And as we grow older, we begin to learn how to love and also how to hate. We learn how to build and how to destroy. We learn how to laugh and how to be angry. Yet, because we have been given such a magnificent physical brain and creative mind, we can do all this and more. "For you have formed my inward parts; You have covered me in my mother's womb. I will praise You, for *I am fearfully and wonderfully made;* Marvelous are Your works, And that my soul knows very well." (Psalm 139:13-14 NIV).

Still, we often take our children for granted. It seems there are those who reason that simply because they had sex with someone of the opposite gender, and nine months later a child is born, there's not a whole lot more they are supposed to do (some men especially think this way). They've done their part or made their mistake, so now, bringing up the kid is up to their spouse, girl friend, boy friend, lover, family, or society. Someone else will just have to take care of it. Well, as any parent reading this book knows, there's a whole lot more to bringing up a child than this!

It's a shame that in our enlightened society so many parents turn over the responsibility of raising their children to some other person or agency. They allow people they don't even know to entertain and teach them. They allow television, music, and films to rear them. Then as time goes by and things in the home begin to worsen, they wonder why their kids become obstinate, hardheaded, bad-tempered, unable to communicate, nasty, rebellious, and turned off only to discover, often after it's too late, that their youngsters have been educated and influenced by those who have little or no real concern for them; by overworked teachers, hired sitters, rebellious peers, daycare centers, and electronic devices. And because the parents neglected to make time for their kids, helping to teach them right from wrong and good from evil, the breakdown of their family and the poor training of their children was completed with their full knowledge and consent! They have no one to blame but themselves!

Let's take a moment to address the following six basic points regarding how parents need to have a deeper understanding about their children if they are ever to succeed in the responsibility of properly rearing them. And let's also look at how children react to their parents:

(1) *CHILDREN EMULATE THEIR PARENTS.* For the most part, the way we live our lives is the way our children will also live their lives. If we love and care for others, chances are our children will also love and care for others. If we cheat and steal, chances are our kids will do like wise. If we smoke, drink, or use illegal drugs as social entertainment, probably so will they. Our children emulate what we say and how we say it; what we do and how we do it! If we don't show respect toward others, then how can we expect our children to respect others? If we constantly find fault, they will also constantly find fault.

A friend told me the following story that might help to illustrate just how much our children emulate us: "When I was younger, I was working on the family car with my dad when my wrench slipped. Well, I thought this was a good time to impress him with something I had learned from him. So I let out with a profanity that he often said whenever he was angry or irritated.

"He wasn't amused at all by my outburst. In fact, his face got pale as he just stood there speechless. He didn't say a word, nor did he have to. How he felt was written all over his face. And of course what he felt was disappointment in me for having said what I said and disappointment in himself for having unconsciously taught me that particular word and its meaning.

"Have you ever noticed a man out with his small son looking at used cars? If you watch for awhile, when the father kicks the tires, so will the son; when the father leans closer to check the paint, so will the son. I had heard my dad say that profane word more than once. I truly admired him; I thought using a word like that meant I was grown up; sort of a macho-maturity thing. So, when I said what I said, I thought my dad would be pleased. But, he wasn't!

"Little children look at us, their parents, as though we are god. In their minds we are everything there is, large or small, good or bad. We provide their food, clothes, entertainment, bath time, stool training. We tell them stories and tuck them in at night. We are god to them! Therefore, one of the most powerful aspects of childrearing is the example we set for our kids!

"When I was a young man beginning to drive, one day I needed to go somewhere, so I asked my dad for the keys to the family car. "Hey, ol' Man," I said, "can I have the keys to the car?"

"I will never forget how my dad looked at me that morning after hearing what I had just said to him, and the way I had said it. I could tell I had really hurt him. He gave me the keys to the car, and I never said the words, "ol' Man" to him again. At that time, saying something like "Dig ya, Daddy'O," "Hey, Pops," or Ol' Man" was supposed to be cool, the thing to say. But I sure discovered that it wasn't the thing to say because it didn't show proper respect for my father.

"A few years ago, the day my dad died, I was talking to him between his bouts of semiconsciousness. I had taken my mom to the nursing home and I had used his car. When he awoke, I held up the keys to the car for him to see and said, "Dad. I've got the keys to your car." Then I told him, "I used your car this morning when I brought mom up to see you. And, I drove just like you taught me. I took real good care of it just like you always wanted me to." When he looked at the keys, I knew he was pleased. You see, no matter how old we get, we always want to please our parents; the parents whose example we want to follow".

Why is it children want to emulate their parents so? Even when parents abuse their kids, they still want to emulate them. This might help to explain why they often grow up abusive of their own children - we simply emulate our parents for good or bad.

If we want our children to be good loyal workers at whatever it is they set out to do, we must show them just what a good loyal worker is by our actions and deeds, not simply by what we say. If we want our kids to speak well and use proper English, without profanities and vulgarities spicing up their speech, we must take care in the way we speak and the words we use. If we want our children to control their tempers and emotions, we must also learn to control our tempers and emotions. If we take care of our things, they will take care of their things.

A story that proves this goes something like this: A little boy went for a drive with his dad one Sunday afternoon and when they got home, his mother asked him, "How was the drive?"

"It was pretty interesting," came his reply.

"What do you mean it was interesting?"

"Well, we met some really interesting people."

"You did?" By now his mother wanted to know more about who he and his father had met during their drive. "Like, who?" She asked.

"Well, we met two dumbbells, one S.O.B., three jackasses and a bastard on a bicycle!" Her smiling son replied. "Yep. We met some pretty interesting people!"

We are a mirror image to our offspring and what we do, they

will do; what we say, they will say.

Children emulating their parents was no different during the time of Jesus Christ. He tells us, "Most assuredly, I say to you, the Son can do nothing of Himself, but what He sees the Father do; for whatever He does, the Son also does in like manner." (John 5:19 NKJV). Emulating our parents is something we seem born to do. It's part of our design, our character, our creation.

If you don't have patience, don't expect your kids to have patience. If you aren't concerned with what they are doing at school or at play, then in the same way, don't expect them to be concerned for their children when they are older. However, just the opposite is also true. If you show love toward your spouse, they will show a similar love toward the one they marry. If you listen to what your children have to say, they will take more time to listen to their children. Really, it's just that simple!

Here's what Dorothy Law Nolte writes.

Children Learn What They Live
By Dorothy Law Nolte

If children live with criticism, in time, they learn to condemn. (If a parent constantly tells a child he or she is worthless; that they don't use their head for anything other than a hat rack; or, they are dumb and stupid and not to be trusted, they will very likely grow up with an attitude problem they will have to fight for the rest of their lives).

If children live with hostility, they soon learn how to fight. (Some kids seem to always be in trouble for fighting simply because they grew up in a hostile environment).

If children live with ridicule, they'll become shy. (Some children have been put down by their parents so often they will grow up to be shy and backward for the rest of their lives. When we are told over and over we can't do something, we soon discover that we can't do it. Over time, constant ridicule will eventually destroy all confidence and self-esteem (worth). However, when children are taught by being encouraged and

316

praised, the likelihood is that they will achieve success in whatever it is they set out to do. If parents see something in their children they appreciate, they should tell them. This is one way to help our kids grow and overcome instead of wilting and fading away into shyness and self doubt.

If children live with shame, chances are they will carry a guilt complex all the days of their lives.

If children live with tolerance, they are likely to show patience and forgiveness.

If children live with courage, they will most likely develop confidence.

When children live with encouragement, they learn to appreciate.

If children live with forgiveness, they learn justice.

If children live with approval, they soon learn to like themselves.

If children live with acceptance and friendship, they learn to find love in the world.

Children are extremely observant! They watch every move their parents make and then they emulate them. An example might be the number of children who grow up attending church with their parents only to stop once they leave home. Why? Probably because they have also seen the hypocrisy committed by their parents on every other day of the week after attending church. Children see not only what we want them to see, they also see many of the things about us we don't want them to see. Our children grow up emulating us whether we want them to or not. So it behooves us to make sure we set the kind of example we want our kids to follow.

(2) *LOVE MUST BE PRACTICED AND IT MUST ALSO BE VERBALIZED!* How will our children ever know how much we love them unless we tell them? When we take care of them and provide their needs, and when we go with them to church, the movies, or a ball game, we show them, by our deeds, that we love them. But, while we're doing all these physical things which demonstrate our abiding love and parental care, we must also verbalize the feelings and love we have for our kids. They need to hear it!

Conversely, words, short of action, are worthless. If we tell our kids how much we love them and then we don't follow through with actions supporting our words, we might as well have kept quiet. What we say just doesn't mean as much if we don't also show our love by our deeds.

What exactly is love? We know that love is "outgoing," away from the self, but to find out what love really is, let's go to the Bible and see just what this remarkable instruction manual has to say about this subject. "...If I have faith that can move mountains, but have not love, I am nothing. If I give all I possess to the poor and surrender my body to the flames, but have not love, I gain nothing. Love is patient, love is kind. It does not envy, it does not boast, it is not proud. It is not rude, it is not self-seeking, it is not easily angered, it keeps no record of wrongs. Love does not delight in evil but rejoices in the truth. It always protects, always trusts, always hopes, always perseveres. Love never fails. But where there are prophecies, they will cease; where there are tongues, they will be stilled; where there is knowledge, it will pass away. For we know in part and we prophesy in part, but when perfection comes, the imperfect disappears. When I was a child, I talked like a child, I thought like a child, I reasoned like a child. When I became a man (woman), I put childish ways behind me. Now we see a poor reflection in a mirror; then we shall see face to face. Now I know in part; then I shall know fully, even as I am fully known. And now these three remain: faith, hope and love. But the greatest of these is love!" (I Corinthians 13:2-13 NIV).

How do we show this type of love to our children? We spend quality time with them: we take them to the park, we fly a kite together, we run and play with them, we share our hopes and dreams together, we talk about those things that interest them. We're there when they need us; we don't fail them. We protect them. We don't seek to always have our own way, but rather, we let our children do those things which are safe, educational, and fun. We help our kids learn how to trust us, and the way we do this is by giving them our unconditional love!

Children need to experience unconditional love! We parents

cannot condition the love for our children based simply on their good behavior. If we did that, how would we ever really be able to love our kids? "Junior, I don't love you right now because you just did something bad." It just doesn't work that way. We must love our children all the time, when they are good as well as when they do something wrong.

Wrong behavior has to be dealt with. And it has to be dealt with in a way where parents are able to help their kids learn how to do what is right even if it means having to punish and discipline them. However, the important thing is that we parents, by our *actions*, *show* our kids that we have unconditional love for them, and, by our *words*, we constantly re-enforce our love for them by *telling* them how much we truly love them!

When a child does a chore such as raking the leaves, what's wrong with telling him or her, "I realize raking the leaves is your responsibility; however, I really appreciate you doing it. It certainly helps us all get our chores over with more quickly. And, afterward, maybe you and I'll run down and grab a hamburger and coke. My treat. Okay?" Words and action!

We need to teach our children what love is. They really don't know what the word means. After all, they didn't come out of the womb with an understanding of what love is or how it applies to their lives. Love is something that must be taught and who better to teach it than their parents!

Take a moment and ask yourself, "When I look at my children, do I see a gift from God? Do I see a physical bundle of love all nicely put together...ready to begin walking life's path? Do I realize my kids are not really mine, that they belong to God? Can I accept the challenge I've been given regarding my responsibility in helping to nurture and train them, even though it's only for a very short period of time? Have I come to the realization that it's my responsibility to prepare my children for adulthood so they can succeed and prosper in life? This is really what parenthood is all about. And the only way we will ever succeed as a parent is by showing our kids how much we love them by our actions and words!

(3) *CHILDREN NEED TO BE ENCOURAGED TO USE THE TALENTS THEY HAVE BEEN GIVEN.* We must never put our children down, but rather, always pick them up and guide them toward success by helping them use their talents and abilities. We want to encourage our kids to do the best with what they've been given, to use their intelligence and their minds while learning how to control and manage their emotions and feelings.

Even if our children don't always win, we parents must encourage them to finish the race. No matter what any coach might tell you, winning is not as important as finishing what we set out to do. And none of us, parents and children alike, can win, or finish a race, without the help from others...we need someone to splash cold water on us when we begin to fall behind; someone to yell, "Get going," when we start to let down; or someone to tell us, "You're doing fine," when we sense anxiety attacking or insecurity beginning to influence our minds. We need that special someone to say, "I love you," when we feel alone and depressed. We need it and so do our kids!

(4) *CHILDREN NEED TO BE TAUGHT ABOUT PROPER HYGIENE, EXERCISE, AND GOOD EATING HABITS.* This is a hard subject to teach. Yet without proper hygiene, how can children ever protect themselves (and others) from disease? Proper hygiene is also important to children because improper hygiene repels the opposite sex. Girls and boys aren't attracted to someone who doesn't take care of his or her body and skin. Junior may have eyes for Betty Lou, but if he smells bad or doesn't brush his teeth or comb his hair, he can forget ever going out with the girl of his dreams.

The word "Hygiene" means "the science of health and its maintenance or a system of sound principles for the preservation of health and prevention of disease, and sanitary practices and cleanliness (D. Webster)." Here we see that when we teach our kids about hygiene, we are helping them to discover sound, basic principles which will, in turn, encourage them to preserve their health while preventing disease. And just as important, a child who understands good hygiene practices will keep his or her body and surrounding environment clean and well-groomed, thus avoiding many diseases that are caused by filthy and unsanitary conditions.

Children who have not been taught proper care of their bodies often become sick and disease-ridden, and this can greatly affect their lives.

Proper nutrition is also very important for young children's growth - both physically and mentally. Diet and exercise will help bolster a child's ability to think, play, perform, and succeed.

When we monitor what our kids eat and how much exercise they get, we help them on their way to a much healthier and more enjoyable life-style, a life-style that will remain with them for the rest of their lives.

So many young people *eat the wrong foods* today. A hamburger every so often is not going to do a lot of harm (as long as it's properly cooked). But eating one every day, or several times a week, will eventually do harm. On top of eating the hamburger, most kids usually want french fries, soda pop, and a sweet desert. They have an insatiable appetite for all the wrong things: sugar, salt, chocolate, candy, soda pop, and ice cream. Put this all together and what have you got? A recipes for physical breakdown! If not now, certainly later!

Do you realize that the problem with our children growing fat and lazy is really our fault and not theirs? We allow our kids to play electronic games instead of making them go outside and play with their friends. We let them eat foods that lack nourishment instead of making them eat wholesome, nutritious grains, and fiber. Also, do you realize physical education is no longer being taught in many schools? Courses regarding hygiene and nutrition are all but extinct. Kids no longer walk or ride their bikes to school - they want their parents to drive them even if they live only a few blocks away! Also, do you realize television has become the "electronic opiate" of the younger crowd? That the family dinner table no longer exists? And who's at fault? Only the parents!

A recent study found that children weighed an average of 11.4 pounds more in 1988 than they did in 1973. Listen to yourself as you read the following: "We're churning out unhealthy kids, who may tragically become unhealthy adults," writes Kenneth Cooper, M.D., M.P.H., *Prevention* advisor and president of Cooper Aerobics Center, and author of *Kid Fitness* (Bantam Books, 1991). "We're already finding higher blood pressure and premature evidence of coronary heart disease among the young!"

If our schools no longer teach our kids about proper health, fitness, hygiene, exercise, and eating right, who will? It's up to us parents to do what is right for our kids. All we need to do is look down the road a few years at what will more than likely be the result of letting our children slide into poor hygiene, exercise, and eating practices - due to our lack of guidance and direction - to see just how important it is that we do something now...beginning today!

(Note: a very good article to read regarding the importance of raising healthy children can be found in the October, 1992, *Prevention Magazine*, page 73, entitled, *"Build A "Healthy Child,"* written as a Special Report).

(5) *CHILDREN NEED TO BE TAUGHT TO CONTROL THEIR EMOTIONS AND TO BE THANKFUL.* Two of the more serious problems our children face today is learning how to control their emotions and being thankful for what they have. When we look at how little control our kids have over their own lives, especially when it pertains to their feelings and emotions, and how little respect and appreciation they show toward those who provide for them, at home and at school, we can only conclude that these are two areas where parents have really dropped the ball!

When children strike out at other children to hurt them, it's usually because they're not in control of their emotions. They allow their anger, pride, envy, insecurity, jealously, and/or bitterness to dictate what they do and how they do it. And the results can at times be disastrous!

322

It takes time and effort to properly teach a child how to maintain control of his or her emotions. It also takes time and effort to teach a child how to be thankful and appreciative. And certainly one of the best ways to teach these important principles (if not the best way) is by the example we set as parents.

If mom and dad are out of control, Junior and Susie probably are too. Maybe they're not out of control in the same way their folks are, but more than likely they will err in judgment and do or say something wrong before too long. Likewise, if mom and dad don't appreciate what they have or what someone may have given them, don't expect Junior or Susie to be all that thankful...it just doesn't work that way. Our kids react to their environment. If their environment is negative, their attitude will usually be more negative than if they live in a positive environment.

We can't tell our kids to appreciate something when, on the other hand, we cuss, ridicule, and put down someone who failed to do something for us exactly the way we wanted it done. Nor can we expect our kids to maintain control of their emotions when we yell and scream at others in our own family, our friends and neighbors, or at some guy driving too close to our rear bumper. How we appreciate others will determine how well our kids appreciate others. How we control our own emotions will greatly influence how well our children control their emotions. And how well they succeed in life!

(6) *CHILDREN NEED TO BE TAUGHT HOW TO RESPECT OTHERS.* We need to teach our children that just because someone wears clothes we think are not stylish; just because another person speaks with a broken dialect and is difficult to understand; just because another person's skin is a different color; just because a neighbor goes to a different church or synagogue; just because a person is old; and just because someone walks with a cane, is blind, has no arms, or may be ill with cancer, heart disease, or AIDS, doesn't mean that they have a lesser value to society, nor does it mean that we have a greater value.

More and more children seem to have less respect for others

today than when we were young. And the sad thing is they also have such little respect for themselves. It's difficult to have respect for someone else when we don't really respect ourselves. Respect is something that has to be taught, and it has to be taught when a child is young.

How can children learn respect for others (or themselves) if parents constantly tell them that they're better (worth more to society) than others who are less fortunate? How will a young daughter or son ever learn to respect value in others if parents overindulge them by providing everything their hearts desire? The answer is, they won't. It just doesn't work that way!

Certainly, parents want their children to have a good life, a better life than they had. But, simply giving a child whatever material objects he or she wants is not the answer. These are only physical things that will soon rot or become discarded whenever something newer and better is introduced to the marketplace. Having a good life doesn't necessarily mean having a lot of material things. Material things are nice to own, but usually they're not all that important. Essentials such as food, shelter, and clothing are important. Having the good life does mean possessing the ability, talent, and character to provide sound direction, tender care, great love, and deep respect both for oneself and others. However, having the good life is not physical, it's spiritual!

Those who experience the wealth of friends, the joy of accomplishment, the love of family, aren't all rich and famous. Most, by far, don't even come close to being rich or famous! The Scout helping an old woman across the street, the doctor attending to starving children in Africa and other parts of the world, the recovering alcoholic working with those who have yet to overcome the disease, the fireman risking his life to save a crippled child in a burning building, the policeman who protects a neighborhood while taking abuse from its citizens and the press, the nurse working with AIDS patients in a hospice, the young man or woman serving his or her country by enlisting in the armed forces - these are the ones who, by giving of themselves, tend to experience the good life.

324

Certainly, no one lives life without facing problems and negative situations that must be overcome on a daily basis. However, when we do those things that help our fellowman, when we give of ourselves to society or when we take a stand for what we believe in (popular or not), we gain self respect which results in our having respect for others. Having the latest electronic gadget, expensive luxury car, the biggest house on the block, or a bank account too large to count, really means nothing when all is said and done. The man who ends up with all the toys really doesn't win!

After we die (and remember we take nothing with us, only our good name), and, later, when our friends, neighbors, co-workers, and family begin to think about us, what is it we really hope they'll remember? Do we want them to remember how successful we were financially or how many cars we owned? Do we want them to recall the number of times we divorced and how it adversely affected our children? Do we hope they'll remember how we rose to such great heights within the company we helped to create? Or, do we want them to remember us for what we gave to society, what we did to help others, how we overcame our own demons of adversity, and, especially, how we raised our kids?

As our children grow into adulthood, shouldn't we be concerned about how well they will do as adult human beings, how much they will add to their society, how much they will give back to their fellowmen, how kind and considerate they will be toward others, how good a parent they will be and how much love they will provide their families? If this is what really concerns us, as parents, we need to begin training and teaching our kids now. If we fail to do so, chances are they will fail to succeed in all of the above!

TWELVE WAYS
TO RAISE A CHILD
TO BE A
DELINQUENT!:

1- Begin in infancy to give a child everything he or she wants so they will grow up believing the world owes them a living.

2- When Junior uses naughty words, laugh at him. This will make him think he's cute in your eyes, and later he'll use words that will probably blow the top of your head off.

3- Never give him any spiritual training. Let him wait until he is older so that he can decide for himself if there is a God or not.

4- Avoid the use of the words "wrong" and "no." After all, you don't want Junior to develop a guilt complex or suffer unduly. Then later, when he's arrested for stealing a car, he can claim that it's all the fault of his parents and society, and that he is simply being persecuted by those who "just don't understand." (A few years ago, a young boy found a wallet with a thousand dollars in it and he turned it in to the authorities. His teacher refused to praise him because she believed that if she did, it would be as though she were telling him that what he had done was right. Her comment was "it's only for the child to decide if what he did was right or not.")

5- Pick up everything your kids leave lying around (books, shoes, clothes) so that later in life, they'll have the experience to throw all responsibility on others.

6- Let them read whatever they want to read, listen to whatever music they want to hear and watch whatever TV show or film they desire to see. Make no attempt to direct or alter their viewing and listening habits. Let whatever garbage they want entering their brain to have free access to their minds. After all, they are certainly wise enough, even in their youth, to make such monumental decisions. Aren't they?

7- Make sure you quarrel and fight with your spouse frequently in the presence of your children. This way they won't be too shocked when the home is finally destroyed and the family is broken up.

8- Give Junior and Susie all the spending money they

want and never let them earn it for themselves. After all, just because you had things tough as a child, why should they?

9- Satisfy their every craving for food, drink and comfort and see that every essential desire is gratified because denial may lead to harmful frustration and maybe even (gasp!) abnormality!

10- Take their part against neighbors, teachers, policemen, and anyone else who may tell you that your children have done something wrong. After all, they are all prejudiced against your kids...aren't they?

11- When your kids get into trouble simply apologize for them by saying, "I never could do anything with them. I mean, he's just like his father or she's just like her mother!" That way you let yourself off the hook!

12- Prepare for a life of grief with your children and, in all likelihood, you'll achieve it!

Anonymous

It always grieves me to contemplate the initiation of children into the ways of life when they are scarcely more than infants.

It checks their confidence and simplicity, two of the best qualities that heaven gives them, and demands that they share our sorrows before they are capable of entering into our enjoyments. *Dickens.*

CHAPTER TWENTY

PARENTING:
A Very Special
PERSPECTIVE!

We now come to the final chapter regarding parents and childrearing. During the last nineteen chapters, we have outlined and discussed some of what it means to be a parent today and including what our children face as they go to school, play with their friends, hang out at the mall, and spend time at home with their families. Some of the things our kids are subjected to in their young lives is not good. Just as their parents, they also live in a society that is going through some very difficult and extreme times, and much of what they experience today, whether good or bad, will greatly influence their lives forever.

While a large number of parents are experiencing layoffs and unemployment, many teenagers, too, are having a hard time finding decent paying jobs. At the same time, crime is escalating in big cities and small towns alike, more and more teenage girls are becoming pregnant and then having abortions to take care of the "problem;" hope is on the decline while fear and anxiety are on the rise, the Dollar, Mark, Yen, Franc or Pound don't go as far today as they did just a few short years ago, health care is completely out of control in the USA (and other nations), and on it goes. On the surface, the quality of life just doesn't seem to be all that good. But it can be!

Let's take a moment and briefly review what we have read and studied in the earlier chapters of this book: In Chapter One: we discussed how it takes more to be a parent today than it did a few years ago. The world is changing, as are our values, principles, and ethics, and this makes a parent's job all the more difficult. Chapter Two: we visualized how children are a little like an assembly line...what we tell them and how we teach them is funneled into their fertile young minds where it stays and grows. Chapter Three: we discussed how important the time is that we spend with our children (it's priceless!). Chapter Four: we explored the way our kids' minds work and, strange as it may seem, they work wonderfully well. Chapter Five: we began to understand the importance of communication with our children (and without it, we are doomed to fail as parents). Chapter Six: we looked at our past to see what went wrong with the family structure and much of our present-day society.

Chapter Seven: we talked about grandparenting. Here, we discovered a very vital and important resource parents can use in their childrearing. Chapter Eight: was about the special needs many single parents have when it comes to raising their children. In this chapter, we looked at some of the problems facing single parents and how they might overcome them. Chapter Nine: this was an important chapter because we saw, more clearly, the need for our involvement in helping our children make wise decisions. Chapter Ten: we discussed some of the qualities of youth and leadership and how our kids, with our help, can grow to become intelligent and honest leaders.

In Chapter Eleven: we paused for a moment to consider some of the things about a child's mind that makes him or her very special. Chapter Twelve: we then pondered the question, "What in the world is success?" And we tried to uncover the true meaning of success; Chapter Thirteen: we discussed an important and very controversial subject regarding childrearing: discipline. Chapter Fourteen: this is a chapter that many of us, looking back at some of the stupid things we did with our money, wish we had been able to read when we were growing up: "Teaching our kids about Money!".

Chapter Fifteen, this was a very important chapter regarding why we should never provoke our children to wrath, and how to avoid it. Chapter Sixteen: here was a chapter that addressed the fear of almost every parent with teenage children: when their kids begin to date! (I'll bet some of you still have goosebumps remembering when your kids first started dating, or, for those of you with small children, thinking into the future when your kids will begin dating).

Chapter Seventeen: we considered how parents go through a time of anticipation - a time when we are concerned mostly about our children's welfare and their future success as adults. Chapter Eighteen: this was a special chapter because we discussed directly with the kids how they can help raise us, their parents. Chapter Nineteen: here was an overview of what we need to do in order to help our children understand us and how we can come to better understand them. And so we now arrive at Chapter Twenty: A very special PERSPECTIVE on childrearing.

Take a moment and think back to when you were a kid. Now compare what you experienced in school and at play with what so many young people are experiencing today. You may or may not have known about drugs (it depends on your age group and where you might have lived), but even if you and your classmates did experiment with all those different drugs that became fashionable during the 60's, 70's and on into the 80's, including LSD, coke, mescaline, and marijuana, what you smoked or dropped doesn't even come close to the potency drugs have today. Some researchers claim that a single marijuana "joint" grown and smoked in the 90's equals approximately 10-20 "joints" smoked in the 60's and 70's. Crack wasn't even heard of in the 60's, and heroin was in a decline. Not so today. Heroin, LSD, and crack are growing in popularity in cities throughout the world. Some difference from just a few years ago!

There may have been a few gangs in your school, but they weren't nearly as violent and ruthless as the gangs are today. Who in your class carried a gun to school? Did you ever hear of one of your friends or teachers getting shot? Killed? How many girls did you know who were pregnant before their sophomore year? How many did you know who had gotten an abortion before graduation? Was gang rape, child abuse, incest, and murder something that you witnessed, read in the morning papers, saw on the evening news, or talked about almost every day? How many kids in your class were homeless, living in shelters with their parents or even alone? And what about AIDS? How many of your friends and classmates in high school and college had the HIV virus or had died of AIDS before reaching their twenty-first birthday? The truth is, we didn't really know that much about heart disease or cancer, let alone a killer called AIDS!

Times, "they are a changing!" And as we project our vision and minds into the future, just a few short years from now, we can begin to see that they really aren't changing for the better!

So, why bring all this negative, gloomy and contrary information to the surface, you ask? Because only when we understand more about ourselves and the problems we face as a people, made up of families both young and old, wealthy and poor, will our society ever gain an attitude of greater wisdom and discernment, including the courage and desire to really change. If we truly believe everything is as good as it can be - that given enough time, things will work out for the best, without any effort, pain, or real sacrifice on our part - we are only fooling ourselves. And by fooling ourselves today, we are creating a very dangerous and uncertain situation for tomorrow!

If older adults were the only ones who would be affected by sticking our heads in the sand - thinking everything is all right when it really isn't, or not wanting to have to face reality by admitting that we have many problems yet to overcome - it probably wouldn't be that big a deal. After all, most of us have lived a good portion of our allotted threescore and ten years already.

However, it is important we remain awake with our heads above the sand - aware of those negative factions that are making our society convulse at the seams while affecting so many of our kids - because the overall effect is not only dangerous, its potentially lethal. The fact is, whenever we, as a society hide our heads in the sand, we affect our very survival as a civilized community of people worldwide...people from every walk of life, every race, color, religion, and creed, young and old!

I'm sure most of you remember the story of the frog and the pot of water. It seems that one day, ol' froggy hopped into a kettle of water thinking to himself, "Great flies flying overhead! This is great!

I'm going to fill my empty belly up with this cool fresh water and, at the same time, I'll take a bath and swim a stroke or two!"

The problem was, ol' froggy didn't know that under the kettle was a slow burning fire. At first he enjoyed the fresh feeling of being able to float on his back in the large kettle filled with cool water. But later, he began to sense that something was wrong. Although he felt very secure and at peace with himself, he was beginning to have a little difficulty moving his arms and legs. He was also beginning to fall asleep.

As the water grew warmer and slowly began to boil, ol' froggy's eyes grew heavier and soon he was in dreamland. So, ol' froggy, without ever waking up, ended up that night on a platter rimmed with garnish and sauce...a meal fit for a french King! Are we as a nation of parents oblivious to the fact that everything is not cool; that we are not safe from influences that can physically harm us? Are we beginning to fall asleep, unaware that a boiling fire rages directly beneath the foundation of our families - a foundation that supports a civilization made up of God-fearing, lawful, caring, and decent people?

The reason we wrote this book is to help parents become better prepared for the challenge of raising their kids in the 21st century. It is the desire of both authors that those parents who have now read this book will become more aware of what their kids are going through in today's world, and that they will do something about it - such as turning the attitude of this country around from its present direction and head toward a more family oriented, ethical, decent, God-worshiping, and compassionate society.

A few pages back, we wrote that even though things are not all that well with the family today, and even though it's certainly more difficult to rear children now than in the past, it doesn't have to be. In the very first chapter, we suggested that everyone reading this book should go before God and ask for guidance and discernment in order to gain a deeper understanding and appreciation of the material and information they would be allowing into their minds...the things they would soon be reading. When we discover such a lack of principles and spiritual values as we have during the last nineteen chapters, it takes great discernment, total commitment, and loving care toward our children for us parents to really want to understand our problems and make a change. And it takes God's intervention and help if we are ever to succeed!

How well we do as parents, and as a society, greatly depends on our personal commitment to a higher standard of principles and morality. More than a few of the problems we are experiencing today have been created and incubated by a massive decline of ethics and integrity over the past several decades. The basis for almost every problem we and our neighbors face as parents, teachers, businessmen, elected officials, and children, is spiritual not physical.

Gangs running loose and doing harm is physical. Parents *lacking the courage* to discipline and control their children, who later become gang members, is spiritual. Breaking the law is physical. *Having the desire* to break the law is spiritual. Having illicit sex resulting in abortion and possible damage to the soul, is physical. *Not having the will or resolve* to abstain from illicit sex, thus avoiding abortion and possible damage to the soul, is spiritual. Going to a movie or listening to music that is violent and evil in context, is physical. *Having the character* to avoid such films and music is spiritual.

The problem is very basic: we have all but done away with God! Some years ago, a large number of those living in the so-called western world - the enlightened and very technological segment of modern civilization - pronounced with great thunder and pageantry that "God is dead!" Apparently, they didn't really understand that only God can provide us, His children, with the spiritual courage, will, resolve, character, faith, and attitude to overcome the heavy pulls and tremendous temptations surrounding every living human being on Earth today...old and young alike!

The other day, I was watching a television talk show and the subject was on childrearing...with emphasis on punishment and discipline. The audience had taken sides with those experts on the stage with whom they felt some type of compatibility; some agreed that children should be disciplined, some didn't. Suddenly, one of the experts said something that really caught my attention.

A woman from the audience had just made a statement that she believed God had given us, in His Word, the Bible, the understanding that parents should certainly punish children whenever they do something bad. Without hesitation, the lady expert on the stage responded, "whoever wrote in the Bible that we should punish our children, doesn't know what he's talking about!" Oh, really?! What a statement! What arrogance!

Take a moment and lay down this book and think about yourself living as a human being on Earth inside a vast universe too large and massive to describe. Start with something you can easily recognize such as that tree just outside your window. By now, you've seen it so many times you probably take it for granted. But, when you look more closely at the way it's roots burrow deep into the soil and how they securely support such a massive, top-heavy piece of creation, doesn't it cause you to wonder just a bit about who you are? Or, who created the tree?

You don't have a tree outside your window? Okay. Tonight look up into the heavens and view the billions upon billions of stars and planets that just seem to be suspended in glittering, shining light. Not only are they beautiful to behold, but when we consider the wisdom behind the way each star remains in its particular orbit and has done so for millions (possibly billions) of years, doesn't this kind of give you cause to want to see more of the workings of God?

No? Well, how about life itself? You and your spouse grew up in childhood living apart. And then one day, you met at a particular place and time. You didn't know you were going to meet, but when it happened, you suddenly knew that this was that special someone you wanted to spend the rest of your life with. You fell in love!

Time goes by and you date and then one day you decide to marry. Has anything other than time, chance and circumstance caused all of this to happen? No? Are you sure? Anyway, let's continue. You both work for a while and then after a trip to the doctor, you discover that in a few months you and your spouse are going to become parents. It seems, one night, after a lovely dinner, when you and your spouse came together in love and passion, a tiny sperm and a minute ovary met and joined together and immediately began reproducing life. Now, has anything caused this all to happen? Still, no? Okay. Nine months later, babies Junior and Susie (twins, no less!) were born to a couple of very happy and proud parents. And suddenly, everyone's life began to change!

Junior and Susie slowly grew from little infants into toddlers, from toddlers into the terrible twos, from the terrible twos into puberty, from puberty into their teens, and from their teens into adulthood. And all the while this was happening, mom and dad were also growing - they were growing older!

Think back at the time when Junior cut his finger and came running for you to "make better!" Remember, how bad the cut was and then a few days later, it had all but disappeared. A miracle? Or, how about the day when Susie came running home from school thinking she was hurt when all that really happened was she had started her menstrual cycle for the very first time. That wonderful thing that happens when a little girl, still in her youth, is being prepared for the time, still to come, when she will reach adulthood and motherhood. A miracle?

The great God who guides and directs His immense universe - keeping everything in order - also provides the water and soil to make the trees grow, keeps in perfect harmony and balance His vast array of stars and planets, heals an injured finger, or prepares a young girl for motherhood when she is older, is the same God who gave us parents His instruction manual in order that we might become His wise and obedient children, while, at the same time, also become loving, caring, and protective parents to our children.

God did not put us on this Earth without providing us with the tools necessary to complete whatever it is we are to do with our lives; how we are to use our talents and abilities. And this includes how we are to raise and care for our kids.

A famous law enforcement officer once remarked, "a child who is taught the laws of God will never have a problem with the laws of the land!" The problem, today, seems to be one where more and more parents are neglecting to teach their children the laws of God! "And these words which I command you today shall be in your heart. You shall teach them diligently to your children..." (Deuteronomy 6:6-7 NKJV).

I am sure almost everyone reading this book has a Bible in their home. It is, after all, the biggest selling book in history. However, just because we have something at our disposal doesn't always mean we use it (or read it). This remarkable information manual of wisdom and knowledge (the Bible), which we have been given to help guide us on our pathway to success as adults and parents, is only going to help us, if we read it and do what it says. It does us no good just sitting on a bookshelf collecting dust!

How do we succeed at what we do on the job? We study. How do we learn to become a physician, nurse, computer operator, dentist, businessman, successful plant manager, student, husband, or wife? We study. How do we acquire the knowledge to teach and instruct others? We study. And, how do we gain the intelligence to master the challenge to become successful parents? We study! And what better book is there to study than your Bible? And what better way to understand what we read in the Bible than to pray for that understanding.

When we decide to use God's Word for our instruction and admonishment, He promises we will be blessed. "If you fully obey the Lord your God and carefully follow all his commands I give you today, the Lord your God will set you high above all the nations on earth." (Deuteronomy 28:1 NIV). He then goes on to describe just what our blessings will be if

337

we obey Him and what will happen if we disobey. Read all of Deuteronomy 28 to find out what course one ought to take if we truly want to be blessed with happy, obedient, and loving children. (Note: it might serve you well to remember that God tells us that He "is the same yesterday, today and forever." He has remained the same throughout history!)

Becoming a loving, devoted and conscientious parent is not easy. It's very difficult! As parents of ten children and twenty three grandchildren (between the two authors), we understand just how difficult and frustrating it can be at times. However, it can also be a lot of fun and very interesting. We can learn so much more about ourselves and the life we live when we properly raise our kids.

Today, children have all the benefits of acquiring new knowledge and understanding because, as a nation of intelligent people, we have created and developed greater technology and more extensive mathematical principles. But learning more about greater technology or mathematical principles isn't nearly as important as is children learning to show love toward their classmates, a kid playing ball with his dad, mom working in the kitchen with her family, dad fixing the car with his son or daughter, grandparents taking an afternoon stroll with their grandchildren, a child overcoming his or her fear of standing up to read in front of the class, parents listening to their toddler's first prayer, going out on a family picnic, watching a child ride a bike for the first time, or holding a son or daughter as they sleep on their parent's lap.

Are all of the things listed above just a figment of some writer's imagination - an illusion? Are they some kind of fantasies we may have read in a book or seen at the movies which were popular years ago? Are they just some faded, worn-out Norman Rockwell sketch we see hanging on our grandparent's wall? No. Not at all! They are not dreams, illusions, or faded paintings. Indeed, we can have the type of family togetherness our parents and their parents had years ago. But in order to do so, we must first of all overcome and turn around some of the negative attitudes and false notions we, as parents, have fallen into during the past several decades; and then we must seek a deeper understanding with greater love and respect toward those in our care...our kids!

If we ever expect to succeed as a society where the family, once again, is more important than any one person or material thing, we must first of all regard the family structure as being our highest priority, having prominence and value above all else. To do this, we must consider those in our family (including those in our worldwide family...our spiritual family) as having greater significance, importance, and worth than any one person has as an individual.

It's impossible to love a child when we only show love toward ourselves! Love is outgoing, not inward. It's impossible to teach and train children right from wrong - good from evil - when we are so busy coveting our own selfish cravings; when we deceive those whom we live and work with; or, when we betray others in order to accomplish our own egotistic desires! When we fail to spend quality time with our kids - working with them, playing with them, teaching them - we not only fail our own children, we fail our children's children. And we fail to do our part for our society!

Living in a society that perpetuates a life-style of fast food, short conversations, meaningless news bites, quarterly financial statements, pornographic and erotic entertainment, instant replay and nightly violence of every type and description, graphically illustrates the way we parents are failing our kids by what we are allowing to happen to them. We need to take more time, quality time, to talk with our kids (as well as with the rest of the family); we need to remember that our society is made up of individuals just like us, and that we are responsible for what we see happening to our families, friends, and children; and we need to "stop and smell the roses" - stopping to rethink what it is we are doing, where we are in history, and how we can help reclaim those things we have lost that have true meaning and value!

So, how do we turn around our lives and begin to take charge of our own destiny as a people, a nation, a parent? It's only going to happen if we begin to do the following things on a regular basis: *if* we accept God as our partner and seek His divine help and guidance in the rearing of our children; *if* we have the courage and will to properly discipline our kids with patience and love; *if* we strive to overcome our own selfish ambitions so that we can make a broader pathway for the needs of our family and children; *if* we begin to learn how to communicate with our kids - communicate as in a dialogue, not simply a monologue; *if* we gain a greater understanding as to where we are in history and then begin to teach our children those things they must know if they are ever to survive and prosper in life; *if* we help our kids make wise decisions - hard decisions - in such a way that doing so becomes second nature to their thinking process;

If we teach our children about money management and how to budget the money they make; *if* we put into practice what we preach; *if* we never provoke our kids to anger, never put them down or ridicule them in front of others (especially their friends); *if* we teach them about proper dating and what it means and how to do it in a way that they will have fun and excitement, while, at the same time, refusing to fall into the temptation of committing fornication and probably ruining their lives; *if* we show them, by our time, love, and patience, how they can help to raise us so that we can become better parents; *if* we, as adults, realize that we must also learn before we can teach - that we must study about how we can become better parents and, at the same time, learn how not to be fearful of what we see happening to our society so that we can grow in faith and courage in order to make those hard, positive decisions that will help solve many of the problems facing society (especially our kids); and, if we always put God in the picture and rely on His Word to help guide and direct our efforts to be the kind of parents He desires us to be - the kind of parents we so desperately want to be - we will, without a doubt, experience

"The JOY

of

RAISING OUR KIDS

in the

21ST CENTURY!"

340

"Hey, Mom and Dad, Thanks for reading this BOOK!"

Dear Reader,

We would like very much to hear from you regarding any comments you would like to make about what you have just read. It is our intention to revise this book from time to time, and any comments you make will help us with these revisions. You can reach us by writing to the address listed on the second page of this book.

Thank you for the time you spent reading this book. We hope that what we have written will help you become an even better parent than you already are.

Yours truly,
Gilbert H. Goethals
L. Raymond Hayes

Index

A

A Guiding Force!, 115
A spirit in man, 137
A spirit of reason and creation, 137
A successful person.", 143
A very important point to ponder, 292
Abel, 37, 210, 213
Abilities, 320
Ability to create, 138
Abortion, 62
Abortions, 263
Abstinence, 248
Abstinence-based programs, 267
Abuse, 36
Academics, 156
Acceptance, 317
Actions and deeds, 315
Adam, 210
Adam and Eve, 37, 38, 57, 2010, 239
Admonish, 36
Adolescence, 284
Adolph Hitler, 60
Adulthood, 284
AIDS, 12, 15, 63, 92, 93, 248, 268
AIDS!, 263
Aims!, 110
Ancestor,. 75
"...And be thankful!", 290
Anger, 130, 214, 217
Angry to be, 208
Ann Landers, 183, 267
Anticipate, 277, 278, 279, 280, 281
Anticipation, 271, 277, 279, 280
Anxiety, 271
Ape, 37
Apologize When You've Done Something Wrong!, 291
Apostle Paul, 285
Apothegm, 51
Appreciate, 317

Appreciative, 323
Approval, 317
Athletics, 156
Attainment of a desired goal, 143
Attilla the Hun, 60
Authority, 115
Avoid sland, 111

B

Bad guy in the black, 130
Bankruptcy, 63
Basic costs of feeding a family!, 192
Beatles the, 62
Beaver the, 122
Be kind, 111
Be neat, 111
Bennett, Elayne, 266
Be polite, 111
Be positive, 111
Be prompt, 111
Become the best, 151
Best Friends Program, 267
Better to be safe than sorry, 150
Bible the, 211, 337
Bible the Living, 115
Big Bang theory, 78
Big Brother, 96
Big lies, little lies; white lies, or dark lies, 272
Bill Vernich, 85
Bio-engineering, 71
Bird, Larry, 153
Black and white, 137
Book of instruction, 172
Bootleg whiskey, 61
Brain the, 135
British Medical Journal, 264
Build A "Healthy Child", 322
Burn your bra, 62

C

C. Simmons, 203
Cain, 37, 38, 2010, 211, 213
Cain and Abel, 209
Cancer, 65, 71, 92
Car-jacking, 63
Catherwood, Carn, 218
Cause and effect, 99
Character, 162
Charlie Shedd, 249
Chaste, 268
Chastise, 278
Career and Vocational Training, 157
Cause, 64
Chicken pox, 71
Child discipline and punishment, 277
Child support, 86
Child violence, 123
Children emulate their parents, 313
Children need to be encouraged
    to use their talents, 320
Children need to be taught about
    proper hygiene, 320
Children need to be taught how
    to respect others, 323
Children need to be taught how
    to control their emotions, 322
Chlamydia, 268
Choices, 267
Cholesterol, 193
Christians, 85
Citizen, good, 112
Citizenship, 156
Colored People (slang), 61
Colossians 3:15 [last part], 290
Colossians 3:21, 163, 216
Columbia, Cocaine, and the DEA!, 63
Commanding, 115
Commandments, Ten, 88
Commitment, 108
Communist Manifesto, 78
Compassion with compassion!, 120
Computer science, 70
Computers, 62
Condom, 264-265
Condom promoters, 263

Condom propaganda, 268
Confidence, 316, 317
Congress, 266
Consistent, 104
Cooper Aerobics Center, 322
Cooper, Kenneth, M.D., 322
Corinthians, 120
Coronary heart disease, 322
Correction, 278
Courage, 317
Court room, 139
Credit card, 62
Credit, credit, credit!, 63
Crips and the Bloods, 63
Criticism, 316
Crowell, Grace Noll, 28
Cultural Awareness, 156
Custody rights, 86

D

"D" word, the big, 161
Daniel Webster, 73, 81, 114, 143, 162,
    176, 208, 235, 247, 277, 320
Dating!, 231, 260
Decisions, 108
Decision making, 108
Defend the weak!, 111
Democritus, 49
Depression the, 61
Desensitized, 209
Deu. 11:19, 1
Deu. 6:6-7, 23
Deuteronomy 28:1, 337
Deuteronomy 4:9, 161
Deuteronomy 6:6-7, 337
Deuteronomy 8:5, 278
Dickens, 328
Diet, 321
Direct, to, 114
Discipline!, 36, 84, 161, 281
Divorce, 62
DNA, 82
Do it with all your might!, 152
Don't manipulate your children,. 133
Do Something Very Special for Your
    Parents Today!, 290

Do you dream?, 137
Don't be afraid of your parents!, 299
Don't be afraid to ask mom and
    dad for advice!, 296
Don't be too strict with mom
    and dad!, 287
Don't think of yourself as
    being perfect!, 294
Dorothy Law Nolte, 316
Dream in color, 137
Dreams, 96, 137
Dreams, spiritual, 137
Drive-by shootings, 63, 89
Drugs, illegal, 71

E

Eating right, 322
Ecclesiastes 5:10, 202
Effect, (Cause and Effect), 64
Electronic opiate, 321
Eliot, G, 49
Elvis, 62
Embarrassment, 277
Emotions, 130, 245, 315, 323
Emulating, 317
Encourage Your Parents Often!, 286
Encouraged and praised, 316
Encouragement, 48, 317
Ephesians 6:1, 207
Ephesians 6:1-3, 286
Ephesians 6:4, 163, 207, 213
Epidemics, 268
ERA, 63
Err and sin, 132
ESP, 72
ET, 73
European friends, 57
Eve, 210
Exasperate (provoke) your
    children, do not, 207
Exercise, 321, 322
Exodus 20:12, 285
Exodus 20:16, 292
Exorcist the, 73

F

F.A.C.T.S, 267
Facing Reality, 267
Fairness, 120
Faith, 214, 277
False advertising, 193
Family, 88
Family genes, 82
Fantasia, 73
Fascism, 78
Father Knows Best, 122
Favorable outcome of an undertaking, 143
Fear and suffering, 58
Finish the race, 320
Fitness, 322
Five dangerous ideas, 265
FM radio, 62
Focus on the Family, 263
For with God nothing will be
    impossible!, 132
Forbes, 146
Ford, Henry, 146
Forgiveness, 317
Free sex, 62
Friendship, 317
Frog, 66
Froggy, The Story of 331
Fury, 208

G

G. Eliot, 49
Garden of Eden, 37, 210
Genesis, 209
Genesis 3:12, 210
Genghis Khan, 60
Getty, J. Paul, 145
Gluttonous, 65
God, 88, 207, 210, 211, 214, 216,
    217, 222, 239, 257, 260, 285,
    290, 293, 336
God's little ones, 27
God's wise plan, 214
Gonorrhea, 268
Goo-goo, gaa-gaa baby talk, 49, 175

Good guys, 130
Good Housekeeping, 32
Grandparent, 69, 71, 73
Greed, 112
Greed is good!, 63
Goodwill store, 79
Grace Noll Crowell, 28
Graham, Mark, 218
Grammar, 49
Grams of fat, 193
Grand, 73
Grandpa Jones, 71
Group Dating!, 237
Guide, 114
Guilt, 277
Guilt complex, 317

H

Haight Ashbury, 62
Harold Morris, 267
Healthcare fraud, 78
Heart attack, 65
Heart disease, 92
Heart failure, 71
Hearts, 245
Heavy Metal, 73
Herpes, 12, 268
High technology, 70
Highlander Boys, 111
HIV, 264, 26
HIV-infected, 264
HIV/AIDS, 263
Homosexuals, Lesbians,
    and Gay rights!, 63
Honest consideration, 277
Honor, 60
Honorable, 212
"Honorable" parents, 212
Horse Ma-gagle, 129
Hosea 4:6, 175, 181
Hosea 4:6, 5
Hostility, 316
How NOT to provoke your child
    to wrath!, 165

How to raise your parents!, 283
HPV, 268
Hugs and kisses, 82
Hygiene, 320, 322
Hypocritical, 133

I

I Corinthians 13:2-13, 318
I Corinthians 13:5, 217
I Timothy 2:9, 253
If it was good enough for Granddad,
    it's good enough for me, 149
Illicit sex, 248
Imagination, 132
In Defense of a Little Virginity!, 263
Incredible brain, 135
Infertility, 268
Influence, 115
Insider Trading, 63
Instruction manual, 172, 285
Integrated circuit, 62
Intellect, 72, 245

J

J. Paul Getty, 145
James 1:27, 90
James Meredith, 62
Japan, 61
Japanese, 57
Jeremiah, 255
Jeremiah 17:9, 245
Jesus Christ, 213, 316
John 15:2, 278
John 5:19, 316
John, Martin, and Bobby, 62
John Ruskin, 56
John Woodin, 148
Jones, Thelma Evelyn, 120
Judge, 139
Junk bonds, 63, 78
Just to be, 120
Justice, 317
Juvenal, 110

K

Kate Douglas Wiggin, 229
Kenneth Cooper, M.D., 322
Kid Fitness, 322
Kind be, 111
King, Jan, 83
King Solomon, 202
King, Steven, 73
KKK, 61

L

Landers, Ann, 183, 267
Larry Bird, 153
Larry Ray, 102
Latex, 264
Law abiding, 112
Leader, 114
Leaders must also have self control!, 131
Leaders must have a sense of humor!, 129
Leverage buyouts, 78
Levitation, 72
Light My Fire, 62
Little blue pill, 65
Linda H. Sigourney, 282
Live Pure, 111
Liver transplants, 71
Lose weight, 65
Love, 60, 121, 318
Love and marriage, 257
Love Chapter, 120
Love must be practiced and it must
   also be verbal, 317
"Love" of money, 203
love with love!, 120
Loving Parent, 112
Loyal workers, 315
LSD, 62
Lying, 272, 274

M

Magic, 72
Magic Johnson, 153

Mahatma Gandhi, 213
Malachi 2:15, 214
Managing money, 185
Mark Graham, 218
Mark Twain, 18
Marriage, 97, 260
Married, 214
Mary Poppins, 62
Materialistic, 112
Maturity, 247
MBA, 62
Me, My World, My Future, 267
Menstrual period, 94
Meredith, James, 62
Military school, 111
Mind of a Child, 135
Minds of our children, 138
Modern medicine, 70
Modesty, 253
Money, 185
Moral considerations, 263
Morality, 112
Morris, Harold, 267
Movie moguls, 268
Multinationals, 63
Municipal court, 139

N

1968, 62
Nana, 81
Nancy, 130
Narcissistic attitude, 112
NASA, 62
Nazi's, 61
Nazism, 78
Neat, to be, 111
Nelson Family, the, 122
Nightshade, 34
Nihilistic to be, 112
Nihilistic Parent, 112
Nixon, Richard, 62
Nolte, Dorothy Law, 316
Number One, 62
Nutrition, 321
Nutritious, 192

O

Obedience, 10
Obey orders, 111
Objective, 120
Old isn't in anymore, 70
Orangutan, 37
Orders, 111
Out of the closet, 63
Out of wedlock, 69
Overweight, 65

P

Pain Threshold, 158
Parent, 74
Parenthood, 319
Parenting skills, 81
Patience, 317
Pay the penalty, 181
Pelvic inflammatory disease, 268
Penicillin, 268
Personal Computer, 63
P ersuasion, 115
Planned Parenthood, 266
Play with children, 280
Play the game square, 111
Polio, 71
Polite be, 111
Positive be, 111
Precepts and Aims, 111
Pregnancy, 264, 268
Premarital sex, 267
Prevention, 322
Prevention Magazine, 322
Prison, 140
Prodigious event, 231
Profanities, 315
Progenitor, 74
Prompt be, 111
Proper health, 322
Proper nutrition, 321
Proper sexual conduct, 257
Properly correct, 281
Prosper, 143
Prostitution, 89
Proverbs, 116, 131

Proverbs 13:24, 163, 171, 175
Proverbs 14:12, 175, 181
Proverbs 15:1, 54
Proverbs 17:6, 301
Proverbs 19:18, 163, 172
Proverbs 20:11, 300
Proverbs 22:15, 163, 172
Proverbs 22:6, 163
Proverbs 23:13, 163, 172, 182
Proverbs 23:14, 172
Proverbs 29:17, 175
Proverbs 29:19, 161
Proverbs 3:11, 161, 278
Proverbs 3:12, 278
Proverbs 3:13-18, 256
Proverbs 5, 257
Provoke our children to wrath
   and anger, do not, 165, 205
Psalms 1:1-3, 146
Psalms 23:4, 172
Psalms 94:12, 278
Psalms 139:13-14, 312
PTA, 96
Puberty, 284
Publilius Syrus, 49
Punishing, 42
Punishment, 42, 106
Pure be, 111
Purity, 60

Q

Quality food, 193

R

Races segregated, 62
Rage, 208
Rape, 140
Ray, Larry, 102
Real leaders, 115
Reasonable Reasons to Wait, 267
Rebellious music, 123
Reject authority, 112
Respect , 324
Respect, Inc., 267
Restriction, 108

Revelation 3:19, 278
Reward, 106
Richter, 302
Ride your success on the shoulders
   of giants, 151, 296
Ridicule, 316
Right a Wrong, 111
Right and proper decisions, 98
Right and wrong, 98
Right from wrong, 60
Robert Louis Stevenson, 138
Rock N' Roll, 62
Rod, 172, 173
Romans 12:17, 293
Rosie the Riveter, 61
Ruskin, John, 56
Russian roulette, 266

S

S&L, 63
Safe sex gurus, 263
Safe sex, 264
Satan, 25, 26, 37, 210
Scouts Boy, 324
Seat of mockers, 146
Secondary virginity, 267
Seed of deception!, 37
Self control, 131, 132, 162
Self doubt, 317
Self-destructive paths, 123
Self-esteem, 316
Selfish pleasure, 112
Sense of humor, 130
Sense of humor!, 129
Seven difficult teen years, 284
Sex, 71, 260
Sex, Love & Choices, 266
Sex Respect, 267
Sexual revolution, 263
Sexually transmitted diseases, 263
Shame, 317
Shebet, 172, 173
Shedd, Charlie, 249
Shy, 316
Shyness, 317
Sigourney, Linda, 282

Simmons, C, 203
Sin, 37
Single Dating!, 237, 245
Single family dwelling, 69
Single mother, 69
Skepticism, 112
Slang, 111
Small Group Dating, 237, 242
Social drugs, 62
Social Security check, 74
Society, 61
Solomon, 202
Somehow these two perfect beings, 37
Soul the, 73
Sound of Music, 62
Southwest Parents Committee, 267
Space, 62
Spare the rod and spoil the child, 171
Speak Truth, 111
Sperm, 264
Spirit, 73
Spiritual, 72
Spiritual Understanding, 157
Star Wars, 73
Steven King, 73
Stevenson, Robert Louis, 138
Storing, and recalling bits and pieces
   of information, 135
Stork is Dead, the, 249
Stroke, 65
Submission to authority, 162
Success, 142
Suicidal, 265
Sullivan, Tom, 155
Syphilis, 268
System of rules, 163

T

Take mom and dad into your
   confidence!, 297
Talents, 320
Talleyrand, 49
Tax dollars, 269
Tax shelters, 63
TB, 92
Teaching, 107

Teaching children about money!, 185
Teen-Aid, 267
Teenager's Bill of Rights, 269
Teens Have the Right, 269
Television, 70
Tell your mom and dad"Thanks"
    at least once a day, 288
Temper, 130, 315
Ten Commandments the, 88
Terrible two's the, 284
Thankful, 323
The best I could be, 152
THE Depression, 61
Thelma Evelyn Jones, 120
Theory of evolution, 78
1Timothy 3:12, 184
Time, chance and circumstance, 57
Tolerance, 317
Tom Sullivan, 155
Tradition, 112
Train, 36
Training, 107
Transistor, 62
Tribute to a good wife!, 119
Trickle down economics, 63
Trump, Donald, 146
Trust, 277
Truth, 60, 111, 293
Turn on and Drop out, 62
Twelve Rules for Raising Children, 183
Twelve ways to raise a child to be
    a delinquent!, 326

U

UFO's, 72
Unconditional love, 277
Unconditional love!, 318
"Unworkable solution", 265

V

VD, 12, 248
Vernich, Bill, 85
Viet Nam, 62
Violent films, 123

Virginity, 269
Virgins, 267
Virtue is a necessity!, 269
Vulgarities, 315

W

Wall, the Berlin, 63
Wall Street, 63
War, 62
War, The Cold, 63
Watergate, 62
We reap what we sow, 150
Weak, 111
Webster, 73, 81, 114, 143, 162, 176,
    208, 235, 247, 277, 320
Webster's dictionary, 3, 72
Webster's New World Dictionary, 72
What goes around comes around, 150
What in the world is success?!, 139
What is a grandparent?, 81
What success is and how to
    obtain it!, 142
What Would You Take?, 32
Wheat, 34
Wiggin, Kate Douglas, 229
White collar crime, 61
Wisdom, 256
Wise decisions, 98
Women's Lib, 62
Woodin, John, 148
Woodstock, 62
Words of anger, 54
World War II, 57
"Worth every effort given
    and minute spent!", 85
Wrath, 131, 208, 209, 217

XYZ

Young Highlander, 111
You're never too young to make
    a difference!, 218

ORDER FORM

If you would like to buy additional copies or give a copy of this book as a gift to your son or daughter, that special person heading for the alter, a high school grad, a newly-wedded couple, a soon-to-be mom, a proud new papa, a grandchild, or a certain friend, please order by completing the following:

- POSTAL ORDERS TO: Bruit Publishing Co., Inc.
  PO Box 927
  Langley, WA 98260 USA

NAME:_____

ADDRESS:_____

CITY:_____STATE:_____ZIP_____

- If this is a gift: please send the book, "The JOY of Raising OUR Kids
  in the 21st Century!"
  TO:

NAME:_____

ADDRESS:_____

CITY:_____STATE:_____ZIP_____

BOOK PRICES:
Hard Cover: No. of books _____ @ $21.95 $_____
Paperback: No. of books _____ @ $16.95 $_____
Shipping/Handling: (Add $3.00 per book) $_____
Sales Tax: Please add 8.0% for books shipped $_____
          to Washington addresses.
Total Amount Inclosed: $_____

PAYMENT: [] Check   [] Money Order

Signature:_____
          Please allow 4-6 weeks for delivery

351